(ex·ploring)

1. Investigating in a systematic way: examining. 2. Searching into or ranging over for the purpose of discovery.

VBA for Microsoft® Office 2016

BRIEF

Series Editor Mary Anne Poatsy

Jason Davidson

Series Created by Dr. Robert T. Grauer

 **Pearson**

330 Hudson Street, NY, NY 10013

Vice President of IT & Career Skills: Andrew Gilfillan

Senior Portfolio Manager: Samantha Lewis

Team Lead, Project Management: Laura Burgess

Project Manager: Barbara Stover

Development Editor: Barbara Stover

Editorial Assistant: Michael Campbell

Director of Product Marketing: Maggie Waples

Director of Field Marketing: Leigh Ann Sims

Product Marketing Manager: Kaylee Carlson

Field Marketing Managers: Molly Schmidt & Joanna Conley

Senior Operations Specialist: Maura Zaldivar-Garcia

Interior and Cover Design: Cenveo

Senior Product Model Manager: Eric Hakanson

Production and Digital Studio Lead: Heather Darby

Media Producer, MyITLab: Jaimie Noy

Course Producer, MyITLab: Amanda Losonsky

Digital Project Manager, MyITLab: Becca Lowe

Media Project Manager, Production: John Cassar

Full-Service Project Management: iEnergizer Aptara®, Ltd.

Composition: iEnergizer Aptara®, Ltd.

Cover Image Credits: cunico/Fotolia (*compass rose*); mawrhis/Fotolia (*checker pattern*); wavebreakmedia/Shutterstock (*students*); Sergey Nivens/Fotolia (*world*); dotshock/Shutterstock (*business people*)

Cataloging-in-Publication data is on file with the Library of Congress.

ISBN 10:   0-13-449708-2
ISBN 13: 978-0-13-449708-2

About the Author

Mary Anne Poatsy, Series Editor

Mary Anne is a senior faculty member at Montgomery County Community College, teaching various computer application and concepts courses in face-to-face and online environments. She holds a B.A. in Psychology and Education from Mount Holyoke College and an M.B.A. in Finance from Northwestern University's Kellogg Graduate School of Management.

Mary Anne has more than 18 years of educational experience. She is currently adjunct faculty at Montgomery County Community College. She has also taught at Gywnedd Mercy University, Bucks County Community College, and Muhlenberg College, as well as conducted personal training. Before teaching, she was Vice President at Shearson Lehman in the Municipal Bond Investment Banking Department.

Jason Davidson, Author

Jason Davidson is a faculty member in the College of Business at Butler University, where he teaches Advanced Web Design, Data Networks, Data Analysis and Business Modeling, and introductory MIS courses. With a background in media development prior to joining the faculty at Butler, he worked in the technical publishing industry. Along with teaching, he currently serves as an IT consultant for regional businesses in the Indianapolis area. He holds a B.A. in telecommunication arts from Butler University and an M.B.A. from Morehead State University. He lives in Indianapolis, Indiana, and in his free time enjoys road biking, photography, and spending time with his family.

Dedications

For my husband, Ted, who unselfishly continues to take on more than his share to support me throughout the process; and for my children, Laura, Carolyn, and Teddy, whose encouragement and love have been inspiring.

Mary Anne Poatsy

I dedicate this book to my beautiful Sarah. You are my greatest achievement.

Jason Davidson

Contents

Customizing Access with VBA

CHAPTER THREE **Access and VBA:**
Customizing Access with VBA **142**

Acknowledgments

The Exploring team acknowledges and thanks all the reviewers who helped us throughout the years by providing us with their invaluable comments, suggestions, and constructive criticism.

Adriana Lumpkin
Midland College

Alan S. Abrahams
Virginia Tech

Alexandre C. Probst
Colorado Christian University

Ali Berrached
University of Houston–Downtown

Allen Alexander
Delaware Technical & Community College

Andrea Marchese
Maritime College, State University of New York

Andrew Blitz
Broward College; Edison State College

Angel Norman
University of Tennessee, Knoxville

Angela Clark
University of South Alabama

Ann Rovetto
Horry-Georgetown Technical College

Astrid Todd
Guilford Technical Community College

Audrey Gillant
Maritime College, State University of New York

Barbara Stover
Marion Technical College

Barbara Tollinger
Sinclair Community College

Ben Brahim Taha
Auburn University

Beverly Amer
Northern Arizona University

Beverly Fite
Amarillo College

Biswadip Ghosh
Metropolitan State University of Denver

Bonita Volker
Tidewater Community College

Bonnie Homan
San Francisco State University

Brad West
Sinclair Community College

Brian Powell
West Virginia University

Carol Buser
Owens Community College

Carol Roberts
University of Maine

Carolyn Barren
Macomb Community College

Carolyn Borne
Louisiana State University

Cathy Poyner
Truman State University

Charles Hodgson
Delgado Community College

Chen Zhang
Bryant University

Cheri Higgins
Illinois State University

Cheryl Brown
Delgado Community College

Cheryl Hinds
Norfolk State University

Cheryl Sypniewski
Macomb Community College

Chris Robinson
Northwest State Community College

Cindy Herbert
Metropolitan Community College–Longview

Craig J. Peterson
American InterContinental University

Dana Hooper
University of Alabama

Dana Johnson
North Dakota State University

Daniela Marghitu
Auburn University

David Noel
University of Central Oklahoma

David Pulis
Maritime College, State University of New York

David Thornton
Jacksonville State University

Dawn Medlin
Appalachian State University

Debby Keen
University of Kentucky

Debra Chapman
University of South Alabama

Debra Hoffman
Southeast Missouri State University

Derrick Huang
Florida Atlantic University

Diana Baran
Henry Ford Community College

Diane Cassidy
The University of North Carolina at Charlotte

Diane L. Smith
Henry Ford Community College

Dick Hewer
Ferris State College

Don Danner
San Francisco State University

Don Hoggan
Solano College

Don Riggs
SUNY Schenectady County Community College

Doncho Petkov
Eastern Connecticut State University

Donna Ehrhart
State University of New York at Brockport

Elaine Crable
Xavier University

Elizabeth Duett
Delgado Community College

Erhan Uskup
Houston Community College–Northwest

Eric Martin
University of Tennessee

Erika Nadas
Wilbur Wright College

Floyd Winters
Manatee Community College

Frank Lucente
Westmoreland County Community
College

G. Jan Wilms
Union University

Gail Cope
Sinclair Community College

Gary DeLorenzo
California University of Pennsylvania

Gary Garrison
Belmont University

Gary McFall
Purdue University

George Cassidy
Sussex County Community College

Gerald Braun
Xavier University

Gerald Burgess
Western New Mexico University

Gladys Swindler
Fort Hays State University

Hector Frausto
California State University Los Angeles

Heith Hennel
Valencia Community College

Henry Rudzinski
Central Connecticut State University

Irene Joos
La Roche College

Iwona Rusin
Baker College; Davenport University

J. Roberto Guzman
San Diego Mesa College

Jacqueline D. Lawson
Henry Ford Community College

Jakie Brown Jr.
Stevenson University

James Brown
Central Washington University

James Powers
University of Southern Indiana

Jane Stam
Onondaga Community College

Janet Bringhurst
Utah State University

Jean Welsh
Lansing Community College

Jeanette Dix
Ivy Tech Community College

Jennifer Day
Sinclair Community College

Jill Canine
Ivy Tech Community College

Jill Young
Southeast Missouri State University

Jim Chaffee
The University of Iowa Tippie College
of Business

Joanne Lazirko
University of Wisconsin–Milwaukee

Jodi Milliner
Kansas State University

John Hollenbeck
Blue Ridge Community College

John Seydel
Arkansas State University

Judith A. Scheeren
Westmoreland County Community College

Judith Brown
The University of Memphis

Juliana Cypert
Tarrant County College

Kamaljeet Sanghera
George Mason University

Karen Priestly
Northern Virginia Community College

Karen Ravan
Spartanburg Community College

Karen Tracey
Central Connecticut State University

Kathleen Brenan
Ashland University

Ken Busbee
Houston Community College

Kent Foster
Winthrop University

Kevin Anderson
Solano Community College

Kim Wright
The University of Alabama

Kristen Hockman
University of Missouri–Columbia

Kristi Smith
Allegany College of Maryland

Laura Marcoulides
Fullerton College

Laura McManamon
University of Dayton

Laurence Boxer
Niagara University

Leanne Chun
Leeward Community College

Lee McClain
Western Washington University

Linda D. Collins
Mesa Community College

Linda Johnsonius
Murray State University

Linda Lau
Longwood University

Linda Theus
Jackson State Community College

Linda Williams
Marion Technical College

Lisa Miller
University of Central Oklahoma

Lister Horn
Pensacola Junior College

Lixin Tao
Pace University

Loraine Miller
Cayuga Community College

Lori Kielty
Central Florida Community College

Lorna Wells
Salt Lake Community College

Lorraine Sauchin
Duquesne University

Lucy Parakhovnik
California State University, Northridge

Lynn Keane
University of South Carolina

Lynn Mancini
Delaware Technical Community College

Mackinzee Escamilla
South Plains College

Marcia Welch
Highline Community College

Margaret McManus
Northwest Florida State College

Margaret Warrick
Allan Hancock College

Marilyn Hibbert
Salt Lake Community College

Mark Choman
Luzerne County Community College

Maryann Clark
University of New Hampshire

Mary Beth Tarver
Northwestern State University

Mary Duncan
University of Missouri–St. Louis

Melissa Nemeth
Indiana University-Purdue University
Indianapolis

Melody Alexander
Ball State University

Michael Douglas
University of Arkansas at Little Rock

Michael Dunklebarger
Alamance Community College

Michael G. Skaff
College of the Sequoias

Michele Budnovitch
Pennsylvania College of Technology

Mike Jochen
East Stroudsburg University

Mike Michaelson
Palomar College

Mike Scroggins
Missouri State University

Mimi Spain
Southern Maine Community College

Muhammed Badamas
Morgan State University

NaLisa Brown
University of the Ozarks

Nancy Grant
Community College of Allegheny
County–South Campus

Nanette Lareau
University of Arkansas Community
College–Morrilton

Nikia Robinson
Indian River State University

Pam Brune
Chattanooga State Community College

Pam Uhlenkamp
Iowa Central Community College

Patrick Smith
Marshall Community and Technical College

Paul Addison
Ivy Tech Community College

Paula Ruby
Arkansas State University

Peggy Burrus
Red Rocks Community College

Peter Ross
SUNY Albany

Philip H. Nielson
Salt Lake Community College

Philip Valvalides
Guilford Technical Community College

Ralph Hooper
University of Alabama

Ranette Halverson
Midwestern State University

Richard Blamer
John Carroll University

Richard Cacace
Pensacola Junior College

Richard Hewer
Ferris State University

Richard Sellers
Hill College

Rob Murray
Ivy Tech Community College

Robert Banta
Macomb Community College

Robert Dušek
Northern Virginia Community College

Robert G. Phipps Jr.
West Virginia University

Robert Sindt
Johnson County Community College

Robert Warren
Delgado Community College

Rocky Belcher
Sinclair Community College

Roger Pick
University of Missouri at Kansas City

Ronnie Creel
Troy University

Rosalie Westerberg
Clover Park Technical College

Ruth Neal
Navarro College

Sandra Thomas
Troy University

Sheila Gionfriddo
Luzerne County Community College

Sherrie Geitgey
Northwest State Community College

Sherry Lenhart
Terra Community College

Sophia Wilberscheid
Indian River State College

Sophie Lee
California State University, Long Beach

Stacy Johnson
Iowa Central Community College

Stephanie Kramer
Northwest State Community College

Stephen Z. Jourdan
Auburn University at Montgomery

Steven Schwarz
Raritan Valley Community College

Sue A. McCrory
Missouri State University

Sumathy Chandrashekar
Salisbury University

Susan Fuschetto
Cerritos College

Susan Medlin
UNC Charlotte

Susan N. Dozier
Tidewater Community College

Suzan Spitzberg
Oakton Community College

Suzanne M. Jeska
County College of Morris

Sven Aelterman
Troy University

Sy Hirsch
Sacred Heart University

Sylvia Brown
Midland College

Tanya Patrick
Clackamas Community College

Terri Holly
Indian River State College

Terry Ray Rigsby
Hill College

Thomas Rienzo
Western Michigan University

Tina Johnson
Midwestern State University

Tommy Lu
Delaware Technical Community College

Troy S. Cash
Northwest Arkansas Community College

Vicki Robertson
Southwest Tennessee Community

Vickie Pickett
Midland College

Weifeng Chen
California University of Pennsylvania

Wes Anthony
Houston Community College

William Ayen
University of Colorado at Colorado Springs

Wilma Andrews
Virginia Commonwealth University

Yvonne Galusha
University of Iowa

Special thanks to our content development and technical team:

Barbara Stover

Janet Pickard

Morgan Hetzler

Steven Rubin

Preface

The Exploring Series and You

Exploring is Pearson's Office Application series that requires students like you to think "beyond the point and click." In this edition, we have worked to restructure the Exploring experience around the way you, today's modern student, actually use your resources.

The goal of Exploring is, as it has always been, to go farther than teaching just the steps to accomplish a task—the series provides the theoretical foundation for you to understand when and why to apply a skill. As a result, you achieve a deeper understanding of each application and can apply this critical thinking beyond Office and the classroom.

The How & Why of This Revision

Outcomes matter. Whether it's getting a good grade in this course, learning how to use Microsoft Office and Windows 10 so students can be successful in other courses, or learning a specific skill that will make learners successful in a future job, everyone has an outcome in mind. And outcomes matter. That is why we revised our chapter opener to focus on the outcomes students will achieve by working through each Exploring chapter. These are coupled with objectives and skills, providing a map students can follow to get everything they need from each chapter.

Critical Thinking and Collaboration are essential 21st-century skills. Students want and need to be successful in their future careers—so we used motivating case studies to show relevance of these skills to future careers.

Students today read, prepare, and study differently than students used to. Students use textbooks like a tool—they want to easily identify what they need to know and learn it efficiently. We have added key features, such as Tasks Lists (in purple) and Step Icons, and tracked everything via page numbers that allow efficient navigation, creating a map students can easily follow.

Students are exposed to technology. The new edition of Exploring moves beyond the basics of the software at a faster pace, without sacrificing coverage of the fundamental skills that students need to know.

Students are diverse. Students can be any age, any gender, any race, with any level of ability or learning style. With this in mind, we broadened our definition of "student resources" to include MyITLab, the most powerful and most ADA-compliant online homework and assessment tool around with a direct 1:1 content match with the Exploring Series. Exploring will be accessible to all students, regardless of learning style.

Providing You with a Map to Success to Move Beyond the Point and Click

All of these changes and additions will provide students an easy and efficient path to follow to be successful in this course, regardless of where they start at the beginning of this course. Our goal is to keep students engaged in both the hands-on and conceptual sides, helping achieve a higher level of understanding that will guarantee success in this course and in a future career.

In addition to the vision and experience of the series creator, Robert T. Grauer, we have assembled a tremendously talented team of Office Applications authors who have devoted themselves to teaching the ins and outs of Microsoft Word, Excel, Access, and PowerPoint. Led in this edition by series editor Mary Anne Poatsy, the whole team is dedicated to the Exploring mission of moving students **beyond the point and click**.

Key Features

The **How/Why Approach** helps students move beyond the point and click to a true understanding of how to apply Microsoft Office skills.

- **White Pages/Yellow Pages** clearly distinguish the theory (white pages) from the skills covered in the Hands-On Exercises (yellow pages) so students always know what they are supposed to be doing and why.

- **Case Study** presents a scenario for the chapter, creating a story that ties the Hands-On Exercises together.

The **Outcomes focus** allows students and instructors to know the higher-level learning goals and how those are achieved through discreet objectives and skills.

- **Outcomes** presented at the beginning of each chapter identify the learning goals for students and instructors.

- **Enhanced Objective Mapping** enables students to follow a directed path through each chapter, from the objectives list at the chapter opener through the exercises at the end of the chapter.
  - **Objectives List:** This provides a simple list of key objectives covered in the chapter. This includes page numbers so students can skip between objectives where they feel they need the most help.
  - **Step Icons:** These icons appear in the white pages and reference the step numbers in the Hands-On Exercises, providing a correlation between the two so students can easily find conceptual help when they are working hands-on and need a refresher.
  - **Quick Concepts Check:** A series of questions that appear briefly at the end of each white page section. These questions cover the most essential concepts in the white pages required for students to be successful in working the Hands-On Exercises. Page numbers are included for easy reference to help students locate the answers.
  - **Chapter Objectives Review:** Appears toward the end of the chapter and reviews all important concepts throughout the chapter. Newly designed in an easy-to-read bulleted format.

End-of-Chapter Exercises offer instructors several options for assessment. Each chapter has approximately 11–12 exercises ranging from multiple choice questions to open-ended projects.

- **Multiple Choice, Key Terms Matching, Practice Exercises, Mid-Level Exercises, Beyond the Classroom Exercises, and Capstone Exercises** appear at the end of all chapters.

Resources

Instructor Resources

The Instructor's Resource Center, available at **www.pearsonhighered.com**, includes the following:

- **Instructor Manual** provides one-stop-shop for instructors, including an overview of all available resources, teaching tips, as well as student data and solution files for every exercise.

- **Solution Files with Scorecards** assist with grading the Hands-On Exercises and end-of-chapter exercises.

- **Prepared Exams** allow instructors to assess all skills covered in a chapter with a single project.

- **Rubrics** for Mid-Level Creative Cases and Beyond the Classroom Cases in Microsoft Word format enable instructors to customize the assignments for their classes.

- **PowerPoint Presentations** with notes for each chapter are included for out-of-class study or review.

- **Multiple Choice, Key Term Matching, and Quick Concepts Check Answer Keys**

- **Test Bank** provides objective-based questions for every chapter.

- **Scripted Lectures** offer an in-class lecture guide for instructors to mirror the Hands-On Exercises.

- **Syllabus Templates**
  - Outcomes, Objectives, and Skills List
  - Assignment Sheet
  - File Guide

Student Resources

Student Data Files

Access your student data files needed to complete the exercises in this textbook at **www.pearsonhighered.com/exploring**.

Available in MyITLab

- **Multiple Choice quizzes** enable you to test concepts you have learned by answering auto-graded questions.

- **eText** available in some MyITLab courses and includes links to videos, student data files, and other learning aids.

- **Key Terms** quizzes enable you to test your understanding of key terms in each chapter.

(ex·ploring)

SERIES

1. Investigating in a systematic way: examining. 2. Searching into or ranging over for the purpose of discovery.

VBA for Microsoft® Office 2016

BRIEF

VBA
Visual Basic for Applications

LEARNING OUTCOMES
- You will use help files to learn more about VBA.
- You will use VBA to automate Excel worksheet calculations.
- You will use VBA to create decision structures in an Access database.

OBJECTIVES & SKILLS: After you read this chapter, you will be able to:

CASE STUDY | Wellington Animal Care

Wellington Animal Care is a local animal hospital, with four locations in Memphis and its surrounding suburbs. Each location offers full-service emergency care, vaccinations, boarding, and grooming. Bill Wellington, the owner of the hospital, manages the business with a series of Microsoft Excel workbooks and an Access database. He currently uses these documents to track client information, billing, health records, and employee information.

As a former intern, you were able to showcase your talents by creating macros to automate simple tasks in Excel and Access. Now you have been hired to help automate several tasks that are currently completed manually each month by using Visual Basic for Applications. You will automate the creation of payroll documents, automate sorting features within animal grooming worksheets, and customize the database with decision-making structures. Although you have limited professional programming experience, you have studied macro syntax (rules that you must follow for constructing code) and have confidence that you can complete the desired tasks.

Getting Started with VBA

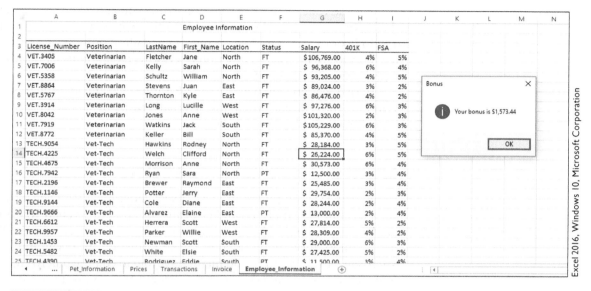

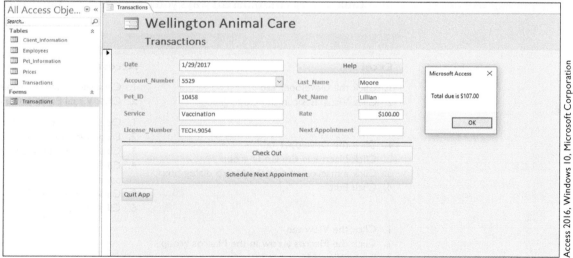

FIGURE 1.1 Wellington Animal Care Documents

CASE STUDY | Wellington Animal Care

Starting Files	Files to be Submitted
v1h1AnimalCare.xlsm	v1h4AnimalCare_LastFirst.xlsm
v1h1AnimalCare.accdb	v1h3AnimalCare_LastFirst.accdb

Introduction to VBA

Visual Basic for Applications (VBA) is a programming language that you can use to create and customize Office applications to enhance their functionality. VBA—which is included with Microsoft Office 2016—is a subset of Visual Basic, a stand-alone robust programming language that is, in turn, part of Visual Studio. Programmers use Visual Basic to create Windows and Web-based applications. Unlike Visual Basic, VBA requires a host application, such as Excel, Access, or PowerPoint.

You can use VBA to customize Excel workbooks or to enhance Access database objects. For example, you might want to modify a command button for exiting an Access database so that the user has an opportunity to cancel the procedure if he or she clicks the button by mistake. You can use VBA to create data entry forms, add custom menus, and hide or display interface elements depending on user access. Office developers also use VBA to create custom functions, perform calculations using variables and constants, and process database records.

In this section, you will use the VBA interface and identify types of code in the Code Window. You will learn then how to create, run, and debug a procedure. Finally, you will learn how to display message boxes.

Using VBA and Getting Help

When you record a macro in Excel, Excel generates VBA code for the actions you take, such as changing margins and clearing cell contents. When you use a wizard to create an Access control, such as a command button, Access creates the VBA code to provide functionality for actions, such as clicking the button. If you have created macros in a Microsoft Office program, you might have had to edit the macro code to add functionality to the macro or to correct an error. To modify macros, you use VBA.

Table 1.1 lists the different ways you can launch VBA in Excel and Access.

TABLE 1.1 Launch VBA	
Excel	**Access**
1. Click the Developer tab* 2. Click Visual Basic in the Code group	1. Click the Database Tools tab 2. Click Visual Basic in the Macro group
1. Click the Developer tab* 2. Click Macros in the Code group 3. Click a macro name in the Macro dialog box 4. Click Edit	1. Open a form or report in Design view 2. Display the Property Sheet 3. Click a specific control (such as a button) 4. Click the Event tab in the Property Sheet pane 5. Click an event, such as OnClick 6. Click Build
1. Click the View tab 2. Click the Macros arrow in the Macros group 3. Select View Macros 4. Click a macro name in the Macro dialog box 5. Click Edit	
1. 1. Press Alt+F11	1. Press Alt+F11

*If the Developer tab is not displayed, click the File tab, click Options, click Customize Ribbon, click the Developer check box in the Main Tabs list, and then click OK.

Pearson Education, Inc.

Use the VB Editor

 The Microsoft Visual Basic for Applications window is called the VB Editor. Figure 1.2 shows the VB Editor for an Excel workbook, and Figure 1.3 shows the VB Editor for an Access database. Notice the similarities between the windows: a menu bar, a toolbar,

Project Explorer, the Properties window, and the Code Window. If these items do not display on your screen, click View on the menu bar and select the item you want to display.

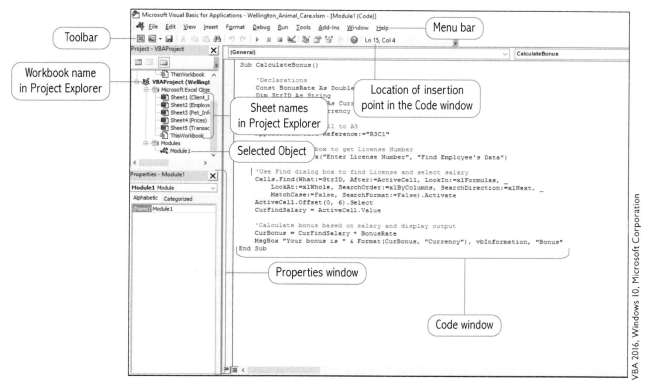

FIGURE 1.2 VB Editor for Excel

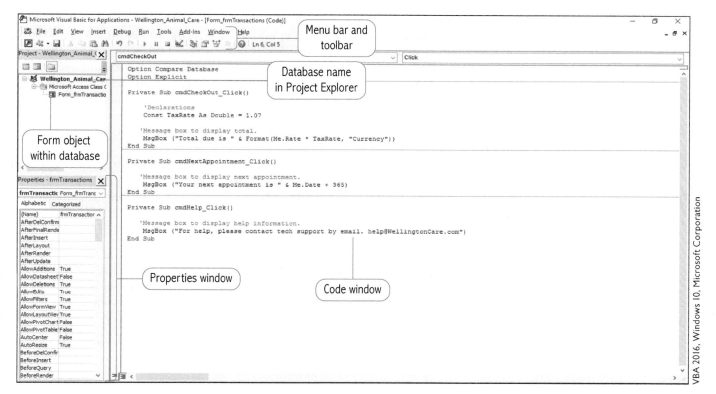

FIGURE 1.3 VB Editor for Access

Menu Bar and Toolbar

The menu bar and toolbar provide access to commands similar to how the Ribbon organizes commands in Excel and Access. The toolbar also indicates the location of the insertion point by line number and column number, such as Ln 15, Col 4 (see Figure 1.2) or Ln 6, Col 5 (see Figure 1.3), within the Code Window.

Project Explorer

The Project Explorer is on the left side of the VB Editor. A **project** is a collection of modules and objects needed to run an application. In VBA, a project is a particular Office file, such as an Excel workbook or an Access database, and its associated modules and macros. The Project Explorer lists all open projects. If three Excel workbooks are open, Project Explorer lists three projects. The project or file includes objects within that file (such as Sheet1 in Excel or Form frmTransactions in Access) and **modules**, which are containers to organize programming code. For example, Excel objects include worksheets, charts, and ranges. In Access, objects include tables, queries, forms, and reports. Click an object or module to display or write code for that selected object or module in the Code Window.

Properties Window

The Properties window displays the **properties** or attributes for the selected object in the Project Explorer. In Figure 1.2, the Properties window shows the properties for Module1 that is selected in Project Explorer. In Figure 1.3, the Properties window shows the properties for the selected Form frmTransactions object. The Properties window is similar to the Property Sheet you use to set properties for database objects in Access. For example, in Access, you can display the Property Sheet to set properties such as the number of decimal points for a calculated field in a query. If the Properties window is not displayed, select View from the menu and select Properties Window.

Code Window

The **Code Window** is a workspace text editor for writing and editing VBA programming statements. When the Code Window is maximized, it takes up most of the screen area. Programming statements include procedures, variable and constant declarations, mathematical expressions, and so on. A module consists of one or more **procedures**, which are named sequences of statements that perform a series of actions for a defined task. When you create several macros in a workbook, Excel stores each macro as a procedure in one module. The macro name becomes the name of an individual procedure in VBA.

When you create a VBA procedure using the VB Editor, you enter your code statements in **design time**, the mode for designing or creating programming code. When you execute a procedure, VBA executes the procedure's code in **runtime**, the mode during which a program is being executed.

TIP: MACRO-ENABLED EXCEL WORKBOOK
When you create macros or write VBA procedures for an Excel workbook, you must save it in the Macro-Enabled Workbook file format (.xlsm), Excel Macro-Enabled Template (.xltm), or Excel Binary Workbook file format (.xlsb). Regular Excel workbooks (.xlsx) cannot store VBA code.

Get Help

Use Help to learn more about VBA, explain terminology, or provide examples of programming code.

> **To get help for VBA, complete the following steps:**
>
> 1. Click Microsoft Visual Basic for Applications on the toolbar or select Help and then select Microsoft Visual Basic for Applications Help. The Microsoft Developer Network will open in a Web browser.
> 2. Type a keyword or phrase in the Search box in the top-right corner of the browser and click Search MSDN, the button on the right side of the Search box.
> 3. Click a link to a topic for more information.

For specific context assistance, select a keyword or function, such as MsgBox, within the Code Window and press F1. The Microsoft Developer Network will open a browser window and display specific help for the function. Figure 1.4 shows Help information about the MsgBox function.

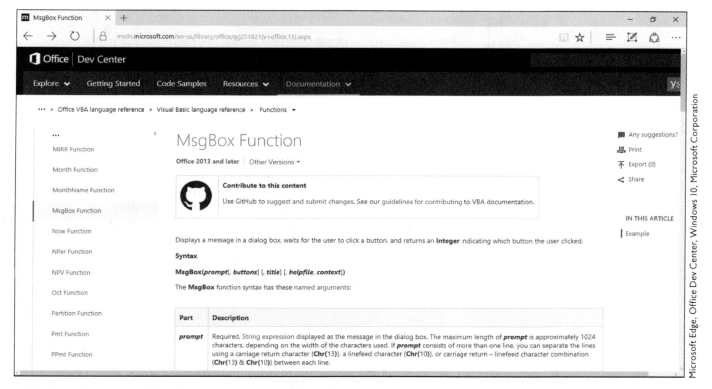

FIGURE 1.4 Help for MsgBox Function

Identifying Code in the Code Window

Before you edit existing code or start to write code, you should learn how to identify different elements in the Code Window. The more you study VBA statements generated by creating macros, the more you will be able to identify the code and start editing it or writing your own code. Programming code must follow proper syntax or rules. Programming syntax is similar to grammar and punctuation rules you follow when writing a paper for an English class. If you do not follow proper programming syntax, the program will fail to execute fully. Figure 1.5 identifies code elements.

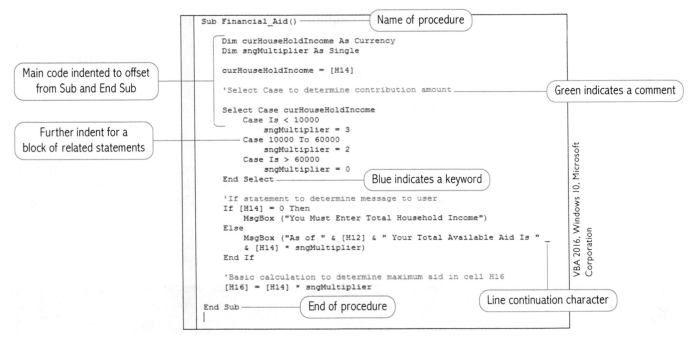

```vba
Sub Financial_Aid()                                    Name of procedure

    Dim curHouseHoldIncome As Currency
    Dim sngMultiplier As Single

    curHouseHoldIncome = [H14]

    'Select Case to determine contribution amount      Green indicates a comment

    Select Case curHouseHoldIncome
        Case Is < 10000
            sngMultiplier = 3
        Case 10000 To 60000
            sngMultiplier = 2
        Case Is > 60000
            sngMultiplier = 0
    End Select                                          Blue indicates a keyword

    'If statement to determine message to user
    If [H14] = 0 Then
        MsgBox ("You Must Enter Total Household Income")
    Else
        MsgBox ("As of " & [H12] & " Your Total Available Aid Is " _
        & [H14] * sngMultiplier)
    End If

    'Basic calculation to determine maximum aid in cell H16
    [H16] = [H14] * sngMultiplier

End Sub                         End of procedure
```

Main code indented to offset from Sub and End Sub

Further indent for a block of related statements

Line continuation character

VBA 2016, Windows 10, Microsoft Corporation

FIGURE 1.5 Programming Code

A procedure begins with Sub and ends with End Sub. Sub includes the procedure name, such as Sub Financial_Aid(). Statements between Sub and End Sub define the tasks that will be executed when you run the procedure. You must define each procedure separately. You cannot nest one procedure within another procedure.

For readability, indent the statements within a procedure to offset them from the Sub and End Sub statements. In addition, if a statement takes up more than one line, indent the continuation lines so that other programmers know at a glance that the carryover lines are part of the same statement. Figure 1.5 illustrates the indented carryover lines for the MsgBox function. You should further indent additional, related blocks of code to indicate coding hierarchy.

Customize the VB Editor

The Code Window color-codes words in black, blue, green, and red. Black indicates properly written programming statements that are free from syntax errors. Red indicates a syntax error. A *syntax error* occurs when you misuse or misspell a keyword, use incorrect punctuation, have not defined a procedure, or violate any other programming rules specific to the language. In addition, the Code Window supports automatic completion of certain statements you enter or adjusts capitalization if needed. Much like other areas of the Office suite, the VB Editor can be customized. Features can be added to the menu bar and the default code colors can be edited.

To customize code colors in the VB Editor, complete the following steps:

1. Click Tools on the menu bar.
2. Click Options.
3. Click Editor Format.
4. Select the desired Code Colors to customize from the list of options.
5. Select the desired Foreground, Background, and Indicator color options.
6. Click OK.

Identify Keywords

Blue words, such as *Sub* and *End Sub*, are keywords. **Keywords** are words or symbols particular to a programming language and have specific purposes. Some general keywords include With, End With, True, False, Do, and Loop.

Keywords are grouped into different categories. For example, procedural keywords include Call, Function, Property Get, and Sub. Decision-control structures use keywords such as Choose, If...Then...Else, Select Case, and Switch. Use Help to learn about the keywords specific to VBA.

Document Code with Comments

Documenting a program is important. As you write programming code, you know what it should do. However, after a few months you might not remember what the code does or if you take over a project from another programmer or are working on a program with multiple programmers, you could spend a considerable amount of time deciphering the code. Therefore, a good programming practice is to include comments within the code. Often programmers in an organization follow a set of coding conventions, such as comments, indenting, and naming techniques, so that all programmers on a development team will create consistent programming code.

A **comment** is a remark or text that documents or explains what a section of code does. Comments are not executable code. A comment appears in green and begins with an apostrophe or the keyword Rem (derived from the word *remark*) followed by a space. Keep comments brief yet descriptive, such as the comment in Code Window 1.1.

```
' Display input box to get percent increase in budget
```

CODE WINDOW 1.1

Identify Objects and Methods

When you create objects, such as Excel macros and Access controls, the host application creates a procedure. Procedures are uniquely named and contain a sequence of programming statements to execute an algorithm. These procedures are contained within modules. VBA has two types of modules: standard modules and class modules. A **standard module** stores procedures that can be used by any object in the application. When you use the macro recorder in some Office applications, such as Excel or Word, or add a module to a workbook, the code for the macro is stored in a standard module.

A **class module** enables you to create an object template along with the properties and methods that decide how the object behaves. These custom objects can have properties and methods similar to the built-in objects, and you can create multiple copies of these objects. Microsoft Access uses class modules to store the procedures associated with objects on a form or report. You can also create class modules in Excel to store procedures for specific objects, such as forms that a VBA procedure displays in a workbook.

VBA is an **object-oriented programming language** in which methods revolve around objects and actions that manipulate those objects. Recall that Excel objects include worksheets, charts, and ranges. In Access, objects include tables, queries, forms, and reports. **Methods** are actions pertaining to the objects. For example, you can Select (method name) an Excel range (object). When you record a macro to select cell A4 or range B4:B10 in an Excel worksheet, the VBA code identifies the object, such as Range("A4") or Range("B4:B10"), and then the action, such as Select. In Access, you can manage macros in dialog boxes. The first line of code in Code Window 1.2 shows how to select a cell or a range in Excel. The second line of code shows how to use the ClearContents method to clear the data in the specified range.

```
Range("A4").Select
Range("B4:B10").ClearContents
```

CODE WINDOW 1.2

In some cases, you need to qualify methods within the hierarchy of objects. For example, a workbook object contains a worksheet object, and a worksheet object contains range objects. When you specify the hierarchy of objects, separate the object names with periods. Code Window 1.3 shows an example of using Excel objects and methods. *ActiveWorkbook* is the main object. Worksheets is an object within the Active Workbook. ("Sheet3") defines which worksheet object you are referring to. The sheet name is enclosed in quotation marks. *Sort* is a method acting on the Sheet3 data, *SortFields* is an object referring to the list of data to sort. The SortField collection is a bundle of SortField objects that allows you to manipulate a sort. *Clear* is a method or an action acting on the SortFields object.

```
ActiveWorkbook.Worksheets("Sheet3").Sort.SortFields.Clear
```

CODE WINDOW 1.3

> **TIP: AUTO LIST MEMBERS**
> When you type a period, the Auto List Members feature displays a list of potential objects, properties, or methods that can logically complete the statement. For example, after you type *Active-Workbook.*, VBA displays a list of applicable items that relate to the active workbook. If you type W, VBA will scroll through the list to the first item starting with a W. You can continue typing the object, property, or method name, press Tab or double-click the word in the list to insert it into the code.

Creating, Running, and Debugging Procedures

Custom applications use VBA to process information or perform actions in response to events. An **event** is an action that occurs when the code is running, such as the user clicking a button that triggers a program instruction at runtime. For example, you can write VBA code to specify what an object does in response to the event. The system triggers some events, such as when Access opens a form. Users trigger other events by performing specific actions, such as selecting an item in a list or a menu option.

VBA supports three kinds of procedures. A **sub procedure** is a procedure that performs an action but does not return a specific value. A **function procedure** is a procedure that performs an action and returns a value, similar to how functions return values in Excel. A **property procedure** is a procedure that creates or manipulates a custom property. Most procedures you create with VBA will be sub procedures or function procedures.

All procedures are either public or private. A **public procedure** is available to any object in an application; the code for an object anywhere in the application can use the code statements. A **private procedure** is available only to a specific object or module. Procedures are public by default, unless the procedure is associated with a specific event, such as clicking a button.

Create a Procedure

STEP 2 ⟩⟩ Sub procedures begin with the Sub statement and end with End Sub. The code for a procedure must be contained between these two statements. In Figure 1.2, the Sub CalculateBonus() statement begins the procedure, which is contained in a standard module. The procedure is public and is available to any object in the Wellington Animal Care workbook. This is useful when more than one procedure must perform the same action, such as changing user preferences or validating an action before closing the application. Rather than writing the code in each procedure that performs the action, you can write the code once and access the procedure from multiple objects.

To create a procedure within the Code Window in the VB Editor, complete the following steps:

1. Type Sub in Excel or type Private Sub in Access, press Spacebar, and type a name for the procedure. The procedure name cannot have spaces. However, you can use Pascal Case (where you capitalize the first letter of each word) to type a multi-word procedure name such as FacultySort.
2. Press Enter, and VBA will enter the End Sub statement automatically.
3. Press Tab to indent the procedure code and type the procedure statements between the Sub and End Sub statements.
4. Click Save on the toolbar.

STEP 3 ⟩⟩ If you are adding a procedure for a control (such as a command button) on an Access form, start the procedure with Private Sub cmdCloseForm_Click(), where cmdCloseForm is the name of the control, such as a command button, and Click is the event to trigger the procedure.

Run and Debug a Procedure

STEP 4 ⟩⟩ After you create a procedure, you can run it. Running a procedure is the process of executing the statements in the procedure.

To run a procedure from within the VB Editor, complete one of the following steps:

*   Click Run Sub/UserForm on the toolbar
*   Click Run from the menu bar and select Run Sub/UserForm

The Debug menu helps you identify errors in programming code by stepping through the code to isolate the specific problem. If a procedure contains an error, you can debug it to identify the error.

To debug a procedure within the VB Editor, complete the following steps:

1. Click within a procedure to position the insertion point within the Code Window, click Debug on the menu bar, and then select Step Into. VBA will highlight the first statement.

2. Click Continue (the same as Run) on the toolbar to step through the procedure statements. VBA displays an error message if a statement contains an error. Figure 1.6 shows an error message if the object variable or with block variable is not set.

3. Click Help to display information about the error, or click Debug to highlight the statement that contains an error so that you can correct it.

4. Look for an error, such as a word that does not start with a capital letter. The lowercase word may indicate an incorrect object, method, or property name.

5. Click Reset on the toolbar to exit debugging mode.

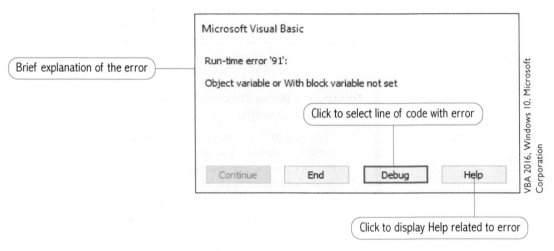

FIGURE 1.6 Debugging Error Message

TIP: DEBUGGING SHORTCUTS
When debugging a lengthy procedure, you can save time by using keyboard shortcuts. Use the keyboard shortcut F8 to quickly Step Into code to isolate an error. Use the variation SHIFT+F8 to Step Over a specific line of code and Ctrl+Shift+F8 to Step Out.

Creating a Message Box

A common task for programmers is to display a message to the user. For example, you might want to display a message that announces that changes were saved to a database table or that the user entered an incorrect value in an Excel cell. Programmers also create message boxes to display intermediate or final calculations in a process. *Message boxes* are small dialog boxes that contain a title bar, a message, an icon, and one or more buttons. During runtime, the program halts until the user clicks a button on the message box. When the user clicks the button, the message box closes, and a specific action programmed to that button executes.

Use the MsgBox Function

To create a message box in VBA, you use the MsgBox function. The MsgBox function can be used either as a function that can return values or as a statement. The *MsgBox statement* displays a message onscreen. This statement is useful when you need to provide a message, such as a confirmed change or error alert, to the user. The default options for a message box include the title of the application in the title bar, the message, and an OK button. The code statement that defines a message box is identical in Access and Excel. Code Window 1.4 illustrates the code to display a message box. Figure 1.7 shows an example of a message box created using the MsgBox statement in Access.

```
Private Sub cmdHelp_Click()

    'Message box to display help information.
    MsgBox ("For help, please contact tech support by email. help@WellingtonCare.com")
End Sub
```

CODE WINDOW 1.4

FIGURE 1.7 Message Box in Access

Using the **_MsgBox function_** displays a message on the screen and returns an integer value indicating which button the user clicked in the message box. Note that although there is only one MsgBox function, arguments are the same if used as a statement or a function, using it as a function provides additional features. The MsgBox function is useful when the program needs to have the user make a choice by clicking a particular button, such as OK or Cancel, and you need to store a specific value depending on that choice. In addition, the MsgBox function enables you to customize the title bar, include an icon, and specify which buttons to display. Like Excel functions, VBA functions include a function name and the arguments. An **_argument_** is a value in the form of a constant, variable, or expression that provides necessary information to a procedure or function, similar to how arguments provide necessary data for Excel functions. The MsgBox function contains four arguments in a specific sequence. If you omit an argument, VBA assigns a default value. The syntax for the MsgBox function is as follows:

MsgBox("prompt" [, buttons] [, "title"] [, helpfile, context])

The prompt argument is the message or information that appears within the main area of the message box. It is called the prompt argument because it prompts the user to click a button within the message box. The title argument is the text that will appear in the title bar of the message box when you run the procedure. You must type the text for the prompt and title arguments within quotation marks.

Prompt is the only required argument; the other arguments—indicated by brackets above—are optional, but typically included. If you omit an optional argument that occurs before another argument you define, you must enter a comma as a placeholder for the omitted argument.

Display Buttons and Icons in a Message Box

The second argument in the MsgBox function enables you to specify buttons and icons you want to display in the message box. Each button requires a different syntax, and some display a set of buttons. For example, the following code will display Yes and No buttons:

```
MsgBox "Welcome to Wellington Animal Care, would you like to login?", vbYesNo, "Welcome"
```

If you want to use the default OK button only but want to specify the message box title, type the prompt, two commas, and then the title. Table 1.2 lists some of the button syntax and the buttons displayed by the syntax.

TABLE 1.2   Message Box Buttons and Icons

Button Syntax	Displays
VbOKOnly	OK
vbOKCancel	OK Cancel
vbAbortRetryIgnore	Abort Retry Ignore
vbYesNoCancel	Yes No Cancel
vbYesNo	Yes No
vbRetryCancel	Retry Cancel
vbCritical	❌
vbQuestion	❓
vbExclamation	⚠
vbInformation	ℹ

Pearson Education, Inc.

You can specify buttons, icons, or both. For example, you might want to display the OK button and the Exclamation icon. Because the default displays the OK button, you can specify only vbExclamation for the second argument. You cannot combine two or more button sets (such as both vbYesNo and vbRetryCancel) or two or more icon sets (such as both vbCritical and vbInformation) in the same statement. However, you can combine a button set with an icon set by typing a + between the button and icon codes, such as vbYesNo+vbExclamation.

The MsgBox function returns an integer value based on which button the user clicks. The statement must do something with that returned value. Often, you will assign that value to a variable. Code Window 1.5 shows three sample buttons or icons and sample combinations. The prompt argument is *Welcome!* in all three lines of code. In the first line of code, the title bar displays *VBA in Access*, and the vbExclamation symbol displays in the message box. Unless you explicitly state a button, OK is the default button that displays. See if you can recognize what will display in the message boxes for the second and third lines of code.

```
Dim intValue As Integer

intValue = MsgBox("Welcome!", vbExclamation, "VBA in Access")
intValue = MsgBox("Welcome!", vbYesNo, "VBA in Access")
intValue = MsgBox("Welcome!", vbYesNo + vbExclamation, "VBA in Access")
```

CODE WINDOW 1.5

Because the MsgBox function returns an integer value based on which button the user clicks, you must assign the returned value to a variable or to do something else with the returned integer. You will learn about the Dim statement and how to assign values to variables in the next section. Table 1.3 lists the buttons and their return values.

TABLE 1.3 Integers Returned by Button

Button	Integer Returned
OK	1
Cancel	2
Abort	3
Retry	4
Ignore	5
Yes	6
No	7

Pearson Education, Inc.

Code Window 1.6 illustrates the use of the MsgBox function. The first argument *"Welcome to Wellington Animal Care!"* contains the text for the message box shown in Figure 1.8. Because the statement is long, divide it into two physical lines by typing the **line-continuation character**, which is a space followed by an underscore (_). The second argument *vbYesNo+vbInformation* creates the Yes and No buttons and the Information icon. The third argument "VBA in Access" displays the text for the message box title bar. When the message box displays, the user clicks Yes or No. If the user clicks Yes, the MsgBox function returns the integer 6. If the user clicks No, the MsgBox function returns the integer 7. The integer is stored in the intMsgBoxReturn variable, and you can execute different statements, depending on the value of 6 or 7 that is stored in that variable.

```
Dim intMsgBoxReturn As Integer
    intMsgBoxReturn = MsgBox("Welcome to Wellington Animal Care!", _
                      vbYesNo + vbInformation, "VBA in Access")
```

CODE WINDOW 1.6

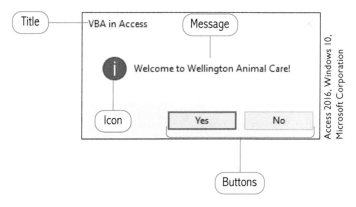

Access 2016, Windows 10, Microsoft Corporation

FIGURE 1.8 Message Box Created by MsgBox Function

1. What default colors are used in the Code Window, and what do these colors mean? *pp. 8–9*

2. What is the difference between a public and private procedure? *p. 11*

3. What is the benefit of using the Step Into feature to debug code? *pp. 11–12*

Hands-On Exercises

Skills covered: Use the VB Editor • Get Help
• Identify Keywords • Document Code with Comments
• Identify Objects and Methods • Create a Procedure
• Run and Debug a Procedure • Use the MsgBox Function
• Display Buttons and Icons in a Message Box

1 Introduction to VBA

Bill provided you with an Excel workbook and an Access database so that you can experiment with implementing VBA code. He wants to make sure you can succeed with some basic VBA commands before having you work on larger files.

STEP 1 ›› **USE VBA AND GET HELP**

You will open an Excel workbook and use the Help menu to find information about VBA and the MsgBox function. Refer to Figure 1.9 as you complete Step 1.

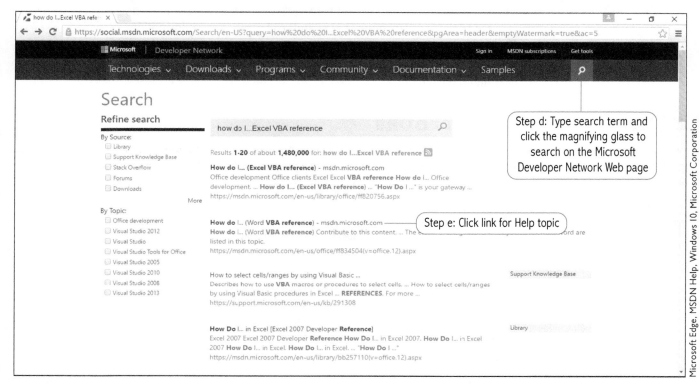

FIGURE 1.9 MSDN Help

> **a.** Start Excel, open *v1h1AnimalCare.xlsm* (an Excel macro-enabled workbook), and save it as **v1h1AnimalCare_LastFirst.xlsm**.

TROUBLESHOOTING: If the Security Warning toolbar displays, click Enable Content. If you make any major mistakes in this exercise, you can close the file, open *v1h1AnimalCare* again, and then start this exercise over.

---

b. Click the **Developer tab** and click **Visual Basic** in the Code group.

The VB Editor opens and shows existing VBA code for a macro.

> **TROUBLESHOOTING:** If the Developer tab is not displayed, click the File tab, click Options, click Customize Ribbon, click the Developer tab check box in the Main Tabs list on the right side, and click OK.

c. Maximize the VB Editor and Code Window.

d. Click **Microsoft Visual Basic for Applications Help** (the question mark) on the toolbar.

The Microsoft Developer Network (MSDN) for Excel Office 2013 and later webpage opens in a browser.

e. Click the magnifying glass, type **How do I...(Excel VBA reference)** in the Search help box and click **Search MSDN** (the magnifying glass).

The results window displays a list of hyperlinked topics.

f. Click the **How do I...(Excel VBA reference)** link to open a window containing a list of tutorials. Scroll through the list and read some of the information.

g. Adapt steps d and e to search for **Create a Procedure** and **MsgBox Function**. Read a few articles from each of the search results. Close the browser window after reading about each topic.

STEP 2 » CREATE A PROCEDURE

The Excel workbook contains a macro to sort the list of employees in alphabetical order by position, and then to further sort in alphabetical order by last name. You will study this macro code to create a new procedure that sorts the list by position, then by status, and then by last name in descending order. Refer to Figure 1.10 as you complete Step 2.

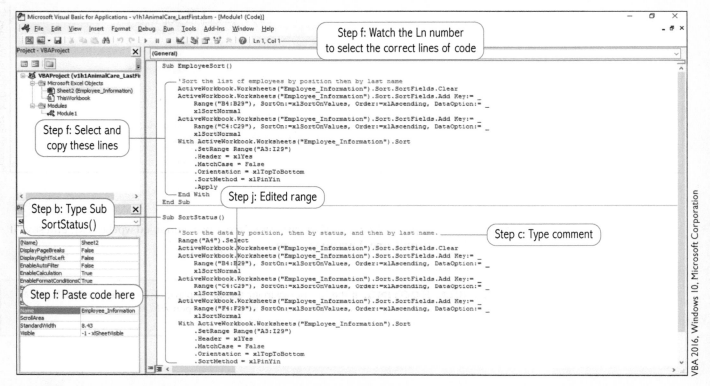

FIGURE 1.10 SortSalary Procedure

a. Position the insertion point in the Code Window, press **Ctrl+End** to position the insertion point on the line below the EmployeeSort procedure End Sub statement, and press **Enter**.

The existing EmployeeSort procedure sorts the list by position and then further by last name.

b. Type **Sub SortStatus()** and press **Enter** twice.

The VB Editor creates a corresponding End Sub statement and displays a horizontal line between the EmployeeSort procedure's End Sub statement and the Sub SortStatus() statement to separate the procedures visually.

c. Press **Tab**, type **'Sort the data by position, then by status, and then by last name.** Then press **Enter**.

The comment displays in green in the Code Window. You indented the main code to offset it from the *Sub* and *End Sub* statements for readability.

d. Type **Range("A4").Select** and press **Enter**.

After you type *Range("A4")*. VBA's Auto List Members feature displays a list of potential items to complete the statement. The Range("A4").Select statement selects a cell in the range to be sorted.

e. Type **ActiveWorkbook.Worksheets("Employee_Information").Sort.SortFields. Clear** and press **Enter**.

After you type *ActiveWorkbook* and the period, VBA displays a list of potential objects that relate to the ActiveWorkbook object. You can select from the list or continue typing the programming statement. This statement clears any prior sort settings in the current Employee_Information worksheet in the active workbook.

f. Select **Ln 5 through the end of Ln 17** of code in the EmployeeSort procedure (look at Figure 1.10 and the toolbar to identify the line numbers), stopping before the *End With* statement, click **Copy** on the toolbar, click below the line of code you typed in the SortStatus procedure (Ln 25), and click **Paste** on the toolbar.

You copied most of the code from the EmployeeSort procedure to the SortStatus procedure to minimize time typing code and to avoid creating syntax errors. Now you need to edit the code so that the procedure will also sort by employee status.

TIP: LOCATION STATUS
Look at the toolbar to identify the lines (Ln) within the Visual Basic Editor to make sure you are copying and editing code as instructed in these steps.

---

g. Select **Ln 29 through the end of Ln 31** and click **Copy** on the toolbar.

You copied three lines of code to use in the modification of the sort procedure.

h. Place the insertion point on **Ln31, Col21**, press **Enter,** and then press **Paste** on the toolbar.

You added the code from the prior sort level to use as a template for the additional sort criteria.

i. Place the insertion point at **Ln32 Col9** and press **Backspace**.

You decreased the indent to make the additional line of code easier to identify.

j. Select **C4:C29** on Ln 33 and type **F4:F29**.

The range F4:F29 contains the employee status information. This portion of the procedure will now sort the data by employee status in ascending order.

k. Click **Save**, close the workbook, and exit Excel.

The Wellington Animal Care database contains five tables and two forms. Currently, the frmTransactions form has five buttons, but only the Quit button works. You have been asked to write the VBA code for the Close Form button. Refer to Figure 1.11 as you complete Step 4.

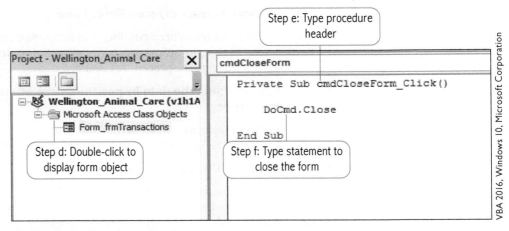

FIGURE 1.11 Close Button Code in Access

a. Start Access, open *v1h1AnimalCare.accdb* (an Access database), and save it as **v1h1AnimalCare_LastFirst.accdb**.

> **TROUBLESHOOTING:** If the Security Warning bar displays, click Enable Content. If you make any major mistakes in this step, you can close the file, open *v1h1AnimalCare* again, and then start this step over.

b. Open the frmTransactions form, and click each button on the form: **Help**, **Check Out**, **Schedule Next Appointment**, **Close Form**, and **Quit App**.

The Quit button is the only button that has been programmed. The Quit button quits or closes the entire database. You will write the code for the Close Form and Help buttons.

c. Click the **Database Tools tab**, and click **Visual Basic** in the Macro group to open the VB Editor.

d. Ensure **Wellington_Animal_Care** is displayed in the Project Explorer and if not already selected, click **Form_frmTransactions**.

The Code Window is now displayed for the Form_frmTransactions.

e. Click in the Code Window and type **Private Sub cmdCloseForm_Click()** and press **Enter** twice.

VBA adds the End Sub statement. You created a procedure with a name that includes *cmdCloseForm*, which is the Close Form button's name (cmdCloseForm). After typing the command button name, you type an underscore and specify the event (Click). Next, you will specify the action to take when the user clicks that button.

f. Press **Tab**. Type **DoCmd.Close** and press **Enter**. Compare your code to the code shown in Figure 1.11.

g. Click **Save** on the toolbar and close the VB Editor.

The frmTransactions form is open in Design view in Access.

h. Right-click the **frmTransactions tab** at the top of the form window and select **Form View** to display the form in Form view. Click **Close Form** at the bottom of the form.

The form closes, but the database remains open (unlike when you click the Quit button).

You want to run the SortStatus procedure to ensure it sorts the list correctly. As you run the procedure, an error message displays. You will correct the error and run the procedure again. Refer to Figure 1.12 as you complete Step 3.

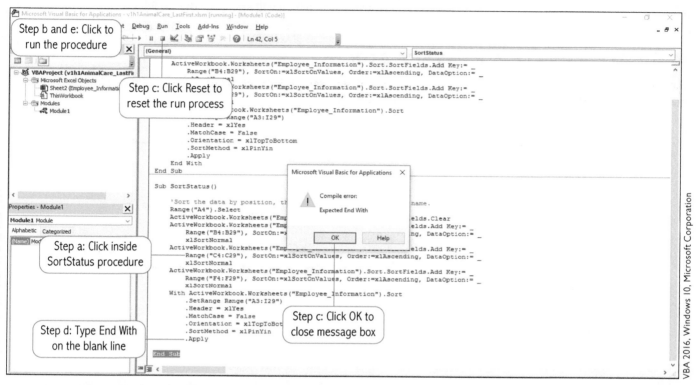

FIGURE 1.12 Run and Debug a Procedure

a. Open the Excel workbook *v1h1AnimalCare_LastFirst*, display the VB Editor, and place the insertion point in the SortStatus procedure you created in step 2.

b. Click **Run Sub/UserForm** (the green triangle) on the toolbar.

A message box displays, informing you that a compile error occurred. The message includes *Expected End With* because the required ending statement was not copied in step b. The VB Editor highlights the procedure name, indicating a problem exists.

c. Click **OK** to close the message box and click **Reset** on the toolbar so that you can correct the error and run the procedure again.

d. Type **End With** on Ln 44 Col 5, the blank line between *.Apply* and *End Sub*. Make sure *End With* is indented to align with the With statement on Ln 37. Click **Save** on the toolbar.

e. Click **Run Sub/UserForm** on the toolbar.

Nothing changes in the VB Editor; however, the procedure runs in the Excel workbook.

f. Minimize the VB Editor and look at the Excel workbook.

The list is sorted in ascending order (largest to smallest) by Position, then by status, and lastly by last name.

g. Click **Macros** in the Code group on the Developer tab, select **EmployeeSort** in the dialog box, and click **Run**.

The list is sorted in alphabetical order by position and then by last name. You can run procedures from either the Macros dialog box or from within the VB Editor.

h. Click **Macros** in the Code group on the Developer tab, select **SortStatus** in the dialog box, and then click **Run**.

The list is sorted in ascending order (largest to smallest) by position, status, and last name again.

i. Save the workbook. Exit Excel, which will also close the VB Editor.

Bill wants a message box to appear in the company database when users click the Help button. You need to add a MsgBox statement to do this. Refer to Figure 1.13 as you complete Step 5.

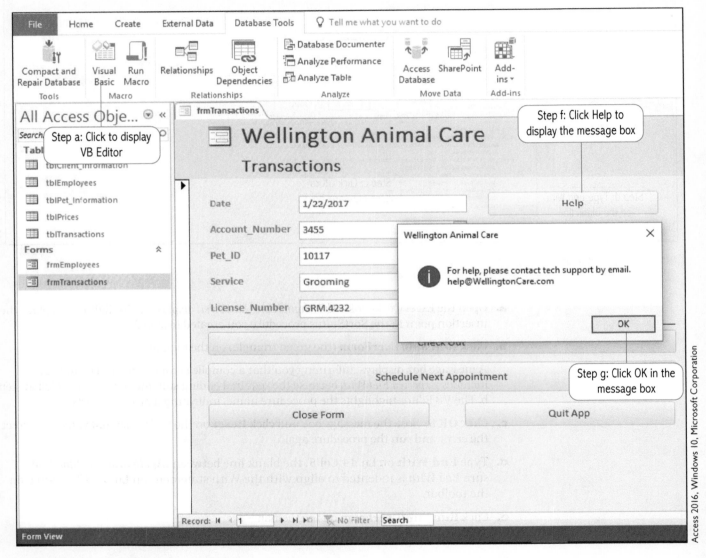

FIGURE 1.13 Message Box for the Help Button

a. Ensure the v1h1AnimalCare database is still open, click the **Database Tools tab,** and click **Visual Basic** in the Macro group.

b. Press **Ctrl+End** to go to the end of the code and press **Enter**.

c. Type **Private Sub cmdHelp_Click()** and press **Enter** twice.

d. Press **Tab**. Type **MsgBox** *"For help, please contact tech support by email. help@ WellingtonCare.com"*, **vbInformation**, *"Wellington Animal Care"*, and press **Enter**.

You created a message box to display tech support contact information.

e. Click **Save** on the toolbar and close the VB Editor.

f. Display the frmTransactions form in Form view. Click **Help** at the top of the form.

The MsgBox statement displays the message, an Information icon, and the title. By default, the message box will also display the OK button.

g. Click **OK** in the message box, click **Close Form** at the bottom of the form, and exit Access.

Variables, Constants, Inputs, and Outputs

When a program is running, it needs to be able to accept input, perform calculations, and then display output. For example, in a payroll program, the inputs need to include an employee's name or ID, the hours worked, and the hourly pay rate. The processing takes the inputs to calculate the regular pay, overtime pay, total gross pay, income taxes and other deductions withheld, and net pay. The output displays the results of the calculations. In addition to specifying the inputs, processing, and outputs, the program needs mechanisms for storing data. Programmers create variables and constants to store values that are then used in other statements to perform calculations or manipulate data during execution.

In this section, you will learn how to declare variables and constants, assign descriptive names, and select appropriate data types. In addition, you will learn how to obtain user input, store the input in variables, and display output.

Declaring and Using Variables and Constants

Variables are programmer-defined names that store values that can change while the application is running. Variables store values in computer memory, and your code statements can change the value at any time. Because variables are stored in computer memory, a value for a variable exists only while a program is running. When the program ends, the ability to access the value in memory is lost. The advantage to using variables is that the value can change. For example, you might originally record an order of one dessert at a restaurant and then change the order to two desserts.

Constants store values that are specified at design time and that remain the same (or constant) while the application is running. Only a programmer can change a constant's value at design time; users cannot change a constant's value during runtime. Declaring and using constants is important in a program because it prevents the use of raw, unidentified values within mathematical expressions. VBA supports three types of constants:

- ***Intrinsic constant*** is a constant specific to an application, such as Microsoft Excel or Microsoft Access. You can use the Object Browser to view constants in the object library. You cannot create a user-defined constant that uses the same name as an intrinsic constant.

- ***Symbolic or user-defined constant*** is a constant created by a programmer.

- ***Conditional compiler constant*** is defined in the host application. The compiler uses it to determine when or if specific Visual Basic code blocks are compiled. (Because this type of constant is more specialized, it will not be discussed or illustrated in this chapter.)

TIP: VARIABLE OR CONSTANT?

When deciding whether to create a variable or a constant, ask yourself if a user should be able to change a value. For example, if you want the user to specify hours worked, create a variable to accept and store that input. If the user should not be changing a value, such as a sales tax rate, create a constant to store the tax rate.

Select a Data Type

All variables and constants have a ***data type***, which refers to the kind of data the variable or constant can hold and how the data is stored in the computer's memory. Data types assigned to variables in programming code are similar to assigning data types to fields in

Access tables. You must specify the type of data that can be stored in an Access table field. Because variables and constants are stored in memory, good programmers select the appropriate data type that uses the least amount of memory necessary to store various kinds of information, such as text and numbers. Because each data type has different memory requirements, you can conserve computer memory, increase the speed of your application, and minimize programming errors by carefully selecting the most appropriate data type for the kind of data your application needs to store. Table 1.4 lists the data types in VBA.

TABLE 1.4 Data Types

Data Type	Data Stored in the Variable	Memory Used
Boolean	Only two possible values: True or False	2 bytes
Byte	A whole number ranging from 0 through 255	1 byte
Currency	Value ranging from −922,337,203,685,477,5808 to 922,337,203,685,477,5807. Use Currency data type to store values that you will use to calculate monetary amounts.	8 bytes
Date	Dates or times	8 bytes
Decimal	Value that contains decimal numbers scaled by a power of 10	12 bytes
Double	Double-precision floating-point numbers with 14 digits of accuracy. See VBA Help for exact value ranges.	8 bytes
Integer	Whole numbers ranging from −32,768 to 32,767	2 bytes
Long	Whole numbers ranging from −2,147,483,648 to 2,147,483,647	4 bytes
Object	A reference to an application object	4 bytes
Single	Single-precision floating-point numbers with six digits of accuracy. See VBA Help for exact value ranges.	4 bytes
String (fixed length)	Alphanumeric data, including letters, numbers, spaces, punctuation, and other characters with a fixed length	1 to approximately 63K characters
String (variable length)	Alphanumeric data, including letters, numbers, spaces, punctuation, and other characters with a variable length	0 to 2 billion characters
Variant	Default type if no specific data type is assigned	Up to 22 bytes plus the length of a text string
Type (user defined)	Structured data that contains data appropriate to the required elements in a range	Size depends on the data definition

Pearson Education, Inc.

How do you determine the appropriate data type? If you need to store a text string such as a person's name, use the String data type. A String data type can be either a fixed length—if you know exactly how many characters are needed—or variable length allowing up to 2 billion characters. If you need to perform calculations on dates, use the Date data type.

For numeric data, such as 100 items in stock, a tax rate of 5%, gross pay of $1,500, or a number expressed as an exponent, such as 3.2×10^{23}, the data type requires more consideration. Table 1.4 shows that the Integer and Long data types store whole-number (non-decimal) values. Because these data types store only whole numbers, they are called *integral data types*. Therefore, if you need to store a whole number value for calculations, such as the number of items in stock or the term of a loan, use an integral data type.

Non-integral data types, such as Single and Double, represent numbers with integer and fractional parts. The Single and Double data types store floating-point numbers. You can use these types to store numbers that are extremely small or extremely large.

Floating-point (Single and Double) numbers have larger ranges but can be subject to rounding errors. Thus, if you use two decimal point numbers in calculations, very small rounding errors might occur. The errors are too small to be of any significance unless you are working with complex monetary calculations. If your application makes complex calculations using money, use the Currency or Decimal data type.

TIP: VARIABLES FOR CURRENCY VALUES

For monetary calculations, such as calculating the value of inventory or a monthly loan payment, some programs perform best if you use the Single data type, whereas others perform best with the Currency data type. This book uses the Currency data type for monetary calculations.

Choosing the appropriate data type for variables is important. Table 1.5 provides examples of the recommended data types for various kinds of data.

TABLE 1.5   Recommended Data Types

Data to Store	Data Type	Example
Employee address	String	100 Elm Street
Number of graduating students	Integer	1234
Marital status	Boolean	0 (married) or 1 (not married)
Speed of light	Double	2.99 10^8
Age of a person in years	Integer	24
Population of a major metropolitan city	Integer	250763
Gross pay for a pay period	Currency	2526.41
Net 30 payment due date	Date	12/01/2018
Term of a loan in months	Integer	360
Total sale amount	Currency	360.27
Constant *pi*	Double	3.1415926535897
Local sales tax rate	Single	0.065
Estimated world population in 2020	Long	7000000000

Pearson Education, Inc.

Name Variables and Constants

In addition to choosing a data type, you must choose a name for your variables and constants. You will then use those names to store and retrieve values to manipulate when the program is running. The standards for naming variables and constants in VBA follow requirements and recommendations.

Requirements

- Use a letter as the first character for a variable or constant name.
- Do not use disallowed characters: space, period (.), exclamation mark (!), @, &, $, and #.
- Create names that are 255 or fewer characters in length.

Recommendations

- Use descriptive names that tell the purpose of a variable or constant and the kind of data it contains.

- Begin the name with the first three characters indicating the data type (in lowercase) and the remainder specifying the variable's purpose (beginning with an uppercase letter). For example, a variable for storing the number of units might be named intQuantity, where *int* indicates the data type (Integer) and *Quantity* is a descriptive name for the values the variable holds (number of units). The first three characters appear in lowercase, with the remaining part of the variable name appearing as descriptive words that begin with uppercase letters. Use Camel Case for descriptive names with more than one word. Table 1.6 lists the Hungarian notation—the three-character designation for each data type—and gives an example of how to apply the Camel Case convention. Some programmers use the Hungarian notation, whereas other programmers omit the three-letter prefix to simplify code. You should use the naming style preferred by your organization.

TABLE 1.6 Variable Prefixes and Sample Names

Data Type	Prefix	Example Variable Name
Boolean	bin	binMaritalStatus
Currency	cur	curNetPay
Date	dtm	dtmNet30
Double	dbl	dblSpeedOfLight
Integer	int	intQuantity
Long	lng	lngPopulation
Object	obj	objCurrent
Single	sng	sngSalesTax
String	str	strAddress

Pearson Education, Inc.

In previous versions of Visual Basic, programmers capitalized constant names and used an underscore between words, such as TAX_RATE. However, the current naming convention for user-defined constants is Pascal Case, such as TaxRate.

Intrinsic constants defined by an application for specific objects use a two-character prefix and mixed-case format. For example, the prefix vb represents a constant in the VBA object library, and xl represents a constant from the Excel object library.

Declare Variables and Constants

STEP 1 ⟩⟩ When you want to define a variable, you must include a declaration statement. The *declaration* statement assigns a name and data type and allocates memory to store a value for the variable or constant. When you declare a variable or a constant, you can specify its accessibility or *scope*. The scope specifies which program statements can access the value stored in the variable or constant. If you declare a variable or constant within a procedure that you want to be available to only that procedure, it is a local variable or constant and has procedure scope. This means that other procedures cannot directly access the variable or constant. If you want to make a variable or constant accessible to any procedure within an Access form, for example, you create a module-level (or form-level) variable or constant, which has module scope.

Declare a local variable at the top of a procedure or declare a module-level variable at the top of the module code in the Code Window using the *Dim* statement, short for Dimension. A declaration statement has the following syntax:

`Dim VariableName As DataType`

After you type the *Dim* keyword, type the variable name, type As, and then type the data type. Code Window 1.7 provides examples of variable declarations.

```
Dim blnMaritalStatus As Boolean
Dim curNetPay As Currency
Dim intQuantity As Integer
Dim strAddress As String
```

CODE WINDOW 1.7

To declare a user-defined constant, start with the keyword *Const* and include the constant name. In addition, you must assign a value that will not change during the runtime of the application. The value must match the data type you specify. For example, if you declare an integer constant, you cannot assign a value of 0.09 to it because integers store whole numbers only. Code Window 1.8 shows sample constant declarations.

```
Const SalesTaxRate As Double = 0.09
Public Const TaxRate As Double = 0.09
Private Const CityTaxRate As Double = 0.09
```

CODE WINDOW 1.8

To be able to use a value stored in a variable or constant in all procedures in a project, use the *Public* statement instead of the *Dim* statement. To ensure that variables are properly declared before being used, you should type the statement **Option Explicit** at the top of the Code Window. If Option Explicit is on, you must explicitly declare a variable before assigning a value to it. If you do not enter that statement, VBA enables you to create variables on the spot, which can lead to errors in an application. It is good programming practice always to declare variables before using them.

By default, constants are private, and cannot be accessed by all procedures in the module, as shown in Code Window 1.8. You cannot change a constant's availability within a procedure. However, in a standard module, you can add the keyword *Public* at the beginning of the declaration statement to make a constant available to "all procedures in all modules." You can limit a constant's availability to a specific module only by including the keyword *Private* at the beginning of the declaration.

TIP: AUTO SYNTAX CORRECTIONS

VBA checks for and corrects some errors for you when the Auto Syntax Check check box is selected in the Options dialog box. For example, if you forget to add a space before and after the assignment operator (=), VBA will insert the spaces for you when you press Enter. Other automatic corrections include changing case, such as changing *as integer* to *As Integer* or making a variable's case match its case in the declaration statement. Select Tools on the menu, and then select Options to verify the Auto Syntax Check setting.

Assign Values to Variables and Constants

As shown in Code Window 1.8, an assignment statement is one that assigns a value to a variable or constant. With constants, the declaration and assignment must occur within one statement because once the constant is declared and assigned a value that value cannot change during runtime. For variables, you create separate declaration and assignment statements. Code Window 1.9 shows examples of variable declaration and assignment statements for an integer and a string. The variable name goes on the left side of the = operator, and the value being assigned goes on the right side of the = operator. When you assign text to a string, you must enclose the text within quotation marks.

When you assign dates to a Date variable or constant, you must type the date in a mm/dd/yyyy (two digits for the month and day, and four digits for the year) format enclosed in pound sign (#) characters, such as #07/01/2018#. This value, known as a date literal, assigns the proper date to the variable or constant.

```
Dim intQuantity As Integer
intQuantity = 100

Dim strLastName As String
strLastName = "Johnson"
```

CODE WINDOW 1.9

Assign Values to Cells and Ranges

While working with VBA in Excel, you will frequently need to reference cells to access or to insert a value. There are several options within VBA to reference a cell. A popular option is using the Cells method. The **Cells method** enables you to reference a cell by using its column and row positions with either index or **R1C1 style** addresses. The index address is similar to the A1 style (column letter, row number) used commonly in Excel; however, it requires the row number to be entered before the column letter. For example, *Cells(3, "B").Value = "Indiana"*, would insert the word *Indiana* in cell B3. The same method would appear in R1C1 style as Cells(3,2), where 3 references the row number and 2 references column B, as it is the second column in the worksheet. Table 1.7 displays examples of A1 style compared to R1C1 style.

TABLE 1.7 A1, Index, and R1C1 Styles

A1 Style*	Index Style	R1C1 Style
B2	Cells(2,"B")	Cells(2,2)
C2	Cells(2,"C")	Cells(2,3)
D5	Cells(5,"D")	Cells(5,4)

*A1 style cannot be used with the Cells method.

> **TIP: A1 STYLE REFERENCES**
> If you are new to R1C1 style and prefer A1 style addresses, square brackets can be used when creating simple references. [D3].Value = "Indiana" and Cells(3,4).Value = "Indiana" will both output the word *Indiana* in cell D3.

When working with multiple cells, the Range Property can be used. The Range Property enables you to define a range that can be used as a reference for input or output. Table 1.8 shows various applications of the Range Property to reference cells in Excel.

TABLE 1.8 Range Property in Excel

Example	Reference
Range("B6:B10")	Cells B6 through B10
Range("B:B")	Column B
Range("B:D")	Columns B through D
Range("7:7")	Row 7
Range("1:10")	Rows 1 through 10
Range("A1:A8, C1:C8")	Cells A1 through A8 and C1 through C8

Creating an Input Box

You need to plan how the data assigned to variables gets into an application. To obtain data from the user, you create an ***input box***. An input box is a dialog box that displays on the screen to prompt the user to enter a value. Like a message box, the program halts after displaying an input box until the user enters data and then clicks OK. Unlike message boxes, input boxes do not have icons.

Programmers use functions to simplify program code statements. VBA includes numerous functions such as the InputBox function to return values. Predefined VBA functions often require one or more arguments similar to Excel functions, such as the IF function. A code statement with a function contains the function name and one or more arguments. The arguments are the values supplied to the function. Arguments can be required or optional. If an argument is required, it must be included in the code statement. As you type a function in the Code Window, the VB Editor displays a pop-up window listing the required functions.

Obtain User Input with the InputBox Function

 The ***InputBox function*** (InputBox) prompts the user to enter a value that the application needs to perform an action. This function returns the value supplied by the user as a string. The syntax for the InputBox function is as follows:

```
InputBox(prompt[, title] [, default] [, xpos] [, ypos] [, helpfile, context])
```

The *prompt* is the message inside the input box and is required. The *title* is an optional argument. When specified, it displays the text that appears on the input box title bar. The optional *xpos* and *ypos* arguments specify the horizontal distance from the left edge of the screen and the vertical distance from the top of the screen, respectively, to display the input box. Code Window 1.10 shows the InputBox function used to get a pet's name, store it in a string variable, and then display a message box that contains a text string and the contents of the strPetName variable. Because the InputBox statement is long, it is divided into two lines by using the line-continuation character. If you do not use a line-continuation character at the end of the first line or if you use a line-continuation within string quotes enclosed within quotation marks, VBA will display an error. To combine two text strings together into one string, type & (the ampersand character) between them. Figure 1.14 shows the input box, and Figure 1.15 shows the resulting message box.

```
'Declare string variable
Dim strPetName As String
    'Display input box, acquire user input, & store variable
    strPetName = InputBox("Please enter the pet's name.", _
                 "Wellington Animal Care")

    'Display results in a message box
    MsgBox "Welcome " & strPetName & " !"
```

CODE WINDOW 1.10

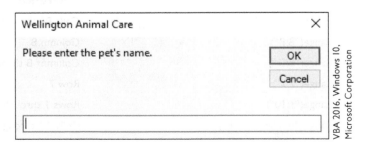

FIGURE 1.14 Input Box

FIGURE 1.15 Message Box

TIP: CONCATENATION CHARACTER

Use the ampersand character (&) or plus sign (+) to **concatenate**, or join, two values, such as MsgBox "Welcome "& strPetName &" !" shown in Code Window 1.10. Figure 1.15 displays the result of the code, Welcome Simba! The message box displays the text string Welcome and the value of the strPetName variable, which in this case is Simba. Concatenation is useful for joining text strings.

Convert Strings to Numeric Values Using the Val Function

When you obtain user input using the InputBox function, the value that the user supplies is returned to the procedure as a text string by default. This is fine for text data, but if you want to perform calculations on numbers entered into an input box, you need to use the **Val function**, which converts the value into numeric data for calculations.

The Val function stops reading the string when it encounters the first character it does not recognize as part of a number. Symbols and characters frequently added to numeric values (like currency symbols and commas) are not recognized. When the Val function encounters a nonnumeric character, it ignores the remaining characters in the string.

You can use the Val function in conjunction with the InputBox function to convert the string value into a numeric value for calculations. For example, Code Window 1.11 shows a procedure that uses the Val function to convert numbers entered as text into numeric values that can be used in calculations. This code declares and assigns text to string variables for the title and the message so that you can use the string variable names in the InputBox() function to simplify that line of code.

```
Dim strMessage As String
Dim strTitle As String
Dim curSalary As Currency

strMessage = "Please enter your annual salary."
strTitle = "Salary Data Entry"

    curSalary = Val(InputBox(strMessage, strTitle, "Type salary here"))
    MsgBox "You entered: " & curSalary
```

CODE WINDOW 1.11

This procedure prompts the user for his or her salary. The title of the input box uses the strTitle variable contents, *Salary Data Entry*, and the message uses the strMessage variable contents, *Please enter your annual salary*. Including *Type salary here* as the third argument in the InputBox function displays that value as a default value in the input box when the program runs. However, the user can type over that value. The Val function converts the user's entry from a text string to a numeric value, assigns it to the variable curSalary, and a message box displays the entry.

Performing Calculations and Formatting Results

To perform calculations within a procedure using variables, you need to create an arithmetic expression. Expressions use operators to perform calculations and join text strings. You can also format the results of calculations.

Use Operators and Order of Precedence

Many of the expressions you create to perform calculations contain functions and operators. An **operator** is a character or combination of characters that accomplishes a specific computation. VBA supports six kinds of operators: arithmetic, assignment, comparison, concatenation, logical, and miscellaneous. Table 1.9 lists the arithmetic operators supported in VBA.

TABLE 1.9 VBA Arithmetic Operators

Operator Symbol	Operator Name	Purpose
^	Exponentiation	Raises a number to the power of another number
*	Multiplication	Multiplies two numbers
/	Division	Divides two numbers and returns a floating point result
\	Integer Division	Divides two numbers and returns an integer result
Mod	Modulus arithmetic	Modulus arithmetic, which divides two integer numbers and returns only the remainder
+	Addition, concatenation	Adds two numbers; also used to concatenate two strings
−	Subtraction, negation	Yields the difference between two numbers or indicates the negative value of a numeric expression
+ or &	String concatenation	Combines two strings

Pearson Education, Inc.

When several operations occur in an expression, each part is evaluated and used in a predetermined order called operator precedence. **Order of precedence** is the order in which arithmetic operations are performed. Understanding operator precedence is important for creating expressions that produce the results you want. VBA performs arithmetic calculations left to right in the order: parentheses, exponentiation, multiplication or division, and finally addition or subtraction.

You can use parentheses to override the order of precedence and force some parts of an expression to be evaluated before others. When you use parentheses, operations within parentheses occur before those outside. Expressions within parentheses are evaluated according to operator precedence (multiplication, division, addition, subtraction). Code Window 1.12 shows example expressions that perform calculations using constants that have already been declared and variable values obtained from worksheet cells.

```
'Declare constants
Const conStTax As Single = 0.065
Const conCityTax As Single = 0.035

'Declare variables
Dim curSaleAmount As Currency
Dim curTotalTax As Currency
Dim curTotalSale As Currency

'Obtain the sale amount
curSaleAmount = Val(InputBox("Enter the sale amount: "))

'Calculate taxes and total sale amount
curTotalTax = curSaleAmount * (conStTax + conCityTax)
curTotalSale = curSaleAmount + curTotalTax

'Display result
MsgBox "The total sale is " & curTotalSale
```

CODE WINDOW 1.12

Given the two constants in Code Window 1.12, if a user enters 123.45 as the sales amount, the result is 135.795. The addition operation within parentheses occurs first: conStTax (0.065) is added to the conCityTax (0.035). The result of 0.1 is then multiplied by the curSaleAmount (123.45) to calculate the curTotalTax (12.345). Then, the curSaleAmount (123.45) is added to the curTotalTax (12.345); the result (135.795) is then stored in the curTotalSale variable and displayed in the message box.

Format Output Results

You should format values that you display onscreen as results. Unformatted results might display more decimal places than required or not include a currency symbol when you are displaying monetary units. For example, the result of the calculation appears as a decimal value with three digits to the right of the decimal: 135.795.

You can use the ***Format function*** to format the results of calculations. This function uses predefined formats to change the appearance of text. In its simplest form, the Format function has the following syntax:

Format (expression, style)

Expression refers to the string you want to format, and style refers to a named format. Table 1.10 lists the named number styles that you can use with the Format function. VBA also includes named formats for dates. Use Help to learn about other named formats.

TABLE 1.10 Named Styles for Number Formats	
Format Name	**Description**
General Number	Displays a value without a comma for the thousand separator
Currency	Displays a value with a dollar sign, a comma as a thousand separator, and displays two digits to the right of the decimal point
Fixed	Displays a value with at least one digit to the left and two digits to the right of the decimal point
Standard	Displays a value with a comma as a thousand separator with at least one digit to the left and two digits to the right of the decimal point
Percent	Displays values multiplied by 100 with two digits to the right of the decimal point with a percent sign (%) on the right side of the value
Scientific	Uses standard scientific notation
Yes/No	Displays the word *No* if the value is 0; displays the word *Yes* for any other value
True/False	Displays the word *False* if the value is 0; displays the word *True* for any other value
On/Off	Displays the word *Off* if the value is 0; displays the word *On* for any other value

Code Window 1.13 illustrates the use of Format functions.

```
Dim curSalary As Currency
Dim sngBonus As Single
Dim blnExempt As Boolean

curSalary = 47000
sngBonus = 0.065
blnExempt = 21

MsgBox "Salary: " & Format(curSalary, "Currency") _
       & Chr$(10) & Chr$(13) _
       & "Bonus: " & Format(sngBonus, "Percent") _
       & Chr$(10) & Chr$(13) _
       & "Exempt: " & Format(blnExempt, "Yes/No")
```

CODE WINDOW 1.13

The procedure in Code Window 1.13 also declares three variables and then assigns each a value. The MsgBox statement returns each variable formatted using a named style. To make the code easier to read, the statement uses the line-continuation character. Figure 1.16 displays the formatted results.

FIGURE 1.16 Message Box

TIP: CHR FUNCTION
The **Chr function** requires an integer as its argument and then returns a character associated with that integer. For example, Chr$(10) returns a line feed, and Chr$(13) returns a carriage return. You can create a hard return in a text string by combining the line feed and carriage return characters, as in the previous code example.

Quick Concepts

4. What is the difference between a variable and a constant? Provide an example of each. *pp. 27–28*

5. What is the difference between an input box and a message box? *p. 30*

6. What is the purpose of the Format function? *pp. 33–34*

Hands-On Exercises

Skills covered: Select a Data Type • Name Variables and Constants • Declare Variables and Constants • Assign Values to Variables and Constants • Assign Values to Cells and Ranges • Obtain User Input with the Input Box Function • Convert Strings to Numeric Values Using the Val Function • Use Operators and Order of Precedence • Format Output Results

2 Variables, Constants, Inputs, and Outputs

Bill asked you to create procedures that perform calculations in the Excel workbook and Access database. You will use your knowledge of message boxes, input boxes, variables, and constants to add the desired functionality. You will create a procedure to automate the Excel workbook so that he can search for an employee by unique ID, locate that person's salary, and then calculate a 6% bonus for that person.

STEP 1 ❯❯ DECLARE VARIABLES AND CONSTANTS

You will create a procedure and declare a constant to store the 6% bonus rate and three variables: License number, salary, and bonus amount. Refer to Figure 1.17 as you complete Step 1.

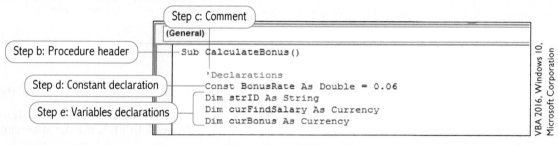

FIGURE 1.17 Declarations

VBA 2016, Windows 10, Microsoft Corporation

a. Open the macro-enabled *v1h1AnimalCare_LastFirst* workbook in Excel, save it as **v1h2AnimalCare_LastFirst**, changing h1 to h2, and display the VB Editor.

> **TROUBLESHOOTING:** If the Security Warning toolbar displays, click Enable Content.

b. Click at the top of the Code Window, type **Sub CalculateBonus()** and then press **Enter** twice.

c. Press **Tab**. Type **'Declarations** and press **Enter**.

It is good programming practice to enter comments for blocks of code.

d. Type **Const BonusRate As Double = 0.06** and press **Enter**.

You declared a constant to store the bonus rate. You must enter 6% as a decimal point equivalent in programming code: 0.06.

e. Type **Dim strID As String** and press **Enter**.

Type **Dim curFindSalary As Currency** and press **Enter**.

Type **Dim curBonus As Currency** and press **Enter**.

Compare your declarations to those in Figure 1.17. You declared a String to store the License Number, a Currency variable to store the employee's salary, and a Currency variable to store the calculated bonus amount.

f. Click **Save** on the toolbar.

STEP 2 〉〉 ## CREATE AN INPUT BOX

The procedure needs to prompt the user to enter a license number, store it in a variable, and use that variable to find the license number in the list. After the procedure finds the license number, it must make the respective salary the active cell. With the salary as the active cell, the procedure saves the salary value in a variable.

```
'Set the active cell to A3
Application.Goto Reference:="R3C1"

'Display input box to get License Number
strID = InputBox("Enter License Number", "Find Employee's Data")
```

CODE WINDOW 1.14

```
'Use Find dialog box to find License Number and select corresponding salary
Cells.Find(What:=strID, After:=ActiveCell, LookIn:=xlFormulas, _
    LookAt:=xlWhole, SearchOrder:=xlByColumns, SearchDirection:=xlNext, _
    MatchCase:=False, SearchFormat:=False).Activate
ActiveCell.Offset(0, 6).Select
curFindSalary = ActiveCell.Value
```

CODE WINDOW 1.15

a. Press **Enter**, type the code shown in Code Window 1.14, and then press **Enter** twice.

The Application.Goto statement is used to set the active cell. It makes the third row (R3) in the first column (C1) the active cell. In VBA, use the abbreviations R and C for row and column respectively.

> **TROUBLESHOOTING:** Look at Code Window 1.14 carefully as you type each statement. Pay close attention to spaces, periods, blank lines, and spelling to avoid syntax errors.

The last line of code in Code Window 1.14 displays an input box with the message *Enter License Number* and the title *Find Employee's Data*.

b. Press **Enter** and type the code shown in Code Window 1.15.

What:=strID is the equivalent of typing a value in the Find dialog box. You want to use the value in the strID variable. LookAt:=xlWhole requires that the entire cell must be identical to the data entered. If you search for 8, it finds 8 and not 86. SearchOrder:=xlByColumns searches down the current (ID) column rather than across by rows.

> **TROUBLESHOOTING:** A syntax error will occur if you forget to use a line-continuation character to continue a line of code. If a line-continuation character is missing, insert it at the end of each line (except the last) of a complete programming statement. In addition, make sure you type the letters xl, not x and the number 1.

The ActiveCell statement keeps the active cell on the same row (0) and moves over to the right by six cells (6) and makes that cell the active cell. That cell contains the salary for the ID you found. The last statement uses the active cell's value and assigns it to the curFindSalary variable.

c. Click **Save** on the toolbar.

To complete the procedure, you add an expression to calculate the bonus amount based on the identified salary and the constant bonus rate. After calculating the bonus, you format it and display it in a message box. Refer to Figure 1.18 and Figure 1.19 as you complete Step 3.

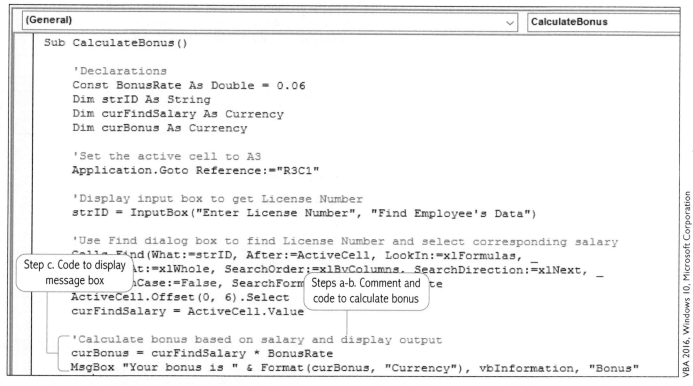

FIGURE 1.18 Code to Calculate and Display the Bonus

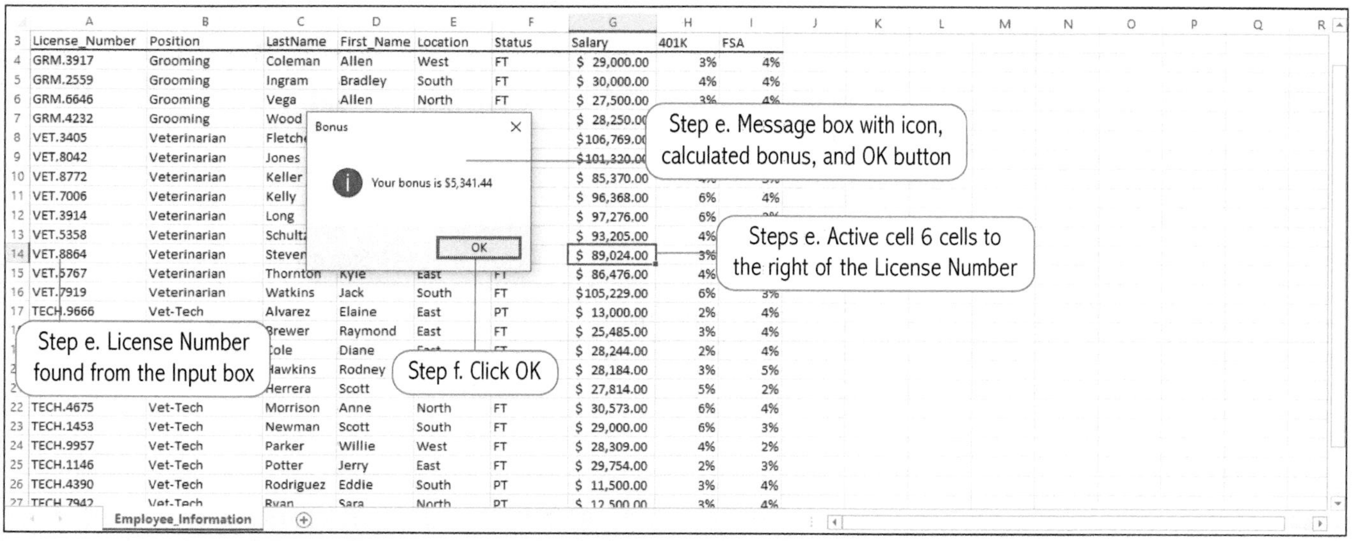

FIGURE 1.19 Bonus Calculated and Displayed

a. Press **Enter** twice after the *curFindSalary = Active.Cell.Value* statement. Type **'Calculate bonus based on salary and display output** and press **Enter**.

b. Type **curBonus = curFindSalary * BonusRate** and press **Enter**.

The expression takes the value in curFindSalary and multiplies it by the value 0.06 in the constant BonusRate. The result is then assigned to the curBonus variable.

c. Type **MsgBox "Your bonus is " & Format(curBonus, "Currency"), vbInformation, "Bonus"** and press **Enter**. Click **Save**.

This statement uses the Format() function to format the curBonus value in Currency format. That result is displayed with the text *Your bonus is* and then displayed in a message box. The message box also contains the Information icon.

> **TROUBLESHOOTING:** Check your code with Figure 1.18 to ensure you entered the statements correctly. The code should contain a space between *is* and the quotation mark to ensure a space displays between the word *is* and the actual salary value.

d. Click **Run Sub/UserForm** on the toolbar.

The Find Employee's Data input box opens.

e. Type **VET.8864** and click **OK**.

The procedure finds VET.8864 in the License_Number column, goes to the right by six cells to find the $89,024 salary, multiplies it by 6%, and displays $5,341.44 in the message box (see Figure 1.19).

f. Click **OK** in the message box. Close the VB Editor, and save and close the workbook.

STEP 4 ▶▶ **USE VARIABLES, CONSTANTS, INPUT, AND OUTPUT IN ACCESS**

You have been asked to expand the frmEmployees form so that it calculates and displays the monthly 401K contribution for an employee. Refer to Figure 1.20 as you complete Step 4.

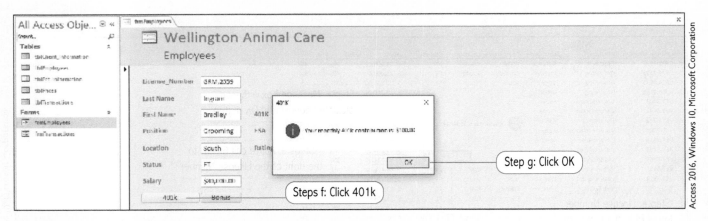

FIGURE 1.20 Message Box with Calculated 401k Value

```
Private Sub cmd401k_Click()
    'Declare three variables
    Dim cur401k As Currency
    Dim curSalary As Currency
    Dim sng401k As Single

    'Obtain values from text boxes on the form
    txtSalary.SetFocus
    curSalary = txtSalary.Text

    txt401k.SetFocus
    sng401k = Val(txt401k.Text) / 100

    'Calculate and display the monthly 401K contribution
    cur401k = curSalary / 12 * sng401k
    MsgBox "Your monthly 401k contribution is: " _
        & Format(cur401k, "Currency"), vbInformation, "401K"
```

CODE WINDOW 1.16

a. Open the *v1h1AnimalCare_LastFirst* database in Access, and save the database as **v1h2AnimalCare_LastFirst**, changing h1 to h2.

b. Click **Enable Content**. Open the frmEmployees form in Design view, click the **cmd401K button** (at the bottom labeled 401k on the form). If not already displayed, click Property Sheet in the Tools group to display the Property Sheet.

c. Select the **On Click event** on the Event tab. Click the **Build button,** select **Code Builder,** and then click **OK**.

This opens the VBE and automatically begins a Private Sub that will run when the cmd401K button is clicked.

d. Press **Tab** and type the code shown in Code Window 1.16.

You declared two Currency variables and one Single variable.

The txtSalary.SetFocus statement moves the focus to the txtSalary box during runtime. That is, when a user clicks the 401k button, the procedure makes the txtSalary box active to select its current value. The curSalary = txtSalary.Text statement uses the Text property, which contains the current value of the txtSalary box and then assigns that value to the curSalary variable.

The txt401K.SetFocus statement then sets the focus to the txt401K box. The sng401K = Val(txt401k.Text)/100 statement uses the Text property that contains the current value in the txt401k box, converts it to a value, divides that value by 100 to convert it to a decimal amount, and then assigns the result to the sng401K variable.

The next statement calculates the 401k value and stores the result in the cur401K variable. The last statement in the procedure displays a message box with the value in the cur401k variable formatted as Currency.

e. Click **Save** on the toolbar and close the VB Editor.

f. Change the view to Form view and click **401k** in the form.

Bradley Ingram's 401K contribution is $100.00 (see Figure 1.20).

g. Click **OK** and exit Access.

Decision Structures

When you customize applications with VBA, you write code using program statements that tell the computer exactly what to do based on a programming structure. A **programming structure** is the sequence in which the program statements execute at runtime. Programmers use programming structures to organize code statements in one of three ways: a sequence structure, a decision structure, or a repetition structure.

The **sequence structure** executes statements in the order that they appear. All of the sub procedures you have written up to this point use the sequence structure because the program statements execute in a direct sequence when the procedure runs—that is, the first statement runs, followed by each successive statement until all statements have run, with no statements skipped. Sequence structures are the simplest programming structures.

In this section, you will learn how to use another programming structure—the decision structure—in VBA procedures. Specifically, you will create procedures that use the If...Then, If...Then...Else, and Select Case decision structures. You will then learn how to use decision structures to perform data validation and how to include logical operators in decision structures.

Using Decision Structures

A **decision structure** is a programming structure that makes a comparison between values, variables, and/or constants. Based on the result of that comparison, the program executes statements in a certain order. If the result of the comparison is true (or yes), one statement executes, but if the result of the comparison is false (or no), an alternative statement executes. Thus, the result of the comparison determines which path the program takes.

By phrasing the conditions in terms of a question, you can determine the appropriate course of action. For example, *Is the curGrossPay value greater than or equal to 500?* A **condition** is an expression that uses a **relational operator** (such as = and <=) to compare two values (through variables, constants, or expressions) and determine whether the result of the comparison is true or false. Recall that an expression is a combination of variables and operators that performs a calculation or returns a value. A comparison that uses relational operators is a **logical test**, which is always contained within a decision structure. In programming, you can use a logical test within your program statements to respond to conditions that vary. VBA uses the relational operators listed in Table 1.11.

TABLE 1.11	**Relational Operators**	
Format Name	**Test Whether the Value of ...**	**Example**
=	Two operands are equal	txtLastName.Text = Lackridge
<>	Two operands are not equal	Val(txtLoanAmount.Text)<>0
<	The first operand is less than the value of the second operand	Val(txtLoanAmount.Text)<25000
>	The first operand is greater than the value of the second operand	Val(txt401k.Text)>100000
<=	The first operand is less than or equal to the second operand	sngConversionResult<=300
>=	The first operand is greater than or equal to the second operand	curGrossPay>=500

Pearson Education, Inc.

Decision structures use relational operators to make comparisons that perform a logical test. You can use a decision statement to test whether a condition is true or false, to test a series of conditions, or to make a selection when a condition is true. Table 1.12 lists the decision structures supported in VBA.

TABLE 1.12	Decision Structures Supported in VBA
Decision Statement	**Use**
If...Then	Performs a logical test. If the test evaluates to true, the program executes a specific statement or block of statements.
If...Then...Else	Performs a logical test. If the test evaluates to true, the program executes a specific statement or block of statements. If the test evaluates to False, the program executes a different statement or block of statements.
Select Case	Compares the same expression to several different values. The Select statement evaluates a single expression only once and uses it for every comparison. When the test evaluates to true, the case is applied.

Pearson Education, Inc.

Create An If...Then Structure

STEP 1 ⟫ The **If...Then structure** represents the simplest kind of decision structure. An If...Then structure performs a logical test; if the test evaluates to True, the program code specifies what action to take. No alternative statements are executed if the logical test is false, however.

Suppose an employer wants to encourage its employees to make a year-end contribution to the company's 401K retirement plan. The standard match is 25%. If an employee contributes more than $500, the company will match the contribution at 50%. You can phrase this decision as a question:

- Is the contribution greater than $500?
- Yes: Match is 50%
- No: Match is 25% (keep the original 25% match)

Code Window 1.17 shows how to implement this decision in a VBA procedure.

```
Sub DecisionStructure()

    Dim curContribution As Currency
    Dim sngMatch As Single
    sngMatch = 0.25

    curContribution = Val(InputBox("Enter the contribution amount", _
                "401k contribution"))

     'Test if contribution is greater than 500
     'If true, assign 0.5 to sngMatch
     'If false, maintain existing value (0.25)
     If curContribution > 500 Then
         sngMatch = 0.5
     End If

    MsgBox "We will match your contribution by " & _
            Format(sngMatch, "Percent")
```

CODE WINDOW 1.17

This procedure declares two variables: a Currency data type for contribution amount and a Single data type for the match percentage, which is assigned a default value of 0.25. An input box prompts the user to enter a contribution amount. The If...Then structure performs the logical test; if the contribution exceeds 500, it assigns a new value to the sngMatch variable. A message box displays the match percentage. For example, if a user types 600 in the input box, the message box will display 50.00%. If the user types 500 in the input box, the message box will display 25.00%.

Create an If...Then...Else Structure

STEP 2 ▶▶ You can use an *If...Then...Else structure* to test for a condition and specify one option if the test evaluates to True and another option if it evaluates to False. Use the If...Then...Else structure to determine the appropriate matching percentage for an employee's 401K contribution. Because the structure tests a condition and specifies a path for a True and a False result, you do not need to set a default value for the sngMatch variable. Figure 1.21 illustrates the process using a flowchart, and Code Window 1.18 shows the code. The code in Code Window 1.18 does the same thing as the code in Code Window 1.17. However, some programmers prefer to assign a value explicitly to a variable instead of relying on the program to maintain a previous value for a variable.

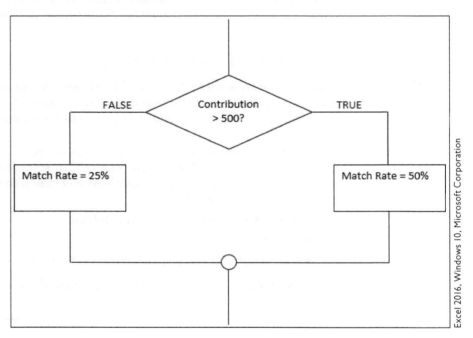

FIGURE 1.21 If...Then...Else Flowchart

```
Dim curContribution As Currency
Dim sngMatch As Single


curContribution = Val(InputBox("Enter the contribution amount", _
              "401k contribution"))

'Test if contribution is greater than 500
'If true, assign 0.5 to sngMatch
'If false, maintain existing value (0.25)
If curContribution > 500 Then
    sngMatch = 0.5
Else
    sngMatch = 0.25
End If

MsgBox "We will match your contribution by " & _
        Format(sngMatch, "Percent")
```

CODE WINDOWS 1.18

The structure begins with *If* and ends with *End If*. The word *Then* must appear after the logical test. In this example, the procedure performs the logical test before assigning a value to the sngMatch variable. Note that the logical test sngContribution > 500 is executed only once. The test evaluates to either True or False. If the result is True, the statement after Then is executed. If the result is False, the statement after the Else is executed.

> **TIP: USING THE ELSEIF STATEMENT**
>
> At times, you need to test additional conditions when the first logical test evaluates to False. You can add additional conditions using the ElseIf statement. You can combine multiple ElseIf conditions as long as the final condition uses the Else statement. You can also nest If statements within one another to test multiple conditions. Because nested If structures can become difficult to manage, the Select Case structure is often used as an alternative.

Create a Select Case Structure

STEP 3 ›› The conditions you need to test sometimes become complex and require one or more If statements nested within another If statement. Suppose Wellington Animal Care pays employees an annual bonus that is a percentage of the employee's salary. The percentage used is determined by the employee's performance rating. Managers rate employee performance on a 10-point scale (see Table 1.13). For example, if an employee gets a rating between 1 and 3, that person earns a 5% bonus.

TABLE 1.13	Ratings and Bonus Percentages
Performance Rating	**Bonus Percentages**
0	No Bonus
1–3	5%
4–8	7.5%
9 and above	10%

Pearson Education, Inc.

You can determine each employee's rating using nested If structures. Figure 1.22 models this decision in a flowchart. The circle at the bottom of the flowchart indicates the end of the algorithm.

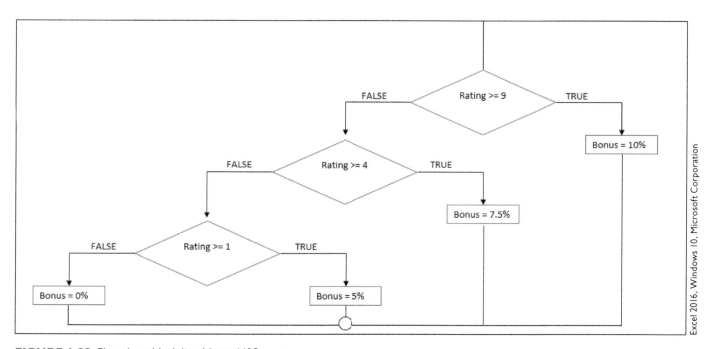

FIGURE 1.22 Flowchart Modeling Nested If Structure

You can nest as many levels of If structures as your application requires; however, nesting too deeply makes code hard to model, write, and manage. The Select Case structure is a good alternative to a nested If structure when you need to test a single variable or expression for multiple values, such as testing for an employee's performance rating and returning one of four possible values depending upon the rating. The Select Case structure is simpler than a nested If structure; the code is more concise for testing one value against multiple conditions.

The **Select Case structure** compares an expression or a value to a case block, which is the set of cases that might apply. A case is an individual condition to test. You can easily code this complex decision structure using the Select Case structure. Figure 1.23 models this decision with a flowchart, and Code Window 1.19 illustrates the use of a Select Case statement.

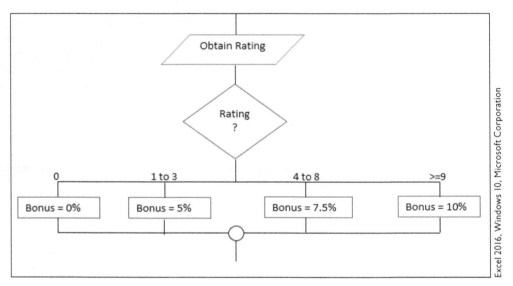

FIGURE 1.23 Flowchart Modeling Select Case Structure

```
Dim CurSalary As Currency
Dim curBonusPay  As Currency
Dim sngBonus As Single
Dim intRating As Integer

CurSalary = InputBox("Enter your salary", "Salary")
intRating = InputBox("Enter your performance rating", "Rating")

Select Case intRating
    Case Is < 1
        sngBonus = 0
    Case 1 To 3
        sngBonus = 0.05
    Case 4 To 8
        sngBonus = 0.075
    Case Is > 8
        sngBonus = 0.1
End Select

curBonusPay = CurSalary * sngBonus
MsgBox "Your bonus is " & Format(curBonusPay, "Currency")
```

CODE WINDOW 1.19

The case block begins with *Select Case* and ends with *End Select*. The Select Case structure uses the case block to determine the appropriate bonus rate based on the performance rating value. When the structure tests a single value, the *Case Is* statement is used. When the structure tests a range of values, the words *Case Is* are followed by the range of values. If a user enters 45500 for the salary and 5 for the performance rating, the calculated bonus is $3,412.50. An optional *Case Else* statement is not shown in the example. You can use this statement after all *Case Is* statements to catch all other conditions and perform an action.

Performing Data Validation

In the decision structures discussed thus far, we have assumed that the data entered into an input box is entered correctly. However, users can inadvertently enter text where a number is required, which can produce unintended results. Because computer output depends on the quality of the data the user supplies, programmers need to check the values entered in Windows forms to make sure the data is appropriate for its intended use.

The process of checking data entered by a user to ensure it meets certain conditions, such as a value within a particular range or values instead of text, is called **data validation**. You can use decision structures to display a message if the user fails to enter the required data or to ensure that users enter numbers where they are needed to perform calculations.

Check for a Required Value

A common data validation task is checking to make sure users input required data. You can use a simple If...Then...Else structure and a message box to confirm the data entered or to warn the user that required data is missing. Code Window 1.20 checks to make sure that users have entered an annual salary greater than 25000.

```
Dim curSalary As Currency

curSalary = Val(InputBox("Enter your salary", "Salary"))
If curSalary > 25000 Then
    MsgBox "You entered " & curSalary
Else
    MsgBox "Not a valid entry", vbCritical, "Invalid Data"
End If
```

CODE WINDOW 1.20

The Val function converts the user's entry into a numeric value. If text is entered instead of a valid number, the function returns a value of zero. The decision structure displays one of two messages, depending upon the value supplied.

Check for a Numeric Value

You have used the Val function to convert data entered into a text box to a numeric value for performing calculations. However, if the Val function encounters an empty text string, it converts the empty string to a value of zero. Therefore, it is important to validate numeric data before performing calculations.

VBA includes a function designed to determine whether data entered is a numeric value. The **IsNumeric function** checks a text string and determines whether it evaluates to a number. If the string does evaluate to a number, the function returns a Boolean value of True; otherwise, the function returns False. The function requires one argument: the expression to evaluate. The required argument can be a variable, a property of a control, or a text string. Code Window 1.21 illustrates the use of the IsNumeric function.

```
Dim varSalary
varSalary = InputBox("Enter your salary", "Salary")

If IsNumeric(varSalary) = False Then
    MsgBox "Enter your salary as a number"
Else
    MsgBox "You entered " & varSalary
End If
```

CODE WINDOW 1.21

This procedure declares a variable for the salary without specifying a data type, so the default data type is variant. The If...Then...Else structure checks the value. If the user has not made an entry or if the user enters invalid characters, the function returns False. A numeric or decimal value returns a Boolean result of True. For example, if the user enters 25000, the return value is True. If the user enters nothing, the return value is False.

Using Logical Operators

You can test for more than one condition in a decision structure by using logical operators. A *logical operator* is an operator that uses Boolean logic to test conditions. The *And operator* requires that all conditions included in the statement evaluate to True in order for the expression value to be true. The *Or operator* requires that any one of the conditions evaluate to True in order for the expression value to be true.

Use the Or Logical Operator

Code Window 1.22 shows a procedure that declares a string variable and prompts the user for a text string to assign to the variable. The procedure then uses the Or operator to validate the text string as being either Full time or Part time.

```
Dim strText As String
strText = InputBox("Enter either 'Full time' or 'Part time'")
If strText = "Full time" Or strText = "Part time" Then
    MsgBox "Your data entry passes the test: " & strText
Else
    MsgBox "Invalid Data", vbCritical, "Error"
End If
```

CODE WINDOW 1.22

If the user enters Full time or Part time, a message informs the user that the data is valid. If the user enters anything else or does not make an entry, a message informs the user that the data is invalid. The text comparisons are case sensitive. If the user enters full time or Full Time, the data entry does not match the text string specified in the logical test; therefore, the Invalid Data message box would appear.

Use the And Logical Operator

 You might need to perform a logical test to ensure that two or more conditions are true. For example, you want the user to enter a value within a particular range. Use the And logical operator to ensure the user input meets the minimum value and another test to ensure the user input does not exceed the maximum value. Code Window 1.23 declares an integer variable and then prompts the user for a value between 10 and 90. The procedure then uses the And operator to validate the entry as being greater than or equal to 10 and less than or equal to 90.

```
Dim intValue As Integer
intValue = InputBox("Enter an integer between 10 and 90")

If Val(intValue) >= 10 And Val(intValue) <= 90 Then
    MsgBox "Your data passed the test: " & intValue
Else
    MsgBox "Invalid Data", vbCritical, "Error"
End If
```

CODE WINDOW 1.23

If the user enters a number that is greater than or equal to 10 and less than or equal to 90, a message appears indicating that the data is valid. If the user enters anything else or does not make an entry, a message appears indicating that the data is invalid.

Quick
Concepts

7. Explain when to use an If...Then...Else structure and a Select Case structure. ***pp. 40–44***

8. In what situation would you use the IsNumeric function? ***p. 45***

9. What is the difference in using the Or and And logical operators in decision structures? ***pp. 46–47***

Hands-On Exercises

3 Decision Structures

Bill wants you to complete the programming code for the buttons on the frmTransactions and frmEmployees forms in the Access database. Specifically, you need to write procedures for the Check out, Schedule Next Appointment, and Bonus buttons.

STEP 1 ▶▶ **CREATE AN IF…THEN STRUCTURE**

Bill wants a confirmation message box to display when the user would like to complete a transaction. When a user clicks Check Out, the procedure should display a message asking for confirmation. If the user clicks Yes, the total based on the rate for the service performed and 6% sales tax will be displayed. Refer to Figure 1.24 as you complete Step 1.

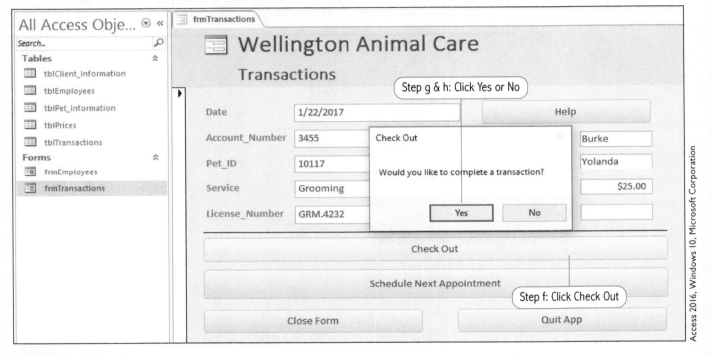

FIGURE 1.24 Message Box

a. Open the *v1h2AnimalCare_LastFirst* database if you closed it at the end of Hands-On Exercise 2 and save it as **v1h3AnimalCare_LastFirst**, changing h2 to h3.

b. Open the form frmTransactions in Design View and ensure that Property Sheet in the Tools group is toggled on and the Property Sheet pane is visible.

c. Select the **cmdCheckOut button** (labeled Check Out). Click the **Event tab**, select **On Click**, and then click **Build**. Select **Code Builder** and click **OK**.

d. Type the code shown in Code Window 1.24. The procedure header and End Sub statements should already exist.

```
Private Sub cmdCheckOut_Click()

    'Declarations
    Const sngTax As Single = 1.06
    Dim intCheckOut As Integer
    Dim curTotal As Currency

    intCheckOut = MsgBox("Would you like to complete a transaction?", vbYesNo, "Check Out")
    curTotal = sngTax * Me.Rate

    'If the user clicks Yes, a message box will appear calculating the total plus 6% sales tax.
    If intCheckOut = 6 Then
        MsgBox ("Total due is : " & Format(curTotal, "Currency"))
    End If

End Sub
```

CODE WINDOW 1.24

The MsgBox function returns an integer that is assigned to the intCheckOut variable. You use the If...Then decision structure to determine if the user clicked Yes, which is assigned an integer value of 6. If so, the procedure calculates the total amount due and displays the value in a message box. If the user clicks No, nothing happens. The database remains open with the form onscreen.

e. Click **Save** on the toolbar and close the VB Editor.

f. Display the form in Form view and click **Check Out** in the form.

g. Click **Yes** and click **OK**.

A message box appears displaying the total due at check out.

h. Click **Check Out** again. Click **No**.

The form and Access remain open.

Your next task is to create a procedure to schedule the next appointment. If the customer's pet was groomed, the next appointment should be scheduled in 30 days; all other appointments should be scheduled for 1 year from the current date. To complete this task, you create an If...Then...Else decision structure. Refer to Figure 1.25 and Code Window 1.25 as you complete Step 2.

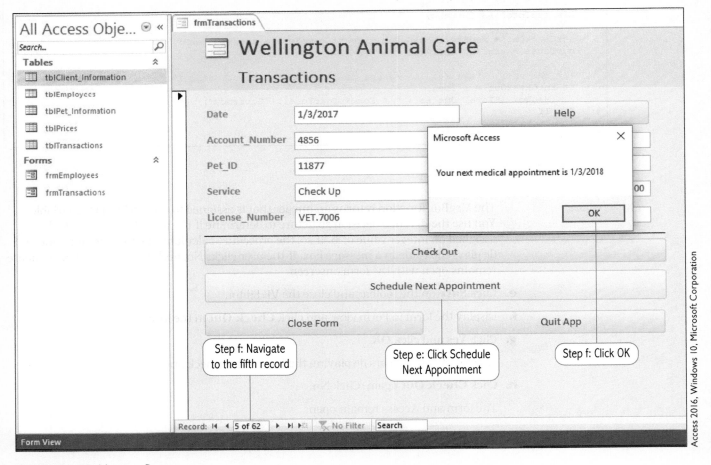

FIGURE 1.25 Message Box

```
Private Sub cmdNextAppointment_Click()

    'Create If...Then...Else statement to schedule next appointment
    If Me.Service = "Grooming" Then
        MsgBox ("Your next grooming appointment is " & Me.Date + 30)
        Me.txtNextAppointment = Me.Date + 30
    Else
        MsgBox ("Your next medical appointment is " & Me.Date + 365)
        Me.txtNextAppointment = Me.Date + 365
    End If

End Sub
```

CODE WINDOW 1.25

a. Open the frmTransactions form in Design view and ensure that the Property Sheet is displayed.

b. Click **cmdNextAppointment** (labeled Schedule Next Appointment). Click the **Event tab**, select **On Click**, and then click **Build**. Select **Code Builder** and click **OK**.

c. Type the code shown in Code Window 1.25. The procedure header and End Sub statement should already exist.

The If...Then...Else statement will use the date and service provided in the frmTransactions form to determine the next appointment. It will also insert the date of the next appointment in the txt.NextAppointment field.

d. Click **Save** and close the VB Editor.

e. Display the form in Form view and click **Schedule Next Appointment** in the form.

Because the first transaction in the database is for grooming, the message box displays 2/21/2017.

f. Click **OK**, navigate to the fifth record in the form, and click **Schedule Next Appointment**.

Because the fifth transaction was for a medical checkup, the next appointment is scheduled for 1/3/2018.

g. Click **OK** to close the message box, save, and close the form.

STEP 3 ⟫ CREATE A SELECT CASE STRUCTURE

Bill wants you to create a set of rules to calculate employees' bonuses based on their respective satisfaction ratings. A rating of 0 means no bonus. A rating of 1–2 earns a 5% bonus, a rating of 3–4 earns a 7.5% bonus, and a rating of 5 earns a 10% bonus. You will create a Select Case decision structure to identify the correct bonus rate and use that rate to calculate the bonus amount. Refer to Figure 1.26 and Code Window 1.26 as you complete Step 3.

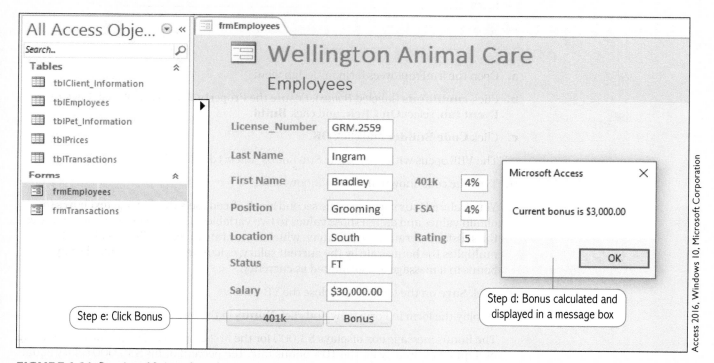

FIGURE 1.26 Results of Select Case Structure

```
Private Sub Bonus_Click()

    'Declare variables
    Dim curSalary As Currency
    Dim intRating As Integer
    Dim sngBonus As Single
    Dim curBonus As Currency

    'Obtain salary and performance ratings
    txtSalary.SetFocus
    curSalary = txtSalary.Text

    txtSatisfaction_Rating.SetFocus
    intRating = txtSatisfaction_Rating.Text

        'Calculates the bonus
        Select Case intRating
            Case Is = 0
                sngBonus = 0
            Case 1 To 2
                sngBonus = 0.05
            Case 3 To 4
                sngBonus = 0.075
            Case Is = 5
                sngBonus = 0.1
            End Select

        'Calculate the bonus and assign to the txtBonus text box
        curBonus = curSalary * sngBonus

        'Message box to display the current bonus
        MsgBox ("Current bonus is " & Format(curBonus, "Currency"))

End Sub
```

CODE WINDOW 1.26

a. Open the frmEmployees form in Design view.

b. Click **cmdBonus** (labeled *Bonus*). Ensure the Property Sheet is displayed. Click the **Event tab**, select **On Click**, and click **Build**.

c. Click **Code Builder** and click **OK**.

   The VBE opens with the Private Sub Bonus_Click() displayed.

d. Type the code shown in Code Window 1.26.

   You declared four variables. The second block of code sets the focus to text boxes to obtain values and assign those values to two variables. The Select Case statement uses the satisfaction rating to determine which bonus rate to select. The last block of code multiplies the bonus rate by the current salary, calculates the bonus, and displays the bonus in a message box formatted as currency.

e. Click **Save** on the toolbar and close the VB Editor.

f. Display the form in Form view and click **Bonus** in the form.

   The Bonus message box displays $3,000 for the first employee. The performance rating of 4 qualifies Bradley for the 10% bonus rate. Ten percent of his $30,000 salary equals his $3,000 bonus.

g. Click **OK** and save the form.

   The procedures you have written to obtain a value from a text box use the SetFocus method to set the focus to the text box and then assign the text value to a variable. In this procedure, you assigned the value of a variable to the Text property of a message box by setting the focus to the text box and then assigning the value of the variable to the Text property of the message box.

Before implementing the database for other users to use, you want to add one data validation structure. You want to make sure the user enters a whole number between 0 and 5 in the Rating text box on the form. If a user enters a negative value or a number higher than 5, you want to display an error message and select the text box contents so the user can try again. Refer to Figure 1.27 and Code Window 1.27 as you complete Step 4.

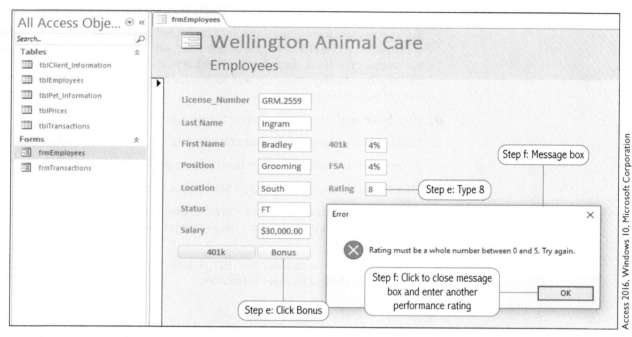

FIGURE 1.27 Results of Select Case Structure

```
'Obtain salary and performance ratings
txtSalary.SetFocus
curSalary = txtSalary.Text

txtSatisfaction_Rating.SetFocus

If Val(txtSatisfaction_Rating) >= 0 And Val(txtSatisfaction_Rating) <= 5 Then

    intRating = txtSatisfaction_Rating.Text

    'Calculates the bonus
    Select Case intRating
        Case Is = 0
            sngBonus = 0
        Case 1 To 2
            sngBonus = 0.05
        Case 3 To 4
            sngBonus = 0.075
        Case Is = 5
            sngBonus = 0.1
    End Select

    'Calculate the bonus
    curBonus = curSalary * sngBonus

    'Message box to display the current bonus
    MsgBox ("Current bonus is " & Format(curBonus, "Currency"))
Else
    MsgBox "Rating must be a whole number between 0 and 5. Try again.", _
        vbCritical, "Error"
    txtSatisfaction_Rating.SetFocus

End If
End Sub
```

CODE WINDOW 1.27

a. Display the VB Editor.

b. Use Code Window 1.27 to insert the If statement between the *txtSatisfaction_Rating. SetFocus* and *intRating = txtSatisfaction_Rating.Text* statements. Press **Enter** before typing the code to leave blank lines before the If statement. Press **Tab** to indent the intRating = txtSatisfaction_Rating.Text statement, and press **Enter** to leave a blank line after the statement.

c. Position the insertion point on the blank line below **Ln38, Col 5**. Use Code Window 1.27 to insert the Else, Message Box, and End If lines of code.

The If structure tests to see if the data contained in the Satisfaction Rating text box is a value between 0 and 5. If so, the data is valid, and the rest of the code to calculate the bonus executes. If the data is not valid (that is, the value is negative or more than 5), a message box displays the error and selects the text box value so that the user can enter a correct value and try again.

d. Click **Save** on the toolbar and close the VB Editor.

e. Select the value in the **Rating text box** on the form, type **8**, and click **Bonus**.

A message box displays because the data you entered is not valid.

f. Click **OK** in the message box, type **5**, and click **Bonus** on the form.

Because the performance rating 5 is valid, the message box does not display. The remaining code in the procedure executes, and the calculated bonus $3,000 displays in the message box.

g. Click OK to close the message box. Exit Access. You will submit this file to your instructor at the end of the last Hands-On Exercise.

Repetition Structures

Programmers use decision structures when an application requires a program to analyze conditions. Sometimes, however, you need to complete an operation a specific number of times while a certain condition is true or until a condition is true. For example, a payroll application may need to calculate employee bonuses for all eligible employees. To accomplish this, you can use a **repetition structure**, which repeats the execution of a series of program statements. You can use two types of statements to define repetition structures: For...Next and Do...Loop.

In this section, you will learn how to use For...Next and Do...Loop repetition structures.

Using the For...Next Structure

STEP 1 ▶▶ The **For...Next structure** repeats a **loop**—a set of statements or a procedure—a specific number of times. As the computer processes the statements, one execution of the loop is an **iteration**. When you use looping, which is the process of repeating a procedure until a condition is met, the statements repeat until the condition is true, until the condition is false, or until they have repeated for a specified number of times.

The For...Next statement requires a **counter variable**, which is used to count the number of times the loop repeats. The counter increases or decreases in value during each repetition of the loop. An increment is an increase in the value of the counter; a decrement is a decrease in the value of the counter. The start value is the value at which it begins incrementing or decrementing. The end value is the final value of the counter. When the counter reaches this value, the loop ends. The **step value** is the amount by which the counter is incremented or decremented during each cycle of the loop. The step value, which is optional, can be positive or negative. If it is omitted, VBA supplies a default value of 1.

Code Window 1.28 shows an incrementing For...Next loop and a decrementing For...Next loop. In the first loop, the intCounter counter variable starts at 1 and ends at 5, incrementing by 1 each time. During each iteration, the loop produces a message box that displays the counter variable's value. After five iterations, the loop ends. In the second loop, the intCount counter variable starts at 5 and ends at 1, decreasing by 1 each time. During each iteration, the loop produces a message box that displays the counter variable's value. After five iterations, the loop ends. When one procedure uses two loops, you should declare two separate counter variables, each with its own name, such as intCount and intCounter.

```
'Counter increases by 1 each time
Dim intCounter As Integer
For intCounter = 1 To 5 Step 1
    MsgBox intCounter
Next

'Counter decreases by 1 each time
Dim intCount As Integer
For intCount = 5 To 1 Step -1
    MsgBox intCount
Next
```

CODE WINDOW 1.28

As you create For...Next loops, it is important to consider under what conditions a loop will never reach the end value. For example, you could inadvertently add a statement that resets the counter, as shown in the following code statements:

```
For intCounter = 1 To 4
    strName = strName & InputBox("Please enter a name.")
    intCounter = 1
Next
```

This loop is infinite, meaning that it will never reach the end value because the counter value is reset to 1 during each iteration of the loop. Avoid introducing an infinite loop into your programs; this is considered a poor programming practice. Test your loops to make sure they will not run endlessly.

Using the Do...Loop Structure

For...Next loops are an appropriate choice when you know how many iterations the loop will require. However, sometimes, you do not know in advance when a loop will end, because the loop will continue until a certain condition is met. Do...Loops are appropriate when you do not know in advance how many times you need to execute the statements in the loop. A *Do...Loop structure* differs from the For...Next structure in that it executes a block of statements while a condition remains true or until a condition is true. In either case, you do not define an end value for the loop. Do...Loop statements execute a series of statements an indefinite number of times, depending on the Boolean value of the condition. The Do...Loop structure uses the keywords *While* or *Until*.

Loop While the Condition is True

Use the While keyword in a Do...Loop to repeat the iterations of the loop *while* the condition is true. VBA provides two ways to use the While keyword to check the condition: by specifying the condition *before* entering the loop, or by checking for the condition *after* the loop runs. Because the loop performs a test to check for the condition, specifying the condition before entering the loop uses a *pretest* to test for the condition, and testing the condition after entering the loop uses a *posttest* to check the condition. In either case, looping continues for as long as the condition remains true.

Code Window 1.29 illustrates pretest and posttest Do While loop structures. In both examples, the loops iterate five times.

```
'Pretest Loop
Dim intCounter As Integer
intCounter = 1
Do While intCounter <= 5
    MsgBox "intCounter is " & intCounter, _
        vbInformation, "Do While Pretest"
    intCounter = intCounter + 1
Loop

'Posttest Loop
Dim intCounter As Integer
intCounter = 1
Do
    MsgBox "intCount is " & intCount, _
        vbInformation, "Do While Pretest"
    intCounter = intCounter + 1
Loop While intCount <= 5
```

CODE WINDOW 1.29

Loop Until a Condition Becomes True

Use the Until keyword in a Do...Loop to repeat the iterations of the loop until the specified condition evaluates to True. The structure is similar to the While keyword. As with the While keyword, you can check the condition before you enter the loop by using a pretest or after the loop has run at least once by using a posttest. In either case, looping continues until the condition evaluates to true.

Code Window 1.30 illustrates pretest and posttest Do Until loop structures. In the pretest loop, the logical test intCounter > 5 is false to start because intCounter starts at 1. The loop iterates until the logical test is true. After the fifth iteration, intCounter is 6.

When the logical test is performed again, the condition is met and the loop does not iterate a sixth time. In the posttest loop, the loop iterates at least one time before performing the logical test. After the first iteration, intCount is 2, the logical test intCount > 5 is false, so the loop iterates again. After the fifth iteration, intCount is 6. When the logical test is performed again, the condition is met, and the loop does not iterate a sixth time.

```
'Pretest Loop
Dim intCounter As Integer
intCounter = 1
Do While intCounter > 5
    MsgBox "intCounter is " & intCounter, _
        vbInformation, "Do Until Pretest"
    intCounter = intCounter + 1
Loop

'Posttest Loop
Dim intCounter As Integer
intCounter = 1
Do
    MsgBox "intCount is " & intCount, _
        vbInformation, "Do Until Posttest"
    intCounter = intCounter + 1
Loop Until intCount > 5

End Sub
```

CODE WINDOW 1.30

Quick Concepts

10. Explain how a For...Next loop structure works. *p. 55*

11. What is the difference between a pretest and posttest in repetition structures? *p. 56*

12. What is an infinite loop? *p. 56*

Hands-On Exercises

Skills covered: Use the For...Next Structure • Use the Loop While the Condition Is True

4 Repetition Structures

Your next assignment is to create two procedures in the Excel workbook to display cumulative monthly salary data. You will use the For...Next loop structure to create a procedure to show cumulative gross salary for a 12-month period. You will then use a Do...Loop structure to display cumulative gross salary, cumulative taxes, and cumulative net pay for a 12-month period.

STEP 1 ›› USE THE FOR...NEXT STRUCTURE

Bill wants a user to enter an employee's License number, look up the salary, and then display a message box that shows the cumulative salary for a 12-month period. You can copy some code you created in Hands-On Exercise 2 to find a salary for a particular License number. Then you need to create a For...Next repetition structure to store the data in a string and display the string in a message box. Refer to Figure 1.28 as you complete Step 1.

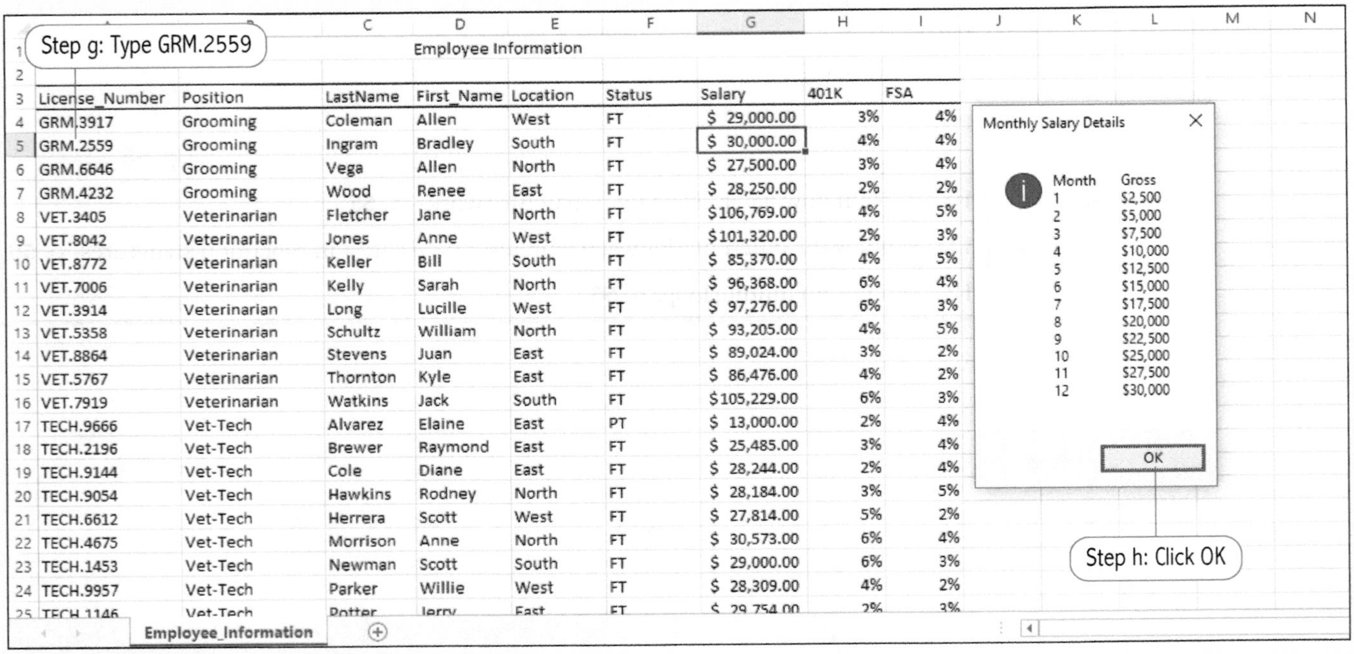

FIGURE 1.28 Results of For...Next Structure

Excel 2016, Windows 10, Microsoft Corporation

a. Open *v1h2AnimalCare_LastFirst.xlsm* in Excel, save it as **v1h4AnimalCare_LastFirst.xlsm**, changing h2 to h4, and open the VB Editor.

b. Position the insertion point before the Sub CalculateBonus() statement. Type the procedure header, comment, and four declarations shown in Code Window 1.31.

```
Sub DisplayMonthlySalary()

    'Declarations
    Dim curSalary As Currency
    Dim curGrossPay As Currency
    Dim intCounter As Integer
    Dim strMessage As String

End Sub
```

CODE WINDOW 1.31

c. Scroll to the CalculateBonus() procedure and start selecting with the comment *Set the active cell to A3* through *curFindSalary = ActiveCell.Value*. Click **Copy** on the toolbar, position the insertion point on the blank line below the declarations in the Sub DisplayMonthlySalary() procedure, press **Enter**, and then click **Paste** on the toolbar.

You copied the statements that set cell A3 as the active cell, display a dialog box to enable the user to find a License number, locate the respective salary for that License, and then save it in a variable.

d. Change *curFindSalary* to **curSalary** in the Sub DisplayMonthlySalary procedure.

The CalculateBonus() procedure declared and used a variable named curFindSalary. However, you need to edit the variable name in the current procedure, which uses curSalary as a variable name instead.

e. Click at the end of the curSalary statement, press **Enter** twice, and then type the rest of the code shown in Code Window 1.32. Leave one blank line between the MsgBox statement and the End Sub statement.

```
'Calculate monthly pay and display cumulative pay
intCounter = 1
curGrossPay = curSalary / 12

For intCounter = 1 To 12
    strMessage = strMessage & vbCrLf & "Month: " & intCounter & " " _
            & Format(curGrossPay * intCounter, "Currency")
Next

MsgBox strMessage, vbInformation, "Monthly Salary"
```

CODE WINDOW 1.32

The code initializes the counter variable, intCounter, to 1 and divides the annual salary by 12 to get a monthly salary. The For...Next loop adds to the existing string, which accumulates during each iteration. The vbCrLf inserts a carriage return within the string, adds the text *Month:*, and enters the current counter variable's value. The monthly salary is multiplied by the current loop's iteration for the month number, formats the value as currency, and adds that to the string.

After the 12th iteration, the loop ends, and a message box displays the cumulative salary by month. You indented the carryover line for the strMessage assignment statement so that the variable name stands out.

f. Click **Save** on the toolbar, click **Run** on the toolbar, and then select **Run Sub/UserForm**.

g. Type **GRM.2559** in the input box and click **OK**.

The procedure finds the License number GRM.2559, identifies and stores the respective salary ($30,000), and uses that salary to calculate the monthly pay and the cumulative pay. The message box displays a string containing the entire 12-month data.

h. Click **OK** in the message box.

The last procedure you created was useful and you have now been asked to create one that displays cumulative taxes and cumulative net pay. You will use the Do While repetition structure this time. Refer to Figure 1.29 as you complete Step 2.

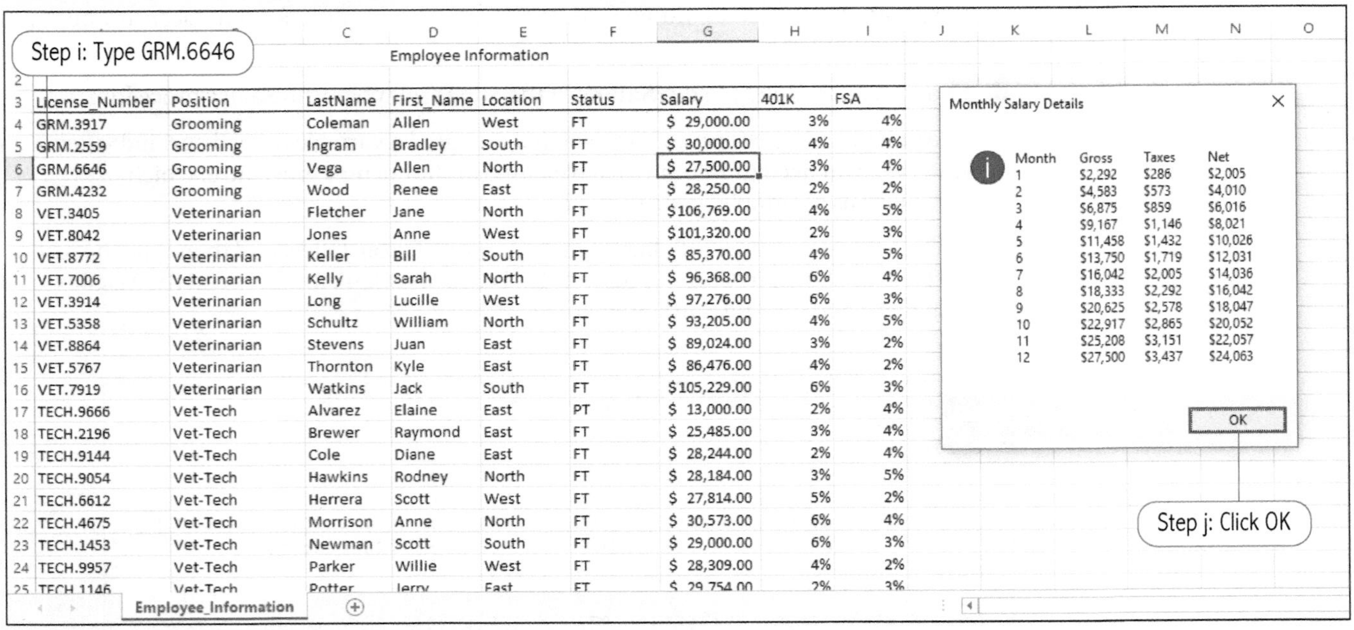

	License_Number	Position	LastName	First_Name	Location	Status	Salary	401K	FSA
					Employee Information				
3	License_Number	Position	LastName	First_Name	Location	Status	Salary	401K	FSA
4	GRM.3917	Grooming	Coleman	Allen	West	FT	$ 29,000.00	3%	4%
5	GRM.2559	Grooming	Ingram	Bradley	South	FT	$ 30,000.00	4%	4%
6	GRM.6646	Grooming	Vega	Allen	North	FT	$ 27,500.00	3%	4%
7	GRM.4232	Grooming	Wood	Renee	East	FT	$ 28,250.00	2%	2%
8	VET.3405	Veterinarian	Fletcher	Jane	North	FT	$106,769.00	4%	5%
9	VET.8042	Veterinarian	Jones	Anne	West	FT	$101,320.00	2%	3%
10	VET.8772	Veterinarian	Keller	Bill	South	FT	$ 85,370.00	4%	5%
11	VET.7006	Veterinarian	Kelly	Sarah	North	FT	$ 96,368.00	6%	4%
12	VET.3914	Veterinarian	Long	Lucille	West	FT	$ 97,276.00	6%	3%
13	VET.5358	Veterinarian	Schultz	William	North	FT	$ 93,205.00	4%	5%
14	VET.8864	Veterinarian	Stevens	Juan	East	FT	$ 89,024.00	3%	2%
15	VET.5767	Veterinarian	Thornton	Kyle	East	FT	$ 86,476.00	4%	2%
16	VET.7919	Veterinarian	Watkins	Jack	South	FT	$105,229.00	6%	3%
17	TECH.9666	Vet-Tech	Alvarez	Elaine	East	PT	$ 13,000.00	2%	4%
18	TECH.2196	Vet-Tech	Brewer	Raymond	East	FT	$ 25,485.00	3%	4%
19	TECH.9144	Vet-Tech	Cole	Diane	East	FT	$ 28,244.00	2%	4%
20	TECH.9054	Vet-Tech	Hawkins	Rodney	North	FT	$ 28,184.00	3%	5%
21	TECH.6612	Vet-Tech	Herrera	Scott	West	FT	$ 27,814.00	5%	2%
22	TECH.4675	Vet-Tech	Morrison	Anne	North	FT	$ 30,573.00	6%	4%
23	TECH.1453	Vet-Tech	Newman	Scott	South	FT	$ 29,000.00	6%	3%
24	TECH.9957	Vet-Tech	Parker	Willie	West	FT	$ 28,309.00	4%	2%
25	TECH.1146	Vet-Tech	Potter	Jerry	East	FT	$ 29,754.00	2%	3%

Step i: Type GRM.6646

Monthly Salary Details

Month	Gross	Taxes	Net
1	$2,292	$286	$2,005
2	$4,583	$573	$4,010
3	$6,875	$859	$6,016
4	$9,167	$1,146	$8,021
5	$11,458	$1,432	$10,026
6	$13,750	$1,719	$12,031
7	$16,042	$2,005	$14,036
8	$18,333	$2,292	$16,042
9	$20,625	$2,578	$18,047
10	$22,917	$2,865	$20,052
11	$25,208	$3,151	$22,057
12	$27,500	$3,437	$24,063

OK

Step j: Click OK

Employee_Information

Excel 2016, Windows 10, Microsoft Corporation

FIGURE 1.29 Results of Do While Repetition Structure

a. Ensure the VB Editor is displayed. Position the insertion point before the Sub DisplayMonthlySalary() statement, and press **Enter** twice.

b. Press **Ctrl+Home** and type the procedure name, comment, declarations, and assignment as shown in Code Window 1.33.

```
Sub DisplayMonthlyDetails()

    'Declarations
    Dim curSalary As Currency
    Dim curGrossPay As Currency
    Dim curTaxes As Currency
    Dim intCounter As Integer
    Const TaxRate As Single = 0.125
    strMessage = "Month" & vbTab & "Gross" & vbTab & "Taxes" & vbTab & "Net"

End Sub
```

CODE WINDOW 1.33

The strMessage assignment statement concatenates the words *Month, Gross, Taxes,* and *Net.* You use the vbTab character constant to insert tabs between the words within the string variable.

c. Select and copy the *'Set the active cell* comment through *curGrossPay = curSalary / 12* in the DisplayMonthlySalary procedure, and paste it below the strMessage assignment statement in the DisplayMonthlyDetails procedure. Check spacing to make sure the pasted code does not continue with existing code. If needed, press **Enter** to separate pasted code from existing code.

d. Edit the first pasted comment to be **Set the active cell to A3 and display input box to get License number**. Delete the blank line below the *Application.Goto* statement and delete the *Display input to get License Number* comment.

e. Position the insertion point after the *curGrossPay = curSalary / 12* statement and press **Enter**. Type **curTaxes = curGrossPay * TaxRate** and press **Enter**.

This expression multiplies the employee's gross pay by the constant tax rate. The product is then stored in the curTaxes variable.

f. Type **curNetPay = curGrossPay – curTaxes** and press **Enter** twice.

This expression subtracts the value in the curTaxes variable from the value in the curGrossPay variable. The result is then stored in the curNetPay variable.

g. Type the comment and the Do While statement block and the MsgBox statement shown in Code Window 1.34. Leave one blank line between the last statement and the End Sub statement.

```
'Calculate, store, and display cumulative salary data
Do While intCounter <= 12
    strMessage = strMessage & vbCrLf & intCounter & " " _
                & vbTab & Format(curGrossPay * intCounter, "$#,###") _
                & vbTab & Format(curTaxes * intCounter, "$#,###") _
                & vbTab & Format(curNetPay * intCounter, "$#,###")
    intCounter = intCounter + 1
Loop

MsgBox strMessage, vbInformation, "Monthly Salary Details"
```

CODE WINDOW 1.34

The loop iterates 12 times, once for each month. The loop continues to add to the existing strMessage variable using the & concatenation character. The vbCrLf character constant inserts a carriage return to store each month's data on a separate line in the string variable.

For each iteration, the current intCounter's value is added to the string to indicate month 1, month 2, and so on. The vbTab character constant inserts tabs between data. The Format function formats values with a custom Currency type: $#,### to avoid zeros for cents. The last line of the loop increments the counter.

After the loop terminates, the MsgBox statement displays the contents of the strMessage.

h. Click **Save** and run the DisplayMonthlyDetails procedure.

i. Type **GRM.6646** in the input box and click **OK**.

j. Click **OK** in the message box, close the VB Editor, and exit Excel. Based on your instructor's directions, submit the following:

v1h3AnimalCare_LastFirst.accdb

v1h4AnimalCare_LastFirst.xlsm

Chapter Objectives Review

After reading this chapter, you will have accomplished the following objectives:

1. **Use VBA and get help.**
   - Use the VB Editor: The VB Editor contains the tools needed to write code or edit macros for Microsoft Office applications. The window contains a toolbar, a menu bar, a Project window, a Properties window, and a Code window.
   - Get help: If you click Help within the VB Editor, the Microsoft Developer Network opens in a web browser so that you can search for information. For specific help on a keyword, click within the keyword and press F1.

2. **Identify code in the Code Window.**
   - Customize the VB Editor: The default colors of the VB Editor can be customized to user-defined preferences.
   - Identify keywords: Keywords are words or symbols particular to a programming language. They appear in blue within the Code window.
   - Document code with comments: Comments are text that explains programming code, but these statements do not execute. Comments start with an apostrophe or Rem and display in green in the Code window.
   - Identify objects and methods: Methods revolve around objects. For example, an Excel workbook contains objects, such as worksheets and charts. You must use the object name followed by a period and a method to perform an action for the object.

3. **Create, run, and debug procedures.**
   - Create a procedure: Start a procedure with the word Sub and end the procedure with End Sub in the Code window.
   - Run and debug a procedure: You can run a procedure directly within the Code window, although the results will display the application window. Use the Debug option to step through a procedure to determine where it contains a problem so that you can fix it.

4. **Create a message box.**
   - Use the MsgBox function: A message box is a dialog box that contains a title bar, message, an icon, and one or more buttons. The prompt argument specifies the text that appears within the message box. The title argument specifies the text that appears on the title bar.
   - Display buttons and icons in a message box: The message box function offers a variety of button options that can be displayed based on user preferences.

5. **Declare and use variables and constants.**
   - A variable stores values that can change during runtime. A constant stores a value declared by the programmer and cannot be changed during runtime.
   - Select a data type: When declaring variables and constants, you should specify a data type, such as integer or double.
   - Name variables and constants: Use a letter to start a variable or constant name, do not use disallowed characters, use descriptive names, and start the name with the designated prefix, such as *int* for integer.
   - Declare variables and constants: Variables are entered using the syntax Dim VariableName As DataType. Constants are private by default and use the prefix *const*. Constants also must have a preassigned value that cannot be changed.
   - Assign values to variables and constants: Use the assignment statement to assign values to variables.
   - Assign values to cells and ranges: Use the Cells method and Range property to work with direct cell values.

6. **Create an input box.**
   - Obtain user input with the InputBox function: An input box prompts the user to enter data. The data is then often stored in a variable.
   - Convert strings to numeric values using the Val function: Use the Val function to convert data entry from an input box to a value before assigning it to a variable.

7. **Perform calculations and format results.**
   - Use operators and the Order of Precedence: The variable name goes on the left side of the assignment (=) operator, and the arithmetic calculation goes on the right side of the operator.
   - Calculations follow the order of precedence: parentheses, exponentiation, multiplication, division, integer division, modulus, addition and concatenation, subtraction and negation, and string concatenation.
   - Format output results: Use the Format function to format values on displayed output.

8. **Use decision structures.**
   - Create an If...Then structure: The If...Then structure performs a logical test. If the test is True, the program code executes specific code. If not, that specific code is not executed.
   - Create an If...Then...Else structure: The If...Then...Else structure tests for a condition. Different code is executed based on the results of the logical test.
   - Create a Select Case structure: The Select Case structure compares an expression or value to a case block. Once the program identifies the correct case, it executes the respective statement.

9. **Perform data validation.**
   - Check for a required value: The process of checking data entered by a user to ensure it meets certain conditions is called data validation.
   - Check for a numeric value: Programmers use If...Then...Else structures to perform data validation to determine if user input contains a value that meets a condition.
   - Programmers also test to determine if users entered a value instead of text for numeric data with the IsNumeric function.

10. Use logical operators.

- Use the Or logical operator: The Or logical operator requires that any of the conditions evaluate to true to execute code.
- Use the And logical operator: The And logical operator requires that all conditions evaluate to true to execute code. Programmers use the And logical operator to ensure a value is both less than a value and greater than another value.

11. Use the For...Next structure.

- The For...Next structure repeats a loop a specific number of times using a counter variable and a step process to increment or decrement the counter during each iteration.

12. Use the Do...Loop structure.

- Loop while the condition is true: Use the Do While... Loop to perform a pretest loop. Use the Do...Loop While to perform a posttest loop.
- Loop until a condition becomes true: Use Do Until...Loop to perform a pretest loop until a condition becomes true. Use a Do...Loop Until to perform a posttest loop that loops until a condition becomes true.

Key Terms Matching

Match the key terms with their definitions. Write the key term letter by the appropriate numbered definition.

a. Comment
b. Constant
c. Design time
d. Do...Loop structure
e. Event
f. For...Next structure
g. If...Then structure
h. Input box
i. Keyword
j. Loop

k. Message box
l. Method
m. Module
n. Project
o. Runtime
p. Select Case structure
q. Sub procedure
r. Syntax error
s. Variable
t. Visual Basic for Applications

1. _____ The mode for designing, writing, and editing programming statements. *p. 6*

2. _____ A dialog box that displays a message of information and contains buttons for the user to click to perform actions. *p. 12*

3. _____ Performs a logical test and executes one or more statements if the test is true. *p. 41*

4. _____ Text or a symbol used for a specific purpose in a programming language. *p. 9*

5. _____ A textual description that explains a section of programming code. *p. 9*

6. _____ A dialog box that prompts the user to enter data. *p. 30*

7. _____ An action at runtime that triggers the execution of code. *p. 10*

8. _____ Stores values that remain the same during runtime. *p. 24*

9. _____ The mode for executing a program. *p. 6*

10. _____ The set of statements that repeat for a repetition structure. *p. 9*

11. _____ A repetition structure that repeats designated statements as long as a condition is true or until a condition is satisfied. *p. 56*

12. _____ Performs an action but does not return a specific value. *p. 10*

13. _____ A repetition structure that repeats statements a specific number of times. *p. 55*

14. _____ A programmer-defined name that stores values that can change or vary during runtime. *p. 24*

15. _____ An action that can be taken for an object. *p. 10*

16. _____ Occurs when code contains a misspelled or misused keyword, incorrect punctuation, or undefined elements. *p. 8*

17. _____ A programming language to enhance the functionality of Office applications. *p. 4*

18. _____ Compares an expression and then executes the code for the matching case. *p. 44*

19. _____ A collection of modules and objects in an Office file. *p. 6*

20. _____ A container to organize programming procedures within a project. *p. 6*

Multiple Choice

1. Which of the following Workbook file extensions does not support macros?

   (a) .xlsm

   (b) .xltm

   (c) .xlsb

   (d) .xlsx

2. What is the default color for keywords in the VB Editor?

   (a) Blue

   (b) Green

   (c) Black

   (d) Yellow

3. What keystroke or combination opens the VB Editor?

   (a) Alt+F12

   (b) F4

   (c) Alt+F11

   (d) Control+Shift+Enter

4. VBA cannot be used to create

   (a) Code in Access.

   (b) Code in Excel.

   (c) Stand-alone applications.

   (d) Code in PowerPoint.

5. Which of the following is an example of R1C1 style?

   (a) A1

   (b) 1A

   (c) 1,1

   (d) J,J

6. A For...Next loop:

   (a) Allows the code to execute from top to bottom.

   (b) Is required in all subroutines.

   (c) Can only be used when incrementing by 1.

   (d) Allows a section of the code to repeat x number of times.

7. Which statement can be used to compare the same expression to several different values?

   (a) InputBox()

   (b) If...Then

   (c) Select Case

   (d) Else...Then

8. The purpose of declaring variables in VBA is

   (a) To make it easier to debug the code at a later date.

   (b) For enhanced memory management.

   (c) To follow standard programming techniques.

   (d) To use the variables later in calculations.

9. The difference between a MsgBox statement and an InputBox statement is

   (a) InputBox allows the user to enter data.

   (b) MsgBox is easier to use.

   (c) Only InputBox can be customized.

   (d) No difference.

10. All of the following are examples of data types *except* which one?

   (a) Decimal

   (b) Boolean

   (c) String

   (d) Simplex

Practice Exercises

1 Library Budget

You have been appointed to the executive board of your local library. As part of your duties, you need to create the budget for the next fiscal year. Using the previous year's budget worksheet, you decide to create a procedure that will ask for the percentage increase (or decrease) from the previous year, and then create the next fiscal year's budget amounts. Refer to Figures 1.30 and 1.31 as you complete this exercise.

```
Sub CopyNextYearsBudget()
    'Check to see if the user wants to continue
    If MsgBox("This procedure will create next year's budget." & vbCrLf & _
        "Do you want to continue?", vbYesNo, "Confirmation") = vbNo Then
        Exit Sub
    End If

    ' Declare variables
    Dim sngIncrease As Single
    Dim strLastCell As String

    ' Set active cell
    Application.Goto Reference:="R5C4"

    ' Display input box to get percent increase in budget
    sngIncrease = Val(InputBox("Enter percent increase (ex. .05 for 5%)", _
            "Enter Percent Increase"))

    ' Use a Do loop to calculate the new amounts for all accounts
    Do Until strLastCell = "Net Budget:"
        ' Set the value of strLastCell
        strLastCell = ActiveCell.Offset(0, -2).Value

        ' Insert new budget amount into first cell
        ActiveCell.FormulaR1C1 = "=RC[-1]"
        ActiveCell = ActiveCell * (1 + sngIncrease)

        ' Move down one row
        ActiveCell.Offset(1, 0).Select
    Loop

End Sub
```

VBA 2016, Windows 10, Microsoft Corporation

FIGURE 1.30 Library Budget Procedure

	A	B	C	D	E	F	G
1	Library Budget						
2							
3	Category	Account	2017	2018	2019	2020	
4	Revenue						
5		Federal Funding	$120,560				
6		Real Estate Tax	$95,000				
7		Local Fundraising	$27,800				
8		Fees	$3,687				
9		Total:	$247,047				
10	Personnel						
11		Librarian	$45,000				
12		Other Professionals	$25,000				
13		Clerical Staff	$15,000				
14		Custodians	$10,500				
15		Benefits	$12,340				
16		Total:	$107,840				
17	Expenses						
18		Books	$50,500				
19		Periodicals	$37,805				
20		Audio/Video	$29,658				
21		Insurance	$3,525				
22		Utilities	$5,988				
23		Maintenance	$7,500				

Excel 2016, Windows 10, Microsoft Corporation

FIGURE 1.31 Library Budget

a. Open the *v1p1Library* Excel workbook, click **Enable Content**, and then save it as **v1p1Library_LastFirst.xlsm**.

b. Type **=C5*1.05** in **cell D5** and press **Enter**.

c. Click the **Developer tab** and click **Visual Basic** in the Code group to open the VB Editor.

d. Type **Sub CopyNextYearsBudget()** in the Code window and press **Enter**. The End Sub statement appears, as shown in Code Window 1.35.

```
Sub CopyNextYearsBudget()
|
End Sub
```

CODE WINDOW 1.35

e. Type the code shown in Code Window 1.36 to verify that the user wants to continue.

```
Sub CopyNextYearsBudget()
    'Check to see if the user wants to continue
    If MsgBox("This procedure will create next year's budget." & vbCrLf & _
        "Do you want to continue?", vbYesNo, "Confirmation") = vbNo Then
        Exit Sub
    End If
```

CODE WINDOW 1.36

f. Press **Enter** and type the code shown in Code Window 1.37. This code declares a variable, sets the active cell, obtains the percentage increase in the budget from the user, and inserts the new amount into the first row.

```
Sub CopyNextYearsBudget()
    'Check to see if the user wants to continue
    If MsgBox("This procedure will create next year's budget." & vbCrLf & _
        "Do you want to continue?", vbYesNo, "Confirmation") = vbNo Then
        Exit Sub
    End If

    ' Declare variables
    Dim sngIncrease As Single
    Dim strLastCell As String

    ' Set active cell
    Application.Goto Reference:="R5C4"

    ' Display input box to get percent increase in budget
    sngIncrease = Val(InputBox("Enter percent increase (ex. .05 for 5%)", _
            "Enter Percent Increase"))

    ' Insert new budget amount into first cell
    ActiveCell.FormulaR1C1 = "=RC[-1]"
    ActiveCell = ActiveCell * (1 + sngIncrease)

End Sub
```

CODE WINDOW 1.37

g. Click **Save** on the toolbar and minimize the VB Editor. Type **0** in **cell D5** and press **Enter** to reset the Federal Funding amount, and click **Visual Basic** on the Ribbon to restore the VB Editor. Make sure the insertion point is within the CopyNextYearsBudget procedure you just created. Click **Run Sub/UserForm** on the toolbar. Click **Yes** to confirm you want to continue, type **.05** in the input box, and then click **OK**. Press **Alt+F11** to preview your results in the worksheet.

h. Press **Alt+F11** to open the VB Editor. Place the insertion point after the Dim sngIncrease As Single statement in the *Declare variables* section and press **Enter**. As highlighted in Code Window 1.38, type **Dim strLastCell As String**.

i. Place the insertion point below the *sngIncrease = Val(InputBox("Enter percent increase (ex. .05 for 5%)", "Enter Percent Increase"))* statement, and press **Enter** twice. Type the remaining code as shown in Code Window 1.38 to create a Do...Loop that will calculate the new budget amounts for all accounts. Save the code.

```
Sub CopyNextYearsBudget()
    'Check to see if the user wants to continue
    If MsgBox("This procedure will create next year's budget." & vbCrLf & _
        "Do you want to continue?", vbYesNo, "Confirmation") = vbNo Then
        Exit Sub
    End If

    ' Declare variables
    Dim sngIncrease As Single
    Dim strLastCell As String

    ' Set active cell
    Application.Goto Reference:="R5C4"

    ' Display input box to get percent increase in budget
    sngIncrease = Val(InputBox("Enter percent increase (ex. .05 for 5%)", _
                "Enter Percent Increase"))

    ' Use a Do loop to calculate the new amounts for all accounts
    Do Until strLastCell = "Net Budget:"
        ' Set the value of strLastCell
        strLastCell = ActiveCell.Offset(0, -2).Value

        ' Insert new budget amount into first cell
        ActiveCell.FormulaR1C1 = "=RC[-1]"
        ActiveCell = ActiveCell * (1 + sngIncrease)

        ' Move down one row
        ActiveCell.Offset(1, 0).Select
    Loop

End Sub
```

CODE WINDOW 1.38

j. Press **Alt+F11** to return to the worksheet and type **0** in **cell D5** in the worksheet to reset the Federal Funding amount. In the VB Editor, make sure the insertion point is within the CopyNextYearsBudget procedure you just created. Click **Run Sub/UserForm** on the toolbar, click **Yes**, enter **.05** in the input box, and then click **OK**. Close the VB Editor.

k. Delete the zeros in **cells D10**, **D17**, and **D26**.

l. Save the workbook and close Excel. Based on your instructor's directions, submit v1p1Library_LastFirst.xlsm.

2 Sun Lake Hardware Rentals

Cindy Kent, the owner of a local hardware store, uses Access to manage clients, transactions, and equipment inventory. Her database is comprised of three tables and a data entry transaction form. She offers discount rates to customers that join the rewards program. She would like you to use VBA to create a message box to automatically calculate the total due based on the 2% discount rate and 7% sales tax. Refer to Figure 1.32 as you complete the exercise.

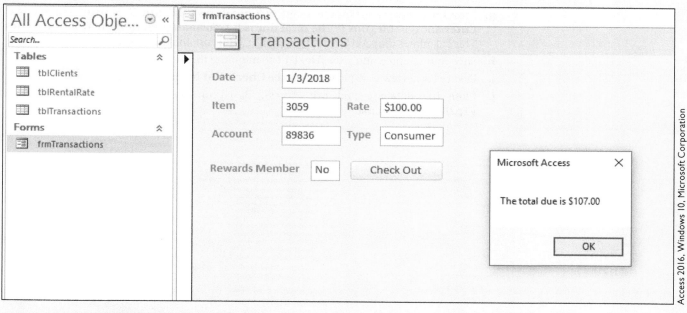

FIGURE 1.32 Sun Lake Hardware Rentals

a. Open the *v1p2Rentals* Access database and save it as **v1p2Rentals_LastFirst**.

b. Click **Enable Content**. Double-click the **frmTransactions** in the Navigation Pane to display the form. On the Home tab, click **Design View** to begin editing the form.

c. Ensure the Property Sheet is visible. Click the **Check Out button** and click the **Event tab** on the Property Sheet. Select **On Click**, click the **Build button**, select **Code Builder**, and then click **OK** to enter the VB editor.

d. Place the insertion point underneath the first line, press **Enter**, and then press **Tab**. Type **'Declarations** and press **Enter**. Enter the 7% tax rate and 2% discount rate as shown in Code Window 1.39 and press **Enter**.

```
Private Sub cmdCheckOut_Click()

    'Declarations
    Const sngTax As Single = 1.07
    Const sngDiscount As Single = 0.002

End Sub
```

CODE WINDOW 1.39

e. Define the rental rate variable as **curRate** with a Currency data type and press **Enter** twice.

f. Type the comment **'Calculates Rental Cost based on rewards program membership** on the current line, and enter the If...Then...Else statement as shown in Code Window 1.40.

```
    'Calculates Rental Cost based on rewards program membership
    If Me.RewardsMember = "No" Then
        curRate = Me.Rate
    Else
        curRate = Me.Rate - Me.Rate * sngDiscount
    End If
End Sub
```

CODE WINDOW 1.40

g. Press **Enter** twice and type the comment **'Calculates total and displays message box**. Press **Enter** and type **MsgBox ("The total due is " & Format(curRate * sngTax, "Currency"))**. This calculates the total by multiplying the rental cost and the constant tax rate.

h. Save your changes and press **Alt+F11** to minimize the VB Editor.

i. Ensure Form view is displayed. Click the **Check Out button** to test your work.

j. Close the database and exit Access. Based on your instructor's directions, submit v1p2Rentals_LastFirst.

Mid-Level Exercises

1 Food Service Company

A food service company wants to increase the price of its products based on category. Categories include Beverages, Condiments, Confections, and so on. The company's database contains a list of products and the corresponding category for each product. You will create a new VBA procedure to display the new price based on the category.

a. Open the *v1m1FoodService* Access database and save the database as **v1m1FoodService_LastFirst**. Enable the content.

b. Open the Categories table and review the categories. Close the table.

c. Open the Products table and review the products. Take note that each product has a CategoryID designation. Close the table.

d. Run the Average Price query to review the average price of products in each category. Close the query.

e. Open the VB Editor.

f. Place the insertion point under *Option Compare Database*, type **Option Explicit**, and then press **Enter**.

g. Type **Sub cmdDisplayNewPrice_Click()** and press **Enter**.

h. Press **Tab**, type **'Declare variables** and then press **Enter**. Type **Dim intCategory As Integer** and press **Enter** twice. Continue typing the remainder of the code shown in Code Window 1.41. This section establishes the VBA category variable.

```
Sub cmdDisplayNewPrice_Click()
    ' Declare variables
    Dim intCategory As Integer

    'Verify that CategoryID is not blank
    If IsNull(Me.CategoryID) Then
        Exit Sub
    End If

    intCategory = Me.CategoryID

End Sub
```

CODE WINDOW 1.41

i. Press Enter and type the comment **'Set the price increase based on category** on the current line. Press **Enter**, type **Select Case intCategory**, and then press **Enter** again. Continue typing the code as shown in Code Window 1.42.

```
Sub cmdDisplayNewPrice_Click()
    ' Declare variables
    Dim intCategory As Integer

    'Verify that CategoryID is not blank
    If IsNull(Me.CategoryID) Then
        Exit Sub
    End If

    intCategory = Me.CategoryID

    ' Set the price increase based on category
    Select Case intCategory

        Case 1 To 4
            MsgBox "New Price: " & Format(Me.UnitPrice * 1.05, "currency"), vbOKOnly, "New Price"

        Case 5, 7, 8
            MsgBox "New Price: " & Format(Me.UnitPrice * 1.03, "currency"), vbOKOnly, "New Price"

        Case 6
            MsgBox "New Price: " & Format(Me.UnitPrice * 1.1, "currency"), vbOKOnly, "New Price"
    Case Else
    MsgBox "New Price not on file."

    End Select

End Sub
```

CODE WINDOW 1.42

j. Save the code and close the VB Editor. Display the Products form in Form view and click the **New Price button** to test the procedure. The new price should appear in a message box. Use a calculator to verify that the new price is correct.

k. Advance to the next record and test the New Price button again. Repeat for several more records.

l. Create a new category in the Categories table and assign any product in the Products table to the new category. Test the New Price procedure to verify it displays the *New Price not on file* message.

m. Close the database and exit Access. Based on your instructor's directions, submit v1m1FoodService_LastFirst.

2 Car Payment Calculation

You have been hired as a financial specialist for Sam's Auto Sales. As part of your daily tasks, you help clients determine how much they can afford when financing a new vehicle. You have decided to use VBA to create a simple payment calculator that uses the payment function along with several client inputs to perform its calculations.

a. Open the Excel workbook *v1m2AutoCalculator* document and save it as **v1m2AutoCalculator_ LastFirst**.

b. Open the VB Editor and in the already created module, create a new procedure named **AutoPayment**, and declare the constant interest rate as **.0375** with the data type Single.

c. Declare variables for the following inputs with the corresponding data types.
- *curPurchasePrice as Currency*
- *intYearsFinanced as Integer*
- *curDownPayment as Currency*
- *curMonthlyPayment as Currency*

d. Assign a value to the curPurchasePrice variable value by creating an input box that requests the purchase price of the vehicle. Use the prompt **Enter Purchase Price** and the title **Price Input**.

e. Assign a value to the intYearsFinanced variable value by creating an input box that requests the users to enter the desired years financed. Use the prompt **Enter Years Financed** and the title **Duration Input**.

f. Assign a value to the curDownPayment variable value by creating an input box that requests the users to enter the Down Payment as a dollar amount. Use the prompt **Enter Down Payment** and the title **Down Payment**.

g. Define the curMonthlyPayment variable by using the built in PMT function as follows **=Pmt(sngInterest / 12, intYearsFinanced * 12, -curPurchasePrice+curDownPayment)**.

h. Create a message box to display the results. Use concatenated text with the words **"Your Total Monthly Payment is:" &** and the value of the curMonthlyPayment variable formatted as Currency.

i. Exit the VB Editor and assign the macro to the **Calculate Monthly Payment** button.

j. Test the button by entering your own information and answer the question that is listed on the Analysis worksheet.

k. Close the workbook and exit Excel. Based on your instructor's directions, submit v1m2AutoCalculator_LastFirst.

Beyond the Classroom

Calculate Financial Aid

GENERAL CASE

You have been hired as a financial aid advisor for incoming freshmen at a local university. To help reduce frequently asked questions regarding financial aid eligibility, you have decided to use VBA in Excel to create a calculator that will determine students' financial aid awards based on household income. To complete this task, you will create a decision structure using Select Case, perform validation with logic, and display the financial award in both a message box and within the student worksheet.

Open the Excel workbook *v1b1FinAid* and save the file as a macro-enabled workbook **v1b1FinAid_LastFirst**. Open the VB Editor. Declare variables for household income as Currency and the aid multiplier as Single. Create a Select Case for the curHouseHoldIncome variable based on the following information.

Any household with an income of less than 10,000 receives a multiplier of 3, any household with an income between 10,000 and 60,000 receives a multiplier of 2, and any household with a total income greater than 60,000 receives a multiplier of 0. Next create an **If...Then...Else** statement that returns the message **"You must enter total household income"** if the cell H14 has a zero value. If the value entered is greater than zero, then the message box should return a statement displaying the amount available as of the current graduation date. Your last step is to use VBA to enter the amount available for aid in **cell H16**. Exit the VB Editor and assign the newly created macro to the **Calculate Financial Aid** button. Based on your instructor's directions, submit v1b1FinAid_LastFirst.

Revise the Scholarship Database

DISASTER RECOVERY

You work as an intern for Lawrence Community School Systems and you have been asked to review the scholarship database to see if you can improve the code. You decide that the message box text could be more efficient if the repeating phrases were assigned to constants. Open the Access database *v1b2Scholarship* file, and save the database as **v1b2Scholarship_LastFirst**. Open the VBA code and review the message box components. Declare a new variable and assign the repeating text phrases to the new variable. Replace the text phrases in the message boxes with the new variable; join the phrase using the "&" character. Test your results and make corrections if necessary. Test the procedure further by introducing an error into the code. Insert a space between the first ElseIf statement so it becomes *Else If*. Click **Debug** in the toolbar and select **CompileVBA4** from the list. The compile process should stop at the Else If error. Correct the error and run the compile process again. Close the database and exit Access. Based on your instructor's directions, submit v1b2Scholarship_LastFirst.

Capstone Exercise

After graduating from college, you have been hired as a data analyst for True Shield Landscaping. True Shield is a local, full-service landscaping company that services Traverse City, Michigan. Currently, True Shield stores all client and service information in an Access database. They also create client invoices in Excel. You have been asked to use VBA to automate several areas of their Access database as well as debug and enhance the VBA in the Service Invoice worksheet, which is currently producing a runtime error.

Run and Debug a Procedure

A coworker has already created a procedure in the Service Invoice worksheet that is currently used. Unfortunately, the procedure produces a runtime error. You will run the procedure and use VBA help to debug the error.

a. Open the Excel the macro-enabled workbook *v1c1Invoice*, click Enable Content, and save as **v1c1Invoice_LastFirst**.

b. Click the **Summary button** on the worksheet, and observe the error produced when the procedure is run.

c. Click **Help** and use the Microsoft Office Dev Center webpage to research the error.

d. Locate the source of the error, add the missing code, and then save the workbook.

e. Run the procedure, and if satisfied with the results, exit the VB Editor.

Create a Procedure

Your next task is to create a procedure to clear the contents of the invoice. This will make using the template more efficient when working with multiple clients.

a. Open the VB Editor and locate the incomplete *Reset* procedure.

b. Place the insertion point at **Ln2, Col 5**, press **Enter**, and type the code as it appears in Code Window 1.43.

```
Sub Reset()

    'Clears contents of the invoice
    ActiveSheet.Range("F6,C18:F26").ClearContents

End Sub
```

CODE WINDOW 1.43

c. Click **Save** and exit the VB Editor.

d. Click the **Reset** button to test the newly created procedure.

e. Save, click OK, and close the workbook.

Declare Constants and Variables

After completing the invoice workbook, your next step is to automate several areas of the company database. Your first task is to automate the calculation of the service rate. The standard rates are listed in the Rates table within the database and clients that are under contract receive a 10% discount on all work completed. You will declare the 10% discount rate as a constant.

a. Open the Access database *v1c1LawnCare*, click Enable Content, and save the database as **v1c1LawnCare_LastFirst**.

b. Open the frmServices in Design View and ensure the Property Sheet in the Tools group is displayed.

c. Select the **Calculate Rate button**, add a new event that is triggered for the On Click event, and click **Build**. Select **Code Builder** and click **OK** to enter the VB Editor.

d. Press **Enter** to add a line, press **Tab** to indent the first line, and then enter the comment '**Declarations.**

e. Press **Enter** and declare the constant sngDiscount with the value **.10** and the data type **Single**. Be sure to use the proper naming conventions for a constant.

f. Press **Enter** and declare the variable curRate as **Currency**. Be sure to use the proper naming convention for a variable.

Use Logical Operators

After declaring the constant discount rate and variable rate, you will use an If...Then...Else statement to determine if the client is eligible for a discount. If the client is under contract, he or she receives a 10% discount. All others pay full price.

a. Enter a comment to document the use of a decision structure in the next statements.

b. Press **Enter** and enter an If...Then...Else statement as it appears in Code Window 1.44.

```
Option Compare Database
Private Sub cmdRate_Click()

    'Declarations
    Const sngDiscount As Single = 0.1
    Dim curRate As Currency

    'If...Then...Else statement to determine discount eligibility
    If Me.Contract = "Yes" Then
        curRate = Me.Rate - sngDiscount * Me.Rate
    Else
        curRate = Me.Rate
    End If

End Sub
```

CODE WINDOW 1.44

Create a Message Box

In the next step, you will create a message box that will display the current rate the client is receiving based on the If...Then...Else statement in the prior step.

a. Place the insertion point at **Ln14** and press **Enter.**

b. Type the comment '**Displays message box with discounted rate** and press **Enter.**

c. Type **MsgBox "The current rate is " & curRate, vbInformation, "Rate Information".**

Format Results

After previewing your results, you determine that the calculations are correct, but the values are not formatted as currency. You will use the Format function to correctly display the data.

a. Open the VB Editor and locate the MsgBox function. Add the **Format function** around the curRate calculation and set the format to **Currency.**

b. Exit the VB Editor, display the frmServices form in Form view, and press the **Calculate Rate button** to test the code.

c. Click OK and save the form.

Obtain User Input with the Input Box Function

You would like to provide a method for users of the database to quickly issue a price quote for a service based on the rates and quantity of services provided. To complete this task, you will obtain the quantity of services requested using an input box. You will then use this value in conjunction with the rate calculations to determine the total price quote.

a. Switch to Design View and ensure the Property Sheet is displayed.

b. Select the **Information button**. Click in the On Click event and click **Build**. Select **Code Builder** and click **OK** to enter the VB Editor.

c. Press **Enter** to add a line, press **Tab** to indent, and then enter the code as it appears in Code Window 1.45.

d. Save and exit the VB Editor.

```
Private Sub cmdInfo_Click()

    'Declarations
    Const sngDiscount As Single = 0.1
    Dim curRate As Currency
    Dim intQuantity As Integer

    intQuantity = InputBox("Enter quantity", "Price Quote")

    'If...Then...Else statement to determine discount eligibility
    If Me.Contract = "Yes" Then
        curRate = Me.Rate - sngDiscount * Me.Rate
    Else
        curRate = Me.Rate
    End If

    'Displays message box with quote
    MsgBox "The total due is " & Format(curRate * intQuantity, "Currency")

End Sub
```

CODE WINDOW 1.45

Test the Buttons

You need to test the buttons to ensure the application works.

a. Display the frmServices form in Form view, click the **Calculate Rate** button and click **OK.**

b. Advance to record 4 and click the **Calculate Rate** button again.

c. Click **OK** and click the **Information button**.

d. Enter a quantity, click **OK**, and then click **OK** again after observing the price quote.

e. Save and close the database. Based on your instructor's directions, submit:

v1c1Invoice_LastFirst
v1c1LawnCare_LastFirst

Excel and VBA

CASE STUDY | Expert Financial Services

Expert Financial Services (EFS) offers home mortgages. The interest rate depends primarily on the amount borrowed and the length of time of the loan repayment. EFS offers fixed interest rates from 4.25% to 5.25%, based on the term (10 to 30 years) and the loan amount ($100,000 to $500,000).

All loans have closing costs, which are fees paid to obtain and process the loan. The origination fees paid vary based on the mortgage scenario. All EFS loans have a 2% origination fee and additional points that vary depending on the loan term and the initial loan amount. Customers who open a personal investment account with EFS qualify for a discount on the origination fees.

Cassandra Wilson, vice president of EFS, asked you to create an Excel application for representing mortgage loan options to customers. You will create an interface to manage customer information, loan details, loan repayment schedule, and so on. You will also create a customer information form and write the VBA code behind it. Next, you will insert buttons and write VBA code on an instructions worksheet to enable users to use the application efficiently. In addition, you will create a loan repayment schedule that lists the monthly principal payment, interest payment, cumulative principal, and cumulative interest payments for each monthly payment until the loan is paid in full. Finally, you will create a Truth-in-Lending disclosure form that summarizes the payments, charges, and due dates.

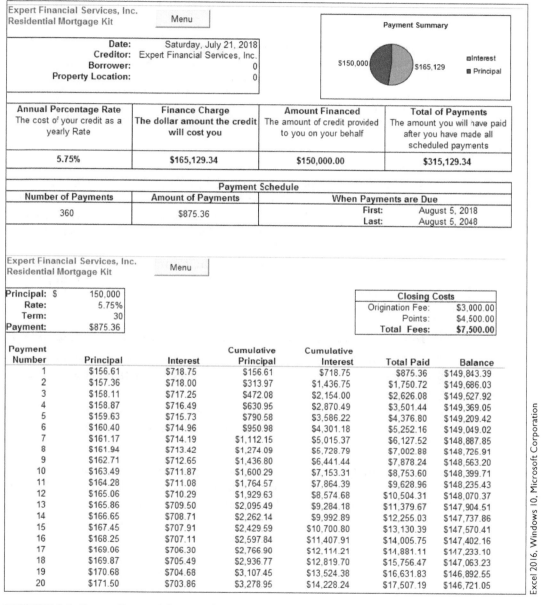

FIGURE 2.1 Expert Financial Services Spreadsheet

Excel 2016, Windows 10, Microsoft Corporation

CASE STUDY | Expert Financial Services

Starting File	File to be Submitted
v2h1Loan	**v2h3Loan_LastFirst**

Forms and Controls

You use forms regularly to enter data into various systems. For example, when you order products from an online store, you enter billing information, such as your name, billing address, credit card number, and expiration date. You can create forms within an Excel worksheet to provide an effective user interface to obtain data from a user. Forms in Excel are similar to forms in Access. However, when you create a form in Excel, you must also write the VBA code behind the controls so that the application can process the data entered.

In this section, you will create a form in a macro-enabled Excel workbook, insert controls, and change the control properties so that you can write VBA code later.

TIP: MACRO-ENABLED WORKBOOK

A regular Excel workbook (.xlsx) cannot store macros and VBA code; however, a macro-enabled workbook (.xlsm) is designed to store macros and VBA code. To save a workbook that contains VBA code for the first time, display the Save As dialog box, click the *Save as type* arrow, and choose Excel Macro-Enabled Workbook.

Creating Forms

An **object** represents an element, such as a worksheet, cell, chart, or a form. All code statements and the Excel objects that you reference in them fit into a logical framework called an **object model.** The object model organizes all objects into an object hierarchy, which defines how objects are related to one another. Objects in the hierarchy are organized in collections. A **collection** is a group of objects with similar characteristics.

The UserForm object contains the Control collection, which manages the individual controls, such as buttons, text boxes, and list boxes that provide a form with its functionality.

To add a UserForm object to an Excel workbook, complete the following steps:

1. Ensure the Developer tab is displayed on the Ribbon by clicking the File tab, clicking Options, clicking Customize Ribbon, clicking the Developer check box in the Main Tabs list, and then clicking OK.
2. Click the Developer tab and click Visual Basic in the Code group.
3. Click Insert on the VBA menu bar and select UserForm.

An empty form and the Toolbox display when you add a UserForm object. Figure 2.2 shows the form after changing the name from UserForm1 to frmLoan, and after changing the caption from UserForm1 to Loan Information.

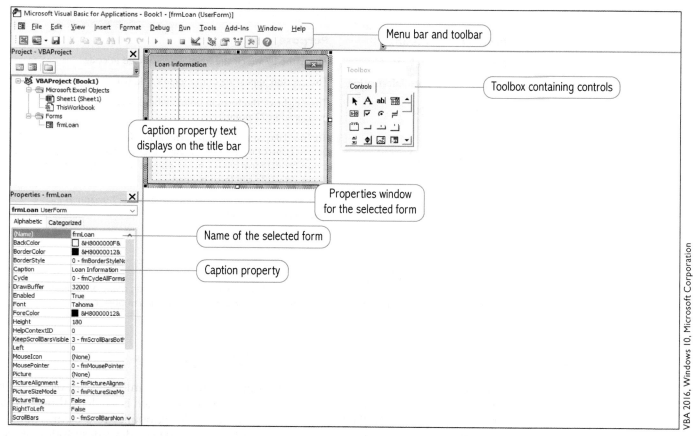

FIGURE 2.2 UserForm Object

VBA 2016, Windows 10, Microsoft Corporation

Set the Form Properties

STEP 1 >> After you insert a new UserForm object, you should set the form's properties. Most of the form properties control the appearance of the form. The Properties window lists the properties and their current values for the selected object—in this case the UserForm object frmLoan (refer to Figure 2.2). If the Properties window is not displayed, click View on the menu and select Properties Window. The Properties window contains two tabs: Alphabetic and Categorized. Click the Alphabetic tab to list property names in alphabetical order, although the Name property remains at the top of the property list, or click the Categorized tab to group the property names into related categories. The first column in the Properties window lists the name of the property; the second column lists the value or setting for the respective property.

The ***Name property*** is a text string that identifies an object, such as a form. The Name property can be used to identify and manipulate an object in VBA code. The naming scheme you choose for objects helps other VBA programmers understand the code better. Names should be meaningful, but short enough to be read easily. Unique names differentiate the objects in your application. The first letter must be an alphabetic character or an underscore. As shown in Figure 2.2, use the three-letter abbreviation *frm* followed by the descriptive name, such as frmLoan, to name a form.

The ***Caption property*** controls the text that appears on the form's title bar. The default name matches the default Name property, such as UserForm1. Unlike the Name property that must not contain spaces, the Caption property allows multiple words. As shown in Figure 2.2, typically, you capitalize the first letter of each word for the caption.

Table 2.1 lists selected properties, their settings, and their purposes for the form shown in Figure 2.2.

Pearson Education, Inc.

TABLE 2.1	Properties of the frmLoan UserForm	
Property	**Setting**	**Purpose**
Name	frmLoan	The name by which the form is referenced in code.
Caption	Loan Information	The caption appearing in the form's title bar.
Height	180	The height of the form in points where one vertical inch is measured in 72 points.
ShowModal	True	The modality setting of the form. A modal form must be closed before control is returned to any other object in the application; a non-modal form allows other objects in the application to be activated while the form is open.
Width	240	The width of the form in points where one horizontal inch is measured in 72 points.

TIP: USERFORM OBJECT

Technically, a custom form is an instance of the UserForm object. However, many developers refer to a UserForm as a form. This chapter uses *form* when referring to a UserForm object.

Adding Controls to Forms

Forms usually contain ***controls*** for entering data, displaying information, or triggering events. You can add controls to a form using the ***Toolbox***, which is a palette that contains the standard controls. Each control provides specific functionality to a form. Table 2.2 lists the control name, shows the icon on the Toolbox, and provides a description of each standard control available in the Toolbox.

TABLE 2.2	Form Controls	
Control	**Icon**	**Purpose**
Select Objects	⌖	Selects a control on a form. After you add a control to a form, use the Selection Tool to select the control to modify it.
Label	A	Appears as text on a form, usually for the purpose of identifying controls. Use this for text that the user will not change.
TextBox	abl	Appears as a box in which text can be entered and changed by the user. A text box is often bound to an object in the application (such as an Excel range).
ComboBox	▦	Combines the functionality of a list box and a text box. The user can either choose an item from the list or enter a value in the text box.
ListBox	▤	Displays a list of items from which the user can make a choice. If there are more items in the list than will fit in the control space, a scroll bar appears.
CheckBox	☑	Creates a square box that can be checked or unchecked, to indicate a yes/no condition or a selection.
OptionButton	⊙	Displays a small circular button for toggling options on or off. When multiple option buttons are used together, only one selection can be made (see *Frame*).
ToggleButton	▤	Displays a button for toggling (turning on or off) a selection.

Pearson Education, Inc.

TABLE 2.2 Form Controls (continued)

Control	Icon	Purpose
Frame		Displays a rectangular panel for grouping other controls. When option buttons are added to a frame, only one selection can be made.
CommandButton		Displays a button that triggers an event when clicked.
TabStrip		Displays tabs along the top of the window so that you can insert different controls on different tabs.
MultiPage		Allows a form to store controls that appear on multiple pages in the form, much like a TabStrip control.
Scrollbar		Enables you to change a set of continuous values using a horizontal or vertical bar. The values are changed by dragging the button appearing in the scroll bar.
SpinButton		Increases and decreases values using up and down arrows. The values in the control are normally bound to a range in an Excel worksheet.
Image		Displays a bitmap, GIF, JPEG, metafile, or icon graphic.
RefEdit		Enables the user to select a range in a worksheet when the button is clicked.

To show or hide the Toolbox, complete one of the following steps:

- Select Toolbox on the View menu to toggle it on or off.
- Click Toolbox on the VB Editor toolbar to show or hide the Toolbox.

Name the Controls

The most common standard for naming controls in Visual Basic is Modified Hungarian Notation. This convention precedes the name of each instance of a control with a three-character prefix to the control and a descriptive title for the control. The prefix appears in lowercase, and the descriptive title starts with an uppercase character. If the descriptive title has more than one word, CamelCase is used to differentiate the words, such as txtFirstName. Table 2.3 lists the naming conventions for common form controls.

TABLE 2.3 Control Naming Conventions

Control	Prefix	Example
Frame	fme	fmeLoan
Label	lbl	lblTitle
TextBox	txt	txtFirstName
ListBox	lst	lstInterestRate
CheckBox	chk	chkSalariedEmployee
CommandButton	cmd	cmdExit
ComboBox	cbo	cboDays
OptionButton	opt	optTerm
Image	img	imgLogo

Insert a Frame Control

STEP 2 **▶▶** When you plan to insert multiple controls on a form, you might want to insert a Frame control first. The **Frame control** displays a frame or border around related controls on the form to increase readability for the user (see Figure 2.3).

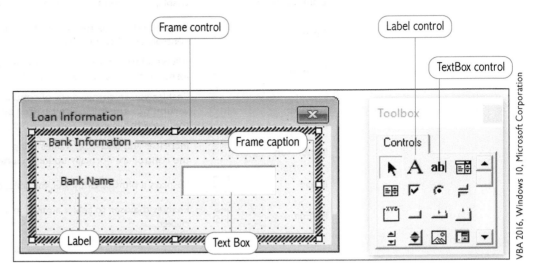

FIGURE 2.3 Frame, Label, and TextBox Controls

To insert a Frame control and change its properties, complete one of the following steps from within the VB Editor:

1. Create a frame control using one of the following methods:
   - Drag Frame from the Toolbox and drop it at the location on the form where you want it and release the mouse button. This approach creates a default-size frame that fills most of the form.
   - Click Frame in the Toolbox to make it the active control. Click and drag within the form to create and size the frame in a specific location.
2. Adjust Frame control properties, such as Name, Caption, Width, and Height.

TIP: FRAME CONTROLS FOR OPTION BUTTONS
Frame controls are mandatory when you need to include more than one set of OptionButton controls on a form. Using Frame controls to separate OptionButton controls enables you to use multiple OptionButton sets in one user form.

Insert Label and TextBox Controls

STEP 3 **▶▶** Because TextBox controls do not have their own caption property, forms usually contain several **Label controls** to identify the purpose of TextBox controls. For example, you might want to insert a **TextBox control** for the user to enter data. However, without a label displaying text, the user will not know what type of data to enter in the text box. The caption for first label in Figure 2.3 is *Bank Name*. A text box is located to the right side of the label so that the user can type the bank name. The **TextAlign property** is a property that specifies the horizontal alignment of a caption appearing in a label.

To insert a Label control and change its properties, complete one of the following steps:

1. Create a Label control using one of the following methods:
   - Drag Label from the Toolbox, drop it at the location on the form where you want it, and release the mouse button. This approach creates a default label that has a Width setting of 72.
   - Click Label in the Toolbox to make it the active control. Click and drag within the form to create and size the label in a specific location.
2. Adjust the properties of the Label control such as Name, Caption, Width, and Height.

TIP: CREATING MULTIPLE LABELS QUICKLY
After you insert and format a Label control, you can copy the control and paste it several times to preserve the formatting property settings. Then you can change the Name and Caption properties of the copied controls as needed.

To insert a TextBox control and change its properties, complete one of the following steps:

1. Create a TextBox control using one of the following methods:
   - Drag TextBox from the Toolbox, drop it at the location on the form where you want it, and release the mouse button. This approach creates a default text box that has a Width setting of 72.
   - Click TextBox in the Toolbox to make it the active control. Click and drag within the form to create and size the text box in a specific location.
2. Type a name (such as txtName) in the Name property of the TextBox and press Enter. Set the values for the Width and Height properties to control the size of the text box. Drag the TextBox control to align it to the right of its respective Label control.

Insert ListBox, CheckBox, and CommandButton Controls

STEP 4 ⟩⟩ Three other common controls include the ListBox, CheckBox, and CommandButton (see Figure 2.4). Insert a **_ListBox control_** to display a list of items from which the user may select. For example, you might want the user to select the number of years for a loan from a list of predefined years.

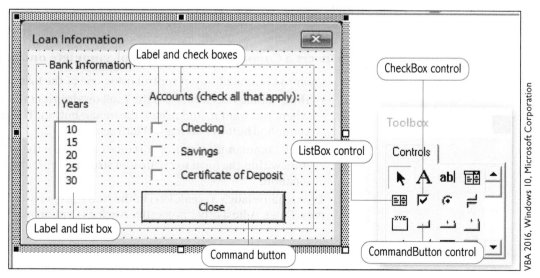

FIGURE 2.4 ListBox, CheckBox, and CommandButton Controls

To insert a ListBox control and change its properties, complete one of the following steps:

1. Create a ListBox control using one of the following methods:
   - Drag ListBox from the Toolbox, drop it at the location on the form where you want it, and release the mouse button. This approach creates a default list box that has a Width setting of 72.
   - Click ListBox in the Toolbox to make it the active control. Click and drag within the form to create and size the list box in a specific location.
2. Type a name (such as *lstTerm*) in the Name property of the ListBox and press Enter. List items can be added to the ListBox by using the RowSource property or loading the items with the ListBox.AddItem method when the form is initialized. Adjust other properties, such as BorderStyle, Width, and Height. (The ListBox control does not have a Caption property.)

Insert **CheckBox controls** when you want the user to select one or more options at the same time. For example, a user might want to select one or more accounts he or she has at a bank, such as Checking, Savings, or Certificate of Deposit.

To insert a CheckBox control and change its properties, complete one of the following steps:

1. Create a CheckBox control using one of the following methods:
   - Drag CheckBox from the Toolbox, drop it at the location on the form where you want it, and release the mouse button. This approach creates a default check box that has a Width setting of 108.
   - Click CheckBox in the Toolbox to make it the active control. Click and drag within the form to create and size the check box in a specific location.
2. Type a name (such as *chkAccount*) in the Name property of the CheckBox control and press Enter. Adjust other properties, such as Caption and Width.

Insert a **CommandButton control** when you want to display a button to execute some action when the user clicks it. For example, you can insert a Close button to accept and apply settings when clicked, and a Cancel button to reject changes made in a form.

To insert a CommandButton control, complete one of the following steps:

1. Create a CommandButton control using one of the following methods:
   - Drag CommandButton from the Toolbox, drop it at the location on the form where you want it, and release the mouse button. This approach creates a default command button that has a Width setting of 72.
   - Click CommandButton in the Toolbox to make it the active control. Click and drag within the form to create and size the command button in a specific location.
2. Type a name (such as *cmdClose*) in the Name property of the CommandButton and press Enter. Adjust other properties, such as Caption and Width.

Adjusting Specialized Properties

After you insert each control, you might want to set many of that control's properties. However, some control properties may rely on other control properties. For these specialized properties, it may save you time to set these properties after you have inserted all the controls.

Set Enabled, TabStop, and TabIndex Properties

STEP 5 ⟩⟩ The ***Enabled property*** determines if a control can receive the focus or if that control can respond to the user. Set the Enabled property to True if you want the control to be able to receive focus or respond to the user. Set the Enabled property to False if you do not want the user to interact with the control when the application starts.

Commands on the Excel Ribbon exhibit Enabled status behavior. For example, the Enabled property of the Cut and Copy commands are set to False until you select something. After you select text, an image, or another object, the Enabled property of Cut and Copy changes to True. You can set a control's default Enabled property value in the Properties window; however, you might want to enable or disable a property based on an action when an application is running. The following code shows how to disable the Enabled property of a control:

```
cmdCut.Enabled=False
```

Some users press Tab to go to another form control to activate it so that they can enter data or select that control. When a control is active, it has ***focus.*** You should make sure the control property values are set correctly to ensure that controls can receive focus and that the form provides a logical flow when a user presses Tab to change focus when entering data on a form. Controls have two properties that determine the order in which the controls are activated as a user tabs through the form: TabStop and TabIndex.

The ***TabStop property***, which accepts a value of True or False, determines whether the control receives the focus when the user presses Tab (True to receive the focus; False to skip the control when tabbing through the controls on the form). The ***TabIndex property***, which accepts an integer value, determines the order in which a control receives the focus. A control with a TabIndex value of 0 receives the focus initially. The control with the next-highest value receives the focus when the user presses Tab. The TabIndex and TabStop properties are often used in conjunction; however, they can also be used independently.

Use Bound and Unbound Controls

A ***bound control*** is a control that is connected to a data source in the host application. In Excel, a bound control typically displays or changes the data in a worksheet cell or range. For example, a form might contain a text box for entering data and assigning the data to a worksheet range object. An ***unbound control*** is a control that is not connected to data in the host application. Labels are common examples of unbound controls because they do not store text that is changed by the user. Another example of an unbound control is the command button, because it always triggers events.

To bind controls to a worksheet range, set the appropriate form properties. ListBox, ComboBox, and TextBox controls all have a ***ControlSource property*** that defines the cell to which the control is bound. VBA provides two ways to set control properties: in the Properties window at design time, or with a code statement that executes at run time. If the ControlSource is set at design time, it cannot be altered with user input. In comparison, if the control source is set by code at run time, user inputs can be used to modify the control source. To set the ControlSource property of a control using the Properties window, type the cell reference, such as A1 or D7, in the row for the ControlSource property. The column reference can be lower- or uppercase.

ListBox and ComboBox controls have a ***RowSource property*** that specifies the range that contains a list of the items that will appear in the list box or combo box control at run time. You can set this property using either the Properties window at design time or in a code statement that executes at run time. The value of the RowSource property is a worksheet range (such as B2:B7) that contains the items that will populate the list. Valid settings include any worksheet range. Just like the ControlSource property, the column references in the RowSource property are not case-specific.

Set Properties for the Loan Application Form

A good practice is to list the controls, their properties, and their desired settings when you plan a form. Doing so helps you remember control names and what properties you need to set. Figure 2.5 shows the EFS Residential Loan Application form that you will work on in Hands-On Exercise 1. Part of the form is created for you, and you will create the rest of it.

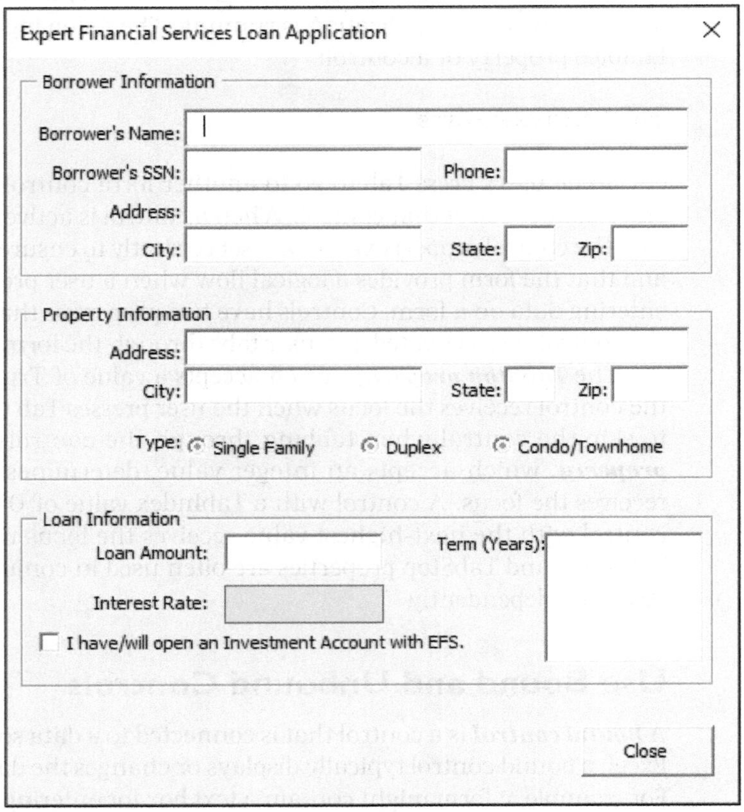

Excel 2016, Windows 10, Microsoft Corporation

FIGURE 2.5 Residential Loan Application Form

The Borrower Information frame groups the controls for entering information about the borrower. The TabStop property for the frame is set to True, and the TabIndex property is set to 0. Table 2.4 lists the property settings for the controls in the Borrower Information frame.

The Property Information frame groups the controls for entering and editing information about the property being financed. This frame has a Name property of fmePropertyInfo and a Caption property of Property Information. Table 2.5 lists the controls and properties used in the Property Information frame.

TABLE 2.4 Properties for Controls in the Borrower Information Frame

Control	Property	Setting
lblName	Caption	Borrower's Name:
txtName	ControlSource	B4
	TabIndex	0
	TabStop	True
lblSSN	Caption	Borrower's SSN:
txtSSN	ControlSource	B5
	TabIndex	1
	TabStop	True
lblAddress	Caption	Address:
txtAddress	ControlSource	B7
	TabIndex	2
	TabStop	True
lblCity	Caption	City:
txtCity	ControlSource	B8
	TabIndex	3
	TabStop	True
lblState	Caption	State:
txtState	ControlSource	B9
	TabIndex	4
	TabStop	True
lblZip	Caption	Zip:
txtZip	ControlSource	B10
	TabIndex	5
	TabStop	True

TABLE 2.5 Properties for Controls in the Property Information Frame

Control	Property	Setting
lblAddress2	Caption	Address:
txtAddress2	ControlSource	B13
	TabIndex	0
	TabStop	True
lblCity2	Caption	City:
txtCity2	ControlSource	B14
	TabIndex	1
	TabStop	True
lblState2	Caption	State:
txtState2	ControlSource	B15
	TabIndex	2
	TabStop	True
lblZip2	Caption	Zip:
txtZip2	ControlSource	B16
	TabIndex	3
	TabStop	True
lblType	Caption	Type:
optSingle	Caption	Single Family
	ControlSource	B17
	TabIndex	4
	TabStop	True
optDuplex	Caption	Duplex
	ControlSource	B17
	TabIndex	5
	TabStop	True
optCondo	Caption	Condo/Townhome
	ControlSource	B17
	TabIndex	6
	TabStop	True

TIP: OPTION BUTTONS
Clicking an option button changes that control's Value to True. The Value property of the remaining option buttons within the same frame is set to False.

The Loan Information frame groups the controls for entering and editing information about the loan. This frame has a Name property of fmeLoanInfo and a Caption property of Loan Information. The TabStop property for the frame is set to True, and the TabIndex property is set to 2. Table 2.6 lists the controls and properties. This frame contains two Label controls for the interest rate. The first displays a descriptive label, and the second will eventually display the calculated interest rate, which is determined by the loan amount (principal), loan term, and whether the applicant has opened or will open an investment account.

TABLE 2.6 Properties for Controls in the Loan Information Frame

Control	Property	Setting
lblPrincipal	Caption	Loan Amount:
	Left	12
	TextAlign	3-fmTextAlignRight
	Top	10
txtPrincipal	ControlSource	F6
	Left	90
	TabIndex	0
	TabStop	True
	Top	6
lblRate	Caption	Interest Rate:
	Left	12
	Top	33
lblRateValue	Caption	None: Delete the default caption
	BackColor	&H00FFFFC0&
	BorderStyle	1-fmBorderStyleSingle
	Left	90
	TextAlign	2-fmTextAlignCenter
	Top	30
lblTerm	Caption	Term (Years):
	Left	186
	Top	6
	Width	51
lstTerm	BorderStyle	0-fmBorderStyleNone
	ColumnWidths	0.15 pt
	Height	60
	Left	234
	TabIndex	1
	TabStop	True
	TextAlign	2-fmTextAlignCenter
	Top	6
chkAccount	Caption	I have/will open an Investment Account with EFS.
	Left	6
	TabIndex	2
	TabStop	True
	Top	48
	Width	200

Inserting Controls on a Worksheet

 In this project, the data entry form is launched from the Instructions worksheet. Therefore, this worksheet needs controls, such as command buttons, so the user can open the form and initialize the application. The first task is to insert a button on the Instructions worksheet that displays and initializes the frmData user form.

To insert a control on a worksheet, complete the following steps:

1. Click the Developer tab and click Insert in the Controls group (see Figure 2.6).
2. Click the icon for the type of control you want to insert on the worksheet.
3. Drag the pointer to insert the control on the worksheet.

   When you add a control to an Excel worksheet, the worksheet is in Design mode, which enables you to edit the control and write VBA code.
4. Click Properties in the Controls group to display the Properties window for the selected control (see Figure 2.7).
5. Click Design Mode to disable Design mode. When the Design mode is disabled and you click a control, the associated VBA code will run.

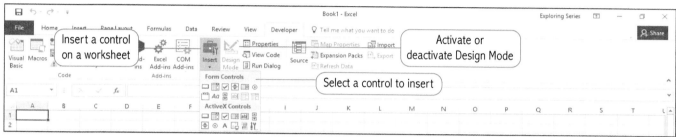

FIGURE 2.6 Inserting a Control on a Worksheet

Excel 2016, Windows 10, Microsoft Corporation

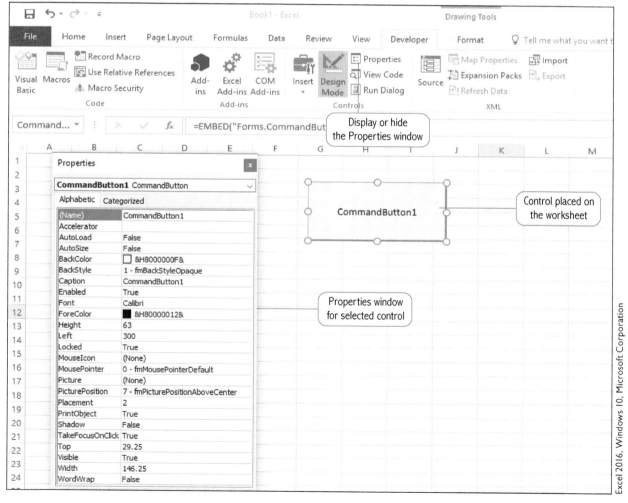

FIGURE 2.7 Properties Window for Control

1. What is the object model framework? *p. 78*

2. Why is it important to assign a Name and a Caption property for an object? *p. 79*

3. What are two methods to add items to a list box? *p. 84*

Hands-On Exercises

Skills covered: Set the Form Properties • Name the Controls • Insert Label and TextBox Controls • Insert ListBox, CheckBox, and CommandButton Controls • Set Enabled, TapStop, and TabIndex Properties • Use Bound and Unbound Controls

1 Forms and Controls

Cassandra's assistant created a workbook with the four main worksheets. In addition, she started to create the Residential Loan Application form. However, Cassandra asked you to finish creating the interface of the form.

STEP 1 » SET THE FORM PROPERTIES

Most of the properties have been set to match the settings listed in Tables 2.4 and 2.5. However, you need to set the Name, Caption, and Height properties for the form. Refer to Figure 2.8 as you complete Step 1.

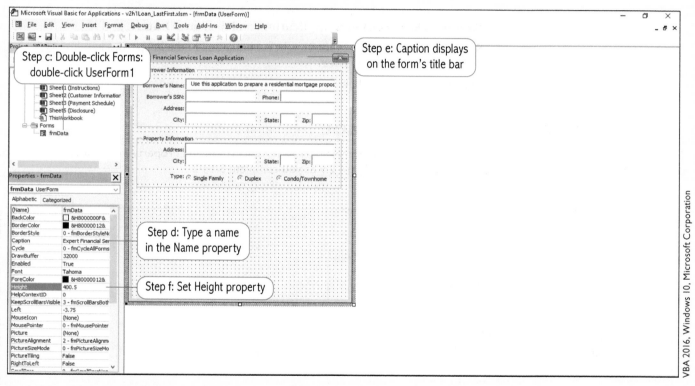

FIGURE 2.8 Form Properties

a. Open *v2h1Loan.xlsm* (an Excel macro-enabled workbook), and save it as **v2h1Loan_LastFirst.xlsm**.

> **TROUBLESHOOTING:** If the Security Warning toolbar displays, click Enable Content. If you make any major mistakes in this exercise, you can close the file, open *v2h1Loan* again, and then start this exercise over.

b. Click the **Developer tab** and click **Visual Basic** in the Code group.

The VB Editor opens. The Project Explorer window shows the worksheet names in the Microsoft Excel Objects section and a Forms folder.

c. Double-click **Forms** in the Project Explorer window and double-click **UserForm1** to display the form, if the form is not already displayed.

The default Name is UserForm1, and the default Caption is UserForm1.

d. Select **UserForm1** in the Name property box in the Properties window, type **frmData**, and then press **Enter**.

e. Select **UserForm1** in the Caption property box in the Properties window, type **Expert Financial Services Loan Application**, and then press **Enter**.

f. Select the existing value in the Height property box in the Properties window, type **400.5**, and then press **Enter**.

g. Click **Save** on the toolbar.

STEP 2 ›› INSERT A FRAME CONTROL

The Residential Loan Application form contains the top two frames: Borrower Information and Property Information. You will add the Loan Information frame and set its properties. Refer to Figure 2.9 as you complete Step 2.

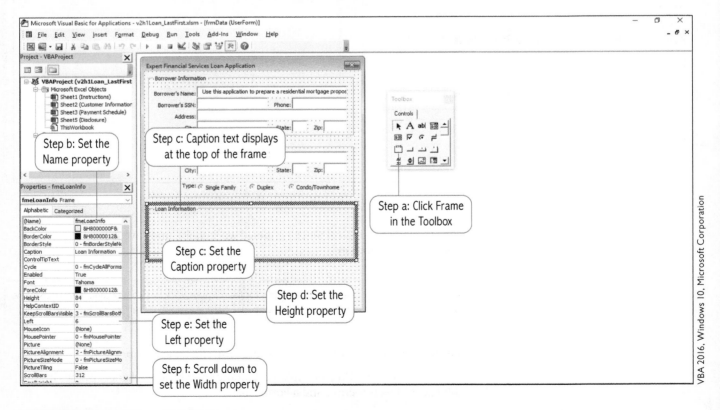

FIGURE 2.9 Loan Information Frame

a. Click the form and click **Toolbox** on the toolbar. Click **Frame** in the Toolbox and click about two dots below the second frame in the form to create a default-sized frame.

> You can drag the Toolbox to the right side of the form so that it is easier to see.

b. Select **Frame1** in the Name property box in the Properties window, type **fmeLoanInfo**, and then press **Enter**.

c. Select **Frame1** in the Caption property box in the Properties window, type **Loan Information**, and then press **Enter**.

> The text *Loan Information:* displays at the top of the frame you created.

d. Select the existing value in the Height property box, type **84**, and then press **Enter**.

> You adjusted the height to be the same as the height of the second frame.

e. Select the existing value in the Left property box, type **6**, and then press **Enter**.

> This setting makes sure the frame aligns on the left side with the other two frames that have a Left property value of 6.

f. Scroll down the Properties window, select the existing value in the Width property box, type **312**, and then press **Enter**.

> You adjusted the width to be the same as the width of the first two frames.

g. Click **Save** on the toolbar.

STEP 3 ▶▶ INSERT LABEL AND TEXTBOX CONTROLS

You need to add Label and TextBox controls for the loan amount and interest rate in the top-left corner of the Loan Information frame you just created. As you insert the controls, you will set their properties. Refer to Figure 2.10 as you complete Step 3.

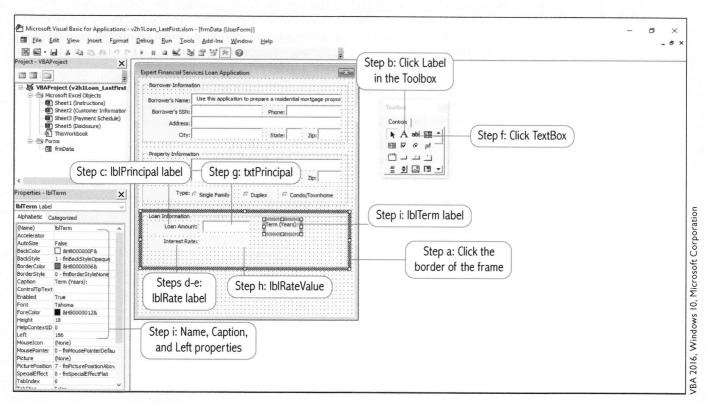

FIGURE 2.10 Label and TextBox Controls

a. Click the border of the Loan Information frame in the form to select it.

b. Click **Label** in the Toolbox and click below the *Loan Information* caption in the frame.

VBA inserts a label within the selected frame.

c. Change the Name property to **lblPrincipal**, change the Caption to **Loan Amount:**, change the Left property to **12**, change the TextAlign property to **3 – fmTextAlignRight**, and then change the Top property to **10**.

You inserted a Label control. The Left property value specifies the distance from the left side of the form. The Top property value specifies the distance from the top edge of the form.

d. Press and hold **Ctrl**, select the label you just created, and then drag down to create a copy below the original label.

The copied label shows the same caption and has the same TextAlign value, but you need to change the Name, Caption, Left, and Top properties.

e. Ensure that the duplicate label is selected, change the Name property to **lblRate**, change the Caption to **Interest Rate:**, change the Left property to **12**, and then change the Top property to **33**.

You want to make sure the label is the same distance from the left side of the form as the first label; however, this label displays farther down from the top edge of the form.

f. Click the **Loan Information frame** to select it, click **TextBox** in the Toolbox, and then click to the right of the *Loan Amount* label.

You inserted a TextBox control to the right of the *Loan Amount* label. The label describes the TextBox because the TextBox does not have a Caption property.

g. Change the Name property to **txtPrincipal**, change the Left property to **90**, and then change the Top property to **6**.

h. Insert a Label control below the TextBox control, change the Name property to **lblRateValue**, delete the default Caption text, change the Left property to **90**, change the TextAlign property to **2-fmTextAlignCenter**, and then change the Top property to **30**.

You inserted two labels for interest rates. The first displays a descriptive label, and the second displays the calculated interest rate, which is determined by the loan amount, loan term, and whether the applicant has opened or will open an investment account.

i. Insert a Label control to the right of the txtPrincipal control, change the Name property to **lblTerm**, change the Caption to **Term (Years):**, change the Left property to **186**, change the Top property to **6**, and then change the Width to **51**.

j. Click **Save** on the toolbar.

To finish the Loan Information frame, you need to insert a ListBox control to list the terms, a CheckBox control for customers to verify they have or plan to open another account with EFS, and a CommandButton to close the form. Refer to Figure 2.11 as you complete Step 4.

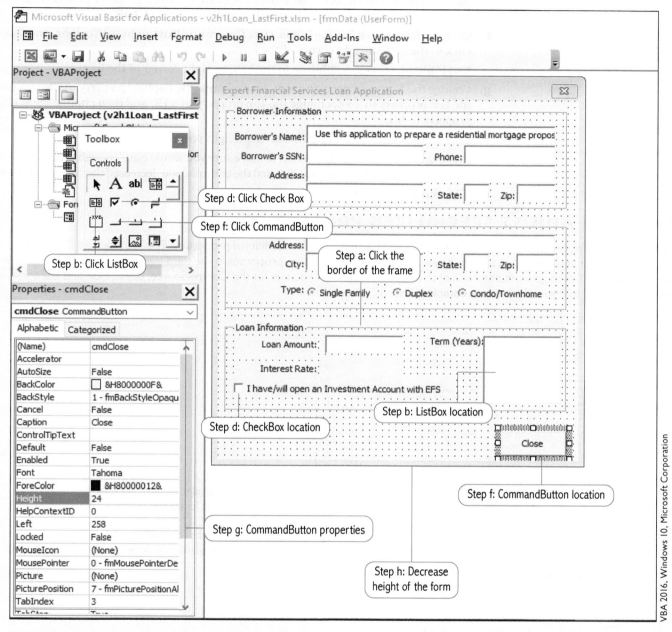

FIGURE 2.11 ListBox, CheckBox, and Button Controls

    a. Select the outer border of the Loan Information frame in the form.

    b. Click **ListBox** in the Toolbox and click to the right of the *Term (Years)* label.

       You inserted a ListBox control to the right of the Term (Years) label. The label is needed because the ListBox control does not have a Caption property to identify the control.

    c. Change the Name property to **lstTerm**, change the Height to **60**, change the Left property to **234**, change the TextAlign property to **2-fmTextAlignCenter**, and then change the Top property to **6**.

> **TROUBLESHOOTING:** Make sure you type a lowercase *l* in the Name instead of the number *1*.

d. Click the Loan Information frame, click **CheckBox** in the Toolbox, and then click below the Interest Rate label.

You inserted a CheckBox control below the Interest Rate label.

e. Change the Name property to **chkAccount**, change the Caption property to **I have/will open an Investment Account with EFS**, change the Left property to **6**, change the Top property to **48**, and then change the Width property to **200**.

f. Click the form instead of the frame, click **CommandButton** in the Toolbox, and then click in the bottom-right corner of the form.

You inserted a CommandButton in the bottom-right corner of the form.

g. Change the Name property to **cmdClose**, change the Caption property to **Close**, change the Left property to **258**, change the Top property to **312**, and then change the Width property to **60**.

h. Click the form to select it and change the Height property to **369.75**.

Previously, you increased the height to make sure you would have enough space to insert the controls. Now that you have inserted the controls, you decreased the height of the form.

i. Click **Save** on the toolbar.

Now that you have inserted all the controls on the form, you need to set additional properties. The TabStop and TabIndex properties are set in the first two frames; however, you need to set these properties in the third frame to provide a logical flow if the user presses Tab to go from one control to another. In addition, you will set the ControlSource, BackColor, and BorderStyle properties. Refer to Figure 2.12 as you complete Step 5.

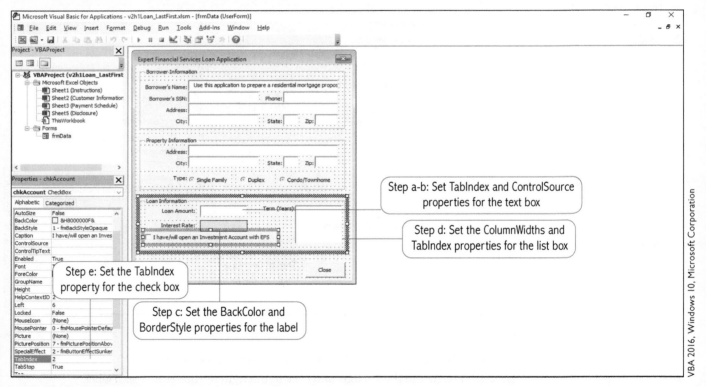

FIGURE 2.12 Set Properties

a. Click the **txtPrincipal control** in the Loan Information frame.

The TabStop property default setting is True.

b. Change the TabIndex property to **0** and change the ControlSource property to **F6**.

To make sure the txtPrincipal is the first control to receive focus within the selected frame, you set the TabIndex value to 0. Finally, you want to use the value stored in cell F6 of the current worksheet as the source for calculations.

c. Click the **lblRateValue control**, click the **BackColor property arrow**, click the **Palette tab**, and then select the **light blue color** (third color from the right on the top row). *H00FFFFC0&* should display in the BackColor property setting now. Set the BorderStyle property to **1-fmBorderStyleSingle**.

You selected a different background color so that the interest rate stands out on the form.

d. Click the **lstTerm** control, set the ColumnWidths property to **0.15**, and then set the TabIndex property to **1**.

Because labels cannot receive focus, you set the lstTerm control to be the second control (indicated by 1) to receive focus in the selected frame.

e. Click the **chkAccount control** and set the TabIndex property to **2**.

You set the chkAccount control to be the third control (indicated by 2) to receive focus in the selected frame.

f. Click **Save** on the toolbar and close the VB Editor.

STEP 6 ▶▶ INSERT CONTROLS ON A WORKSHEET

The Instructions worksheet displays instructions for entering customer and loan information, calculating and displaying a loan repayment schedule, and displaying the Truth-in-Lending disclosure worksheet. You need to insert three command buttons on the Instructions worksheet. Later, you will write VBA code for each button. Refer to Figure 2.13 as you complete Step 6.

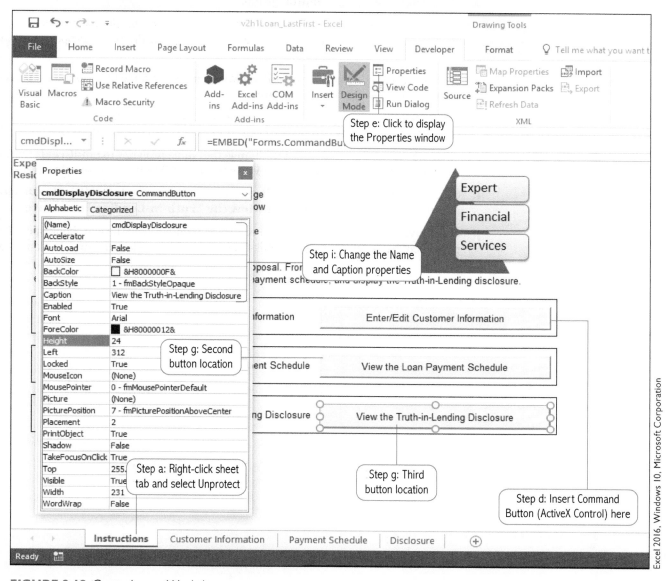

FIGURE 2.13 Controls on a Worksheet

a. Right-click the **Instructions sheet tab** and select **Unprotect Sheet**.

Excel prevents you from inserting controls on a protected worksheet. You must temporarily unprotect the worksheet to insert a control on it.

b. Click the **Developer tab** and click **Insert** in the Controls group.

c. Click **Command Button (ActiveX Control)** in the ActiveX Controls section in the gallery.

The pointer looks like a plus sign, indicating you are ready to drag to draw the control on the worksheet.

> **TROUBLESHOOTING:** If you click Button (Form Control) instead of Command Button (ActiveX Control), you will not be able to code the button correctly. You must delete the Button control and click Command Button (ActiveX Control) in the gallery to create the correct type of control.

d. Drag to create a command button to approximate the size and location within the top box as shown in Figure 2.13.

e. Click **Properties** in the Controls group.

The Properties window displays so that you can set the properties for the selected command button. You can increase the height and the width of the Properties window, if needed.

f. Change the Name property to **cmdDisplayForm** and change the Caption property to **Enter/Edit Customer Information**.

g. Press **Ctrl+C** to copy the selected button and press **Ctrl+V** twice to paste two copies of the button. Drag the two duplicate buttons to their respective locations (see Figure 2.13).

h. Click the second button to select it. Change the Name property to **cmdCreateSchedule** and change the Caption property to **View the Loan Payment Schedule**.

i. Click the third button to select it. Change the Name property to **cmdDisplayDisclosure** and change the Caption property to **View the Truth-in-Lending Disclosure**.

j. Click **Save** on the toolbar. Close the Properties window. Keep the workbook open if you plan to continue with the next Hands-On Exercise. If not, close the workbook and exit Excel.

Procedures and Functions for Form Controls

After you create a form, insert controls on the form, and set the properties for the controls, you are ready to start writing the code. The code should enable the form to accept user input, store data into variables, perform calculations if needed, and display output.

In Chapter 1, you learned the foundational structures for creating procedures. In this section, you will write procedures that are attached to controls. In addition, you will learn how to create and call function procedures.

Adding a Procedure to a Control

STEP 1 ►► The CommandButton control is probably the most common control for which you need to write code. Typically, you write code specifically for a button that executes a procedure when the user clicks the button. The process of writing code is similar to how you created procedures in Chapter 1. The difference is that the procedure name matches the button's name, includes an underscore, and includes the name of the event that triggers the code, such as Click.

> **To add a procedure to a control that is on a worksheet, complete the following steps:**
>
> 1. Click Design Mode in the Controls group on the Developer tab.
> 2. Right-click the control and select View Code. VBA creates a procedure that handles the button's Click event. The procedure includes the button's name, an underscore, and the event name. For example, if the button's name is cmdDisplayForm, VBA creates the procedure header Private Sub cmdDisplayForm_Click().
> 3. Type the code for the control's procedure.

After creating the procedure for the control, click Design Mode to deactivate the Design mode and click the button to make sure the procedure runs as you intended.

Use Object Hierarchy

Understanding how objects relate to one another is essential to working with VBA, because VBA statements refer to objects by name and in order according to their position in the object hierarchy.

Assume you are creating a VBA procedure that needs to obtain a value from the Payment worksheet in a workbook named Loan Calculator. The worksheet is a member of the Worksheets collection. Therefore, you specify the Worksheets object with the worksheet object name enclosed in quotation marks within the parentheses. If you are working with two workbooks that both have a worksheet named Payment, you must indicate which worksheet you want to manipulate by specifying the name of the workbook. When you reference multiple objects in a hierarchy, the top-level object is referenced first. A period (dot) separates the object references. To refer to a specific cell or group of cells, use the Range object after the Workbooks and Worksheets objects.

The object highest in the hierarchy is the Application object. To reference every object in the hierarchy to which a specific cell belongs (such as a specific worksheet range), your code must include the Application object. Code Window 2.1 displays four statements that illustrate different levels of depth in referencing objects. To ensure the correct object is being used from the correct worksheet in a specific workbook, you can explicitly or directly state the entire hierarchy.

```
'Only one workbook open with a Payment worksheet
Worksheets ("Payment")

'Two or more workbooks open, each with a Payment worksheet
Workbooks("Loan Calculator.xlsm").Worksheets ("Payment")

'A range in a particular worksheet object
Workbooks("Loan Calculator.xlsm").Worksheets("Payment").Range ("B9")

'Explicit statement showing hierarchy
Application.Workbooks("Loan Calculator.xlsm").Worksheets("Payment").Range ("B9")
```

CODE WINDOW 2.1

The way you reference an object depends on several factors. First, determine whether other objects in the application have a similar name. For example, referencing a cell range in a worksheet when two workbooks with different names are open and both workbooks have a worksheet with the same name requires an explicit or complete reference that names the workbook, the worksheet, and the range. If your object references omit any part of the hierarchy, Excel uses the active object. For that reason, most programmers do not include a reference to the Application object in code, because by default the application is running. The best principle is to keep your code as simple as possible while also anticipating how the code will run when multiple workbooks might be open. The more explicit you are in specifying the hierarchy, the less the potential for conflicts, but more coding is required. Therefore, you should explicitly include as many elements in the hierarchy as you think the application will require for typical usage.

Manipulate Object Properties, Methods, and Events

You need to know about the characteristics of objects (properties), the actions that objects can perform (methods), and the actions that cause program statements to act upon objects (events).

As detailed earlier, a property is an attribute of an object that defines one of the object's characteristics. To change an object's characteristics, you can use an assignment statement to set the value of a property. The object reference and property name are separated by a period, and an equal sign assigns a value to the property.

A method is an action that an object can perform while the application is running. For example, Worksheet objects have an *Activate* method, which makes a specified worksheet the active sheet. Range objects have a *Clear* method, which clears all the cells in a range.

An event is an action occurring at run time that triggers a program instruction. Recall that VBA is an event-driven language in which program statements execute at run time to process information or perform actions in response to events. The code specifies what the object will do in response to the event. The system triggers some events, such as when a user opens a workbook. Users trigger other events, such as clicking the mouse or pressing a key.

Code Window 2.2 illustrates several statements that manipulate object properties, methods, and events.

```
'Use the Value property to assign 150000 to cell B5 in the active workbook
Workbook("Loan Calculator.xlsm").Worksheets("Payment").Range("B5").Value = 150000

'Move the active cell to the same row (0) and to the right by one cell (1)
ActiveCell.Offset(0, 1).Activate

'Assign a value stored in a variable to the active cell
ActiveCell.FormulaR1C1 = strFirst

'Use the Activate method to make a particular worksheet active
Worksheets("Customer Information").Activate

'Set the RowSource property for a combo box and a list box
cboInvestment.RowSource = "E2:E47"
lstYears.RowSource = "F2:F21"
```

CODE WINDOW 2.2

The first statement changes the value in a range (cell B5) in a specific worksheet (Payment) in a specific workbook (Loan Calculator).

The second statement uses ActiveCell.Offset to move the active cell to the same row (0) and to the right one cell (1) and uses the Activate method to activate that cell.

The third statement uses ActiveCell.FormulaR1C1 to assign the content of the variable strFirst to the active cell.

The fourth statement uses the Activate method to activate a specific worksheet (Customer Information).

The fifth statement populates a combo box by using the values in the range E2:E47 and assigning the range to the RowSource property.

The sixth statement uses the values in the range F2:F21 to populate the RowSource property of the lstYears list box.

At times, you do not want a worksheet to display the values used to populate a list in a ListBox or ComboBox control, because displaying these ranges clutters the user interface. If the list obtains its value from a worksheet range, you can hide the worksheet column containing the range. You can also add items to a list at run time using the AddItem method in a code procedure. For example, a form can include a procedure to initialize the control with a list of items when the application loads the form into memory. Code Window 2.3 contains an example of an initialization procedure.

```
'Populate the combo box and list box controls on the form
cboInvestment.AddItem = "8000"
cboInvestment.AddItem = "10000"
cboInvestment.AddItem = "12000"
cboInvestment.AddItem = "14000"
cboInvestment.AddItem = "16000"

lstYears.AddItem = "1"
lstYears.AddItem = "2"
lstYears.AddItem = "3"
lstYears.AddItem = "4"
lstYears.AddItem = "5"

lstContribution.AddItem = "25"
lstContribution.AddItem = "50"
lstContribution.AddItem = "75"
lstContribution.AddItem = "100"
```

CODE WINDOWS 2.3

Show, Hide, Close, and Unload Forms

STEP 2 ⟩⟩ When you add custom forms, you decide how to display the form, when to close it, and how to set the initial values when the form opens. In the EFS loan application, you write code procedures to initialize, display, and close the form for entering borrower, property, and loan information. The form displays when the user clicks a button on the Instructions worksheet. The procedure that displays the form also initializes the application by activating the Customer Information worksheet, disabling the worksheet protection, and setting the initial values: $160,000 for the principal, 30 years for the term, and 5.75% as the interest rate. Changing the principal or the term calls a custom procedure that calculates the interest rate and displays the updated rate in the lblRateValue control. Closing the form enables the worksheet protection and activates the Instructions form.

The command button that displays the data entry form handles a click event on the Instructions worksheet that opens the form. The form displays as a modal form. A modal form disables all other worksheet objects until the form is closed. All data entry and editing must be done while the form is open.

The *Show* method displays the form. The *Close* method closes the form and removes it from memory. The *Hide* method closes the form, but does not remove it from memory. If you use frmForm.Show again, the form will display with its previous values entered. To unload a form from memory, use the statement *Unload frmForm*, substituting the form's actual name.

1. Click the Object arrow at the top of the form, and then select UserForm. The Object shows the currently selected object for which you are writing code. If you are unsure which arrow is the Object arrow, position the pointer of the arrow to display a ScreenTip, such as Object.

2. Click the Procedures or Methods arrow at the top of the form, and then select Initialize from the Methods list. When you position the pointer over the Methods arrow, the ScreenTip displays *Procedure* or *Method*.

3. Initialize controls. For example, if you want to ensure previously entered data is cleared, you can adapt the following to clear a text box:

   txtName.Text=" "

Creating and Calling a Function Procedure

You have used implicit functions in VBA procedures. Implicit functions are predefined VBA functions. For example, the Val function converts a number stored as text into a numeric value for calculations, the Format function formats a value for display, the Input function displays a text box for user input, the MsgBox function displays information in a dialog box, and the IsNumeric function verifies that a value is a number. These are all examples of implicit functions, or functions that are a part of the VBA programming environment. Previously, you created sub procedures to perform actions. For example, you have created sub procedures to display message boxes. Function procedures, however, perform an action (such as obtaining user input and converting it to values) and return a value (such as calculating the monthly payment).

A function procedure begins with the keyword *Function* and ends with *End Function*. A function can receive arguments passed to the function by a procedure that calls the function. A procedure that calls a function is called the **calling procedure**. One advantage of function procedures is that you can create the procedure once and call it from multiple procedures. Code Window 2.4 illustrates a function procedure (LoanPayment) and the calling procedure (Loan_Payment).

```
'Function to calculate the loan payment
Function LoanPayment(Principal, Rate, Term)

    LoanPayment = Principal * (Rate / (1 - (1 + Rate) ^ -Term))

End Function

Sub Loan_Payment()

    'Declare variables
    Dim curPrincipal As Double
    Dim sngRate As Single
    Dim intTerm As Integer
    Dim curPayment As Currency

    'Obtain input and assign to variables
    curPrincipal = Val(InputBox("Please enter the loan principal"))
    sngRate = Val(InputBox("Please enter the annual interest rate")) / 12
    intTerm = Val(InputBox("Please enter the term")) * 12

    'Call the function and pass arguments to it
    curPayment = LoanPayment(curPrincipal, sngRate, intTerm)

    'Format and display the results
    MsgBox ("The monthly payment is: " & Format(curPayment, "Currency"))

End Sub
```

CODE WINDOW 2.4

Create the Main Procedure with the Calling Statement

The Loan_Payment procedure is the main procedure. It declares four variables, displays input boxes to obtain the values from the user, and converts the data to values before storing the values in the declared variables. Within the first InputBox statement, the APR is divided by 12, and within the next InputBox statement, the term is multiplied by 12, because the clients make 12 monthly payments.

The second-to-the-last statement contains LoanPayment(curPrincipal, sngRate, intTerm), which calls the LoanPayment function and passes the values stored in the curPrincipal, sngRate, and intTerm variables to that function. The function contains code to process the values and returns a value back to the calling procedure, which is then assigned to the curPayment variable.

> **TIP: CALLING PROCEDURES**
> The statement that calls a function always receives a value back from the function. The calling procedure statement cannot start with the function name. The program must do something with the return value, such as displaying it onscreen or storing the value in a variable. Therefore, the variable or output is typed at the left side, followed by the assignment operator =, and then the calling statement is on the right side of the assignment operator.

Create the Function Procedure

The LoanPayment function procedure receives the three arguments using the alias or similar names *Principal*, *Rate*, and *Term*. Often programmers use similar names for the argument names instead of identical names of the variables being passed to the argument. In this case, the function uses the name *Principal* instead of the original variable name *curPrincipal*. The function has one statement to calculate the loan payment. When the term and rate are expressed in monthly payment periods (the years multiplied by 12 months per year for the term and the annual interest divided by 12 months per year), the statement assigns the calculated result to the function name *LoanPayment*. The LoanPayment function then returns that value back to the calling procedure statement in the Loan_Payment sub procedure.

Process the Returned Value from the Function

The calling statement must do something with the returned value. In this case, it assigns the returned value to the curPayment variable. The Loan_Payment sub procedure then displays the formatted monthly payment in a message box.

If a user enters 160000 in the input box when prompted for the principal, 0.0645 in the input box that prompts for the interest rate, and 15 in the input box that prompts for the term, the resulting message box will display *The monthly payment is: $1,389.38.*

> **TIP: PASSING ARGUMENTS BY VALUE AND BY REFERENCE**
> You can pass arguments to procedures in two ways: by reference and by value. The default is by *reference*, which means that the value is passed by referencing the variable, and the procedure has access to the variable itself, and can potentially change its value. You can also pass arguments to a procedure by *value*, meaning that the procedure references a copy of the variable, and its value cannot be changed.

Quick Concepts

4. Explain the object hierarchy requirements for writing code. *p. 99*

5. What is the difference between a method and an event? *p. 100*

6. What is the purpose of a function? Why does the function calling statement have to have an assignment? *p. 102*

Hands-On Exercises

Skills covered: Manipulate Object Properties, Methods, and Events • Use Object Hierarchy • Show, Hide, Close, and Unload Forms • Create the Main Procedure with the Calling Statement • Create the Function Procedure • Process the Returned Value from the Function

2 Procedures and Functions for Form Controls

Previously, you inserted controls on the Loan Application form and changed some of the properties. In addition, you inserted a button control directly on a worksheet. You are now ready to start writing the code that displays the form, performs calculations based on input, and closes the form.

STEP 1 ›› ADD A PROCEDURE TO A CONTROL

You need to write code procedure for the cmdDisplayForm button that you inserted on the Instructions worksheet. The code will activate and unprotect the Customer Information sheet, populate a list box on the form, set initial values in the form, and use worksheet data to complete the form. Refer to Figure 2.14 as you complete Step 1.

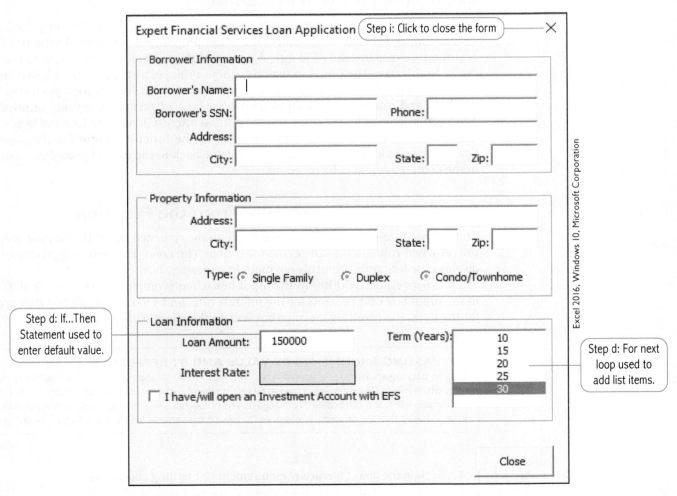

FIGURE 2.14 Form after Coding the Control

a. Open the macro-enabled *v2h1Loan_LastFirst* workbook if you closed it at the end of Hands-On Exercise 1 and save it as **v2h2Loan_LastFirst**, changing h1 to h2.

b. Click the **Developer tab** and click **Design Mode** in the Controls group to activate Design mode.

c. Right-click the **Enter/Edit Customer Information command button** on the worksheet and select **View Code**.

   VBA creates a procedure that handles the button's Click event.

d. Type the code shown in Code Window 2.5. Press **Enter** twice and type the code in Code Window 2.6.

```
Private Sub cmdDisplayForm_Click()

    'Activate the worksheet
    Worksheets("Customer Information").Activate
    Worksheets("Customer Information").Unprotect

    'Clear and populate the list box
    frmData.lstTerm.Clear
    Dim intItem As Integer
    For intItem = 10 To 30 Step 5
        frmData.lstTerm.AddItem (intItem)
    Next

    'Set the initial values
    If frmData.txtPrincipal.Text = "" Then
        frmData.txtPrincipal.Text = 150000
        Worksheets("Customer Information").Range("F6") = 150000
    End If

    If Worksheets("Customer Information").Range("F10") <> "" Then
        Dim intTerm As Integer
        intTerm = Val(Worksheets("Customer Information").Range("F10"))
    Else
        intTerm = 30
    End If

    Select Case intTerm
        Case 10
            frmData.lstTerm.Selected(0) = True
        Case 15
            frmData.lstTerm.Selected(1) = True
        Case 20
            frmData.lstTerm.Selected(2) = True
        Case 25
            frmData.lstTerm.Selected(3) = True
        Case 30
            frmData.lstTerm.Selected(4) = True
    End Select
```

CODE WINDOW 2.5

```
    Worksheets("Customer Information").Range("F10") = intTerm
    frmData.txtName.SetFocus

    'Display the form
    frmData.Show

End Sub
```

CODE WINDOW 2.6

The first two statements activate the Customer Information worksheet and then unprotect it so that the rest of the procedure can add data on the worksheet.

You can use a repetition structure to add items to a list box at run time. In this case, the procedure for initializing a form uses a repetition structure and a selection structure. The For...Next loop populates the list box with a range of values from 10 to 30, at intervals of 5.

The Select Case structure uses the value assigned to the intTerm variable to assign the value of True to the appropriate list box item so that it is selected. The frmData.txtName.SetFocus statement, gives the txtName box Focus. The last statement, frmData.Show, displays the form onscreen.

e. Click **Save** on the toolbar and close the VB Editor.

f. Right-click the **View the Truth-in-Lending Disclosure button** and select **View Code**.

g. Press **Enter**, press **Tab**, type **Worksheets("Disclosure").Activate**, and then press **Enter**. Click **Save** on the toolbar and close the VB Editor.

h. Click **Design Mode** in the Controls group on the Developer tab in Excel to deactivate Design mode.

i. Click the **Enter/Edit Customer Information button** to view the form. Click the **Close button** in the top-right corner of the form to close it. (The Close command button will not close the form because you have not created the code behind it yet.)

> **TROUBLESHOOTING:** If the form does not open when you click the command button, display the VB Editor and then check your code carefully. Make any necessary corrections to the code, click Save, and exit the VB Editor. Then repeat steps h–i again.

j. Click the **Instructions sheet tab** and click the **View the Truth-in-Lending Disclosure button** to activate the Disclosure worksheet. Click the **Instructions sheet tab**. Save the workbook.

STEP 2 ›› ADD A PROCEDURE TO CLOSE A FORM

You need to add a procedure to the Close button on the form so that it will close the form. In addition, you need to add a command button on the Customer Information worksheet to return to the Instructions worksheet. Refer to Figure 2.15 as you complete Step 2.

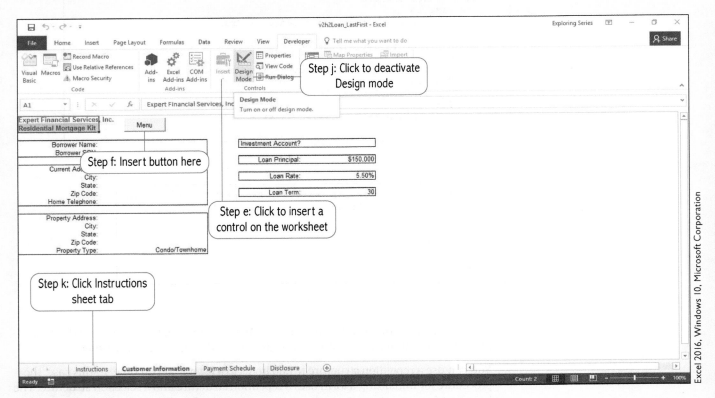

FIGURE 2.15 Customer Information Worksheet

a. Open the VB Editor and display the frmData form.

b. Right-click the **Close button** and select **View Code**.

c. Type the code shown in Code Window 2.7 between the Sub and End Sub statements.

```
Private Sub cmdClose_Click()

    'Determine property type; add to worksheet
    If optSingle.Value = -1 Then
        Worksheets("Customer Information").Range("B17") = "Single Family"
    ElseIf optDuplex.Value = -1 Then
        Worksheets("Customer Information").Range("B17") = "Duplex"
    Else
        Worksheets("Customer Information").Range("B17") = "Condo/Townhome"
    End If

    'Update interest rate, set protection, hide form
    Worksheets("Customer Information").Range("F8") = frmData.lblRateValue.Caption
    Worksheets("Customer Information").Protect
    frmData.Hide

End Sub
```

CODE WINDOW 2.7

The If...ElseIf statement determines which option button is selected. For each logical test, you compare a specific option button's Value property to –1, which is the value assigned by VBA to the selected option button. When a particular option button's Value property equals –1, a text entry will be entered in cell B17 on the Customer Information worksheet.

Next, the caption value in the lblRateValue control is then copied to cell F8 in the Customer Information worksheet. After the data is copied into cell F8, the procedure protects the Customer Information worksheet from further changes. Finally, the frmData.Hide statement hides the form but does not remove it from memory.

d. Save the code and minimize the VB Editor.

e. Click the **Customer Information sheet tab** and click **Design Mode**. Click **Insert** in the Controls group on the Developer tab and click **Command Button (ActiveX Control)**.

f. Click to the right side of the Expert Financial Services heading on the left side of the worksheet to create a command button. Refer to Figure 2.15 for placement and size.

g. Click **Properties** in the Controls group. Change the Name property to **cmdReturn** and the Caption property to **Menu**.

h. Close the Properties window, right-click the **Menu button**, and then select **View Code**.

VBA creates the Private Sub cmdReturn_Click() and End Sub lines.

i. Press **Enter**, press **Tab**, type **Worksheets ("Instructions").Activate** and then press **Enter**. Save and close the VB Editor.

j. Click **Design Mode** in the Controls group to deactivate Design mode.

k. Click the **Instructions worksheet tab** to make it the active sheet. Click the **Enter/Edit Customer Information button** you created earlier. When the form opens, click **Close** in the bottom-right corner.

The form closes now that you have created a procedure for the Click event.

l. Click the **Menu button** you created at the top of the Customer Information worksheet.

The Click event procedure activates the Instructions worksheet again.

m. Save the workbook.

STEP 3 » CREATE AND CALL A FUNCTION PROCEDURE

You need to create a function procedure that calculates the interest rate based on the term or principal. If a term is 10 years or if the principal is greater than or equal to $500,000, the interest rate is 4.75%. If the term is 15 years or if the principal is greater than or equal to $400,000, the interest rate is 5%. If the term is 20 years or if the principal is greater than or equal to $300,000, the interest rate is 5.25%. If the term is 25 years or if the principal is greater than or equal to $200,000, the interest rate is 5.5%. All other terms or principal amounts require a 5.75% interest rate. After you create the function procedure, you will create a calling procedure. Refer to Figure 2.16 as you complete Step 3.

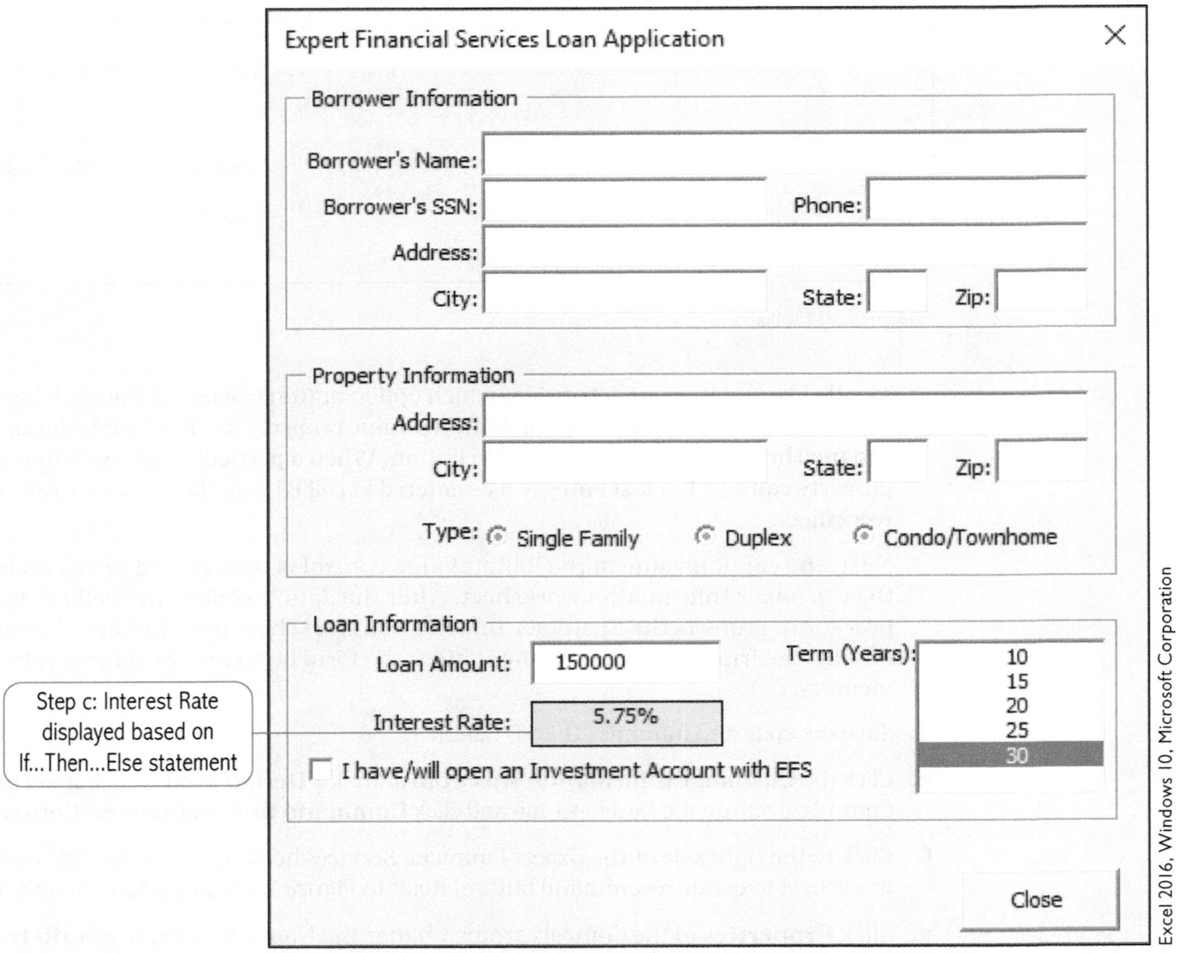

FIGURE 2.16 Interest Rate Displayed

a. Display the VB Editor, right-click the **frmData form** in the Project Explorer, and then select **View Code**.

b. Press **Ctrl+Home**, type **Option Explicit** and then press **Enter** twice.

c. Use Code Window 2.8 to create the Calculate procedure.

TROUBLESHOOTING: Remember to type a lowercase l not the number 1 in *lstTerm.Text*. Remember to indent the statements within the If...ElseIf statement block for readability.

```
Sub CalculateRate()
    'Declare variables
    Dim curPrincipal As Currency
    Dim intTerm As Integer

    'Obtain values
    curPrincipal = Val(frmData.txtPrincipal.Text)
    intTerm = Val(lstTerm.Text)

    'Display interest rate
    If intTerm = 10 Or curPrincipal >= 500000 Then
        frmData.lblRateValue.Caption = "4.75%"
    ElseIf intTerm = 15 Or curPrincipal >= 400000 Then
        frmData.lblRateValue.Caption = "5.00%"
    ElseIf intTerm = 20 Or curPrincipal >= 300000 Then
        frmData.lblRateValue.Caption = "5.25%"
    ElseIf intTerm = 25 Or curPrincipal >= 200000 Then
        frmData.lblRateValue.Caption = "5.50%"
    Else
        frmData.lblRateValue.Caption = "5.75%"
    End If

End Sub
```

CODE WINDOW 2.8

The procedure declares two variables and uses the Text property of the text box and the list box controls to store the current values from the Text properties into the respective variables. You used an If...ElseIf statement block to handle the multiple logical tests. Each If and ElseIf test evaluated to see if either the term was equal to a value or if the principal was greater than or equal to a monetary value.

d. Use the Code Window 2.9 to create the calling procedures immediately after the CalculateRate procedure's End Sub statement.

```
Private Sub lstTerm_Click()

    CalculateRate

End Sub

Private Sub txtPrincipal_AfterUpdate()

    'Declare string variable
    Dim strMessage As String
    strMessage = "Please enter a value between 100000 and 700000"

    'Validate entry
    If Val(frmData.txtPrincipal.Text) < 100000 Or _
       Val(frmData.txtPrincipal.Text) > 700000 Then
            MsgBox strMessage, vbCritical, "Invalid Loan Principal"
    Else
        CalculateRate
    End If

End Sub
```

CODE WINDOW 2.9

The procedure declares a string variable and then assigns text to it to avoid having a lot of extra text in the MsgBox statement. The code then checks to determine if the value entered is either too low or too high. If either condition exists, a message box displays an error to the user. The last statement calls the CalculateRate procedure.

TROUBLESHOOTING: Remember to use the line-continuation (space and underscore) for long statements that carry over to a second line. If you forget the line-continuation character, a VBA error message will appear.

e. Click **Save** on the toolbar and close the VB Editor.

f. Click the **Instructions worksheet tab** and click the **Enter/Edit Customer Information button** in the worksheet.

The Loan Application form displays 5.75% in the Interest Rate label because the term is 30 years.

g. Click the **Close button** on the form. Save the workbook. Keep the workbook open if you plan to continue with Hands-On Exercise 3. If not, close the workbook and exit Excel.

Loan Payment Schedule and Disclosure Worksheets

The loan payment schedule and disclosure worksheets are important to provide additional details about loans to EFS clients. To complete these worksheets, you will incorporate a variety of VBA statements that you have previously learned. For example, you will create procedures that use the object model, declare variables, initialize variables, create a repetition structure, call a custom function procedure, and return a value from a function back to the calling statement.

In this section, you will create a loan payment schedule using variables, If statements, repetition statements, financial functions, and the Excel object model. Furthermore, you will complete a loan disclosure worksheet that includes financial and date functions. Finally, you will complete the entire EFS application by setting workbook options to protect the worksheets against unauthorized data entry.

Creating a List in a Worksheet

You can write VBA code that creates a list in a worksheet. For example, you might want to create an amortization table that lists each monthly payment's details for a particular loan. To create such a list, use a repetition structure (i.e., a loop) where, through each iteration, data is entered on the next blank row in the worksheet.

A loan payment schedule provides information for each monthly payment until a loan is paid in full. When you make a residential mortgage payment, you pay the same amount each month, but the portion of the payment that applies to the loan principal varies each month. For the initial payments, a greater portion of each payment applies to the interest charged for the loan, but as the payments continue, a greater portion of the monthly payment applies to the outstanding loan principal. A loan repayment schedule is useful for displaying the details of each monthly payment and determining the outstanding balance at any time during the loan.

The EFS workbook includes the Payment Schedule worksheet to display the loan principal, term, rate, monthly payment, and closing costs. It also displays the following details for each monthly payment: the payment number, the amount of the monthly payment that applies to the loan principal, the amount of the monthly payment that applies to the loan interest, the principal paid to date, the interest paid to date, the total principal and interest paid to date, and the outstanding loan balance.

Prepare the Worksheet and Obtain Input

STEP 1 ›› Before writing code to populate a list on a worksheet, you need to prepare the worksheet. This process may include creating a control that will run the code, declaring variables, and obtaining input from a data-entry section on a worksheet or from a form.

> **To prepare the worksheet and obtain input, complete the following steps:**
>
> 1. Insert a Command Button (ActiveX Control) on a worksheet. The button will be used to execute the VBA code.
> 2. View the code for the control.
> 3. Write the code to unprotect a worksheet and clear an existing range from any previous lists.
> 4. Declare variables to store data obtained from a worksheet, calculated values, a counter variable to store the current row number of the list, and a counter variable to control the iterations.
> 5. Use the Worksheets.Range code to obtain values from appropriate cells in a worksheet and assign the values to variables.
> 6. Perform any calculations that will be needed before the loop begins.

Code Window 2.10 declares intCurrentRow, a counter variable to store the value of the current row number where you want to enter data in the list. This value will change during each iteration of the loop. The intCounter is a counter variable that controls the number of times the loop iterates. For example, if a user takes out a 5-year loan with monthly payments, the intCounter variable will be set to 60 (5 years with 12 months each).

```
'Current row number for entering data in the list
Dim intCurrentRow As Integer

'Counter variable to control loop iterations
Dim intCounter As Integer
```

CODE WINDOW 2.10

Write Code to Create a List

STEP 2 ▶▶ After preparing a worksheet, declaring variables, and obtaining input, you are ready to write the code to create a list. The code should include a statement that primes the loop—that is, you should set the value of the variable that will control which row the data will be entered in the worksheet. Then, create a loop that will iterate the number of times needed to populate the list.

> **To write code to create a list, complete the following steps:**
>
> 1. Assign a value of the first row for which you want to enter data. This variable will increment each iteration so that data will be entered on the next empty row in the list.
> 2. Create the loop header using a For statement. Specify the starting value of the counter variable, such as 1, and specify its termination value using a variable to iterate enough times based on the data. For example, if you are making monthly payments on an automobile loan for 5 years, the loop needs to iterate 60 times. Do not hard-code 60, because the number of monthly payments will vary based on whether the user takes out a 4-, 5-, or 6-year loan.
> 3. Create the body of the loop to enter data on the current row. For the first iteration, the current row should be the starting row of the list.
> 4. Write the code for the last line of the loop before the Next statement to increment the row number. The counter variable controlling the iterations should automatically increment because of the For header.

Code Window 2.11 illustrates a loop to enter data on a worksheet. The statement before the loop, intCurrentRow = 10 makes sure the first data is entered on row 10 in the worksheet. The header starts the intCounter variable at 1. During each iteration, the value increases until it reaches the total of payment periods, indicated by the value stored in intTerm.

```
'Specify starting row number for the list
intCurrentRow = 10

'Loop through each monthly payment to calculate & display values
For intCounter = 1 To intTerm
    'Enter current payment number in Column A of current row
    Worksheets("Payment Schedule").Range("A" & intCurrentRow) = intCounter

    'Calculate monthly payment and enter it in Column B of current row
    curPpmt = PPmt(dblRate, intCounter, intTerm, -curPrincipal)
    Worksheets("Payment Schedule").Range("B" & intCurrentRow) = curPpmt

    'Calculate current interest and enter it in Column C of current row
    curIpmt = IPmt(dblRate, intCounter, intTerm, -curPrincipal)
    Worksheets("Payment Schedule").Range("C" & intCurrentRow) = curIpmt

    'Increment the row number for the next row in the worksheet
    intCurrentRow = intCurrentRow + 1

Next
```

CODE WINDOW 2.11

To make sure the data gets entered in the correct cells, the Range argument specifies the column letter in quotation marks. For example, to enter the payment number in the first column, use Range ("A" & intCurrentRow). The & concatenates the column letter A with the value in the intCurrentRow variable. During the first iteration, the data starts in cell A10. The comments explain the calculations and what data is entered in columns B and C. The last statement increments the intCurrentRow by 1 and saves that value back to the intCurrentRow variable. At the end of the first iteration, intCurrentRow contains the value 11 so that during the next iteration, data will be placed on row 11.

Understand Other Sections on the Payment Schedule Worksheet

The range B4:B7 summarizes the loan details. Because some of this information is already displayed on the Customer Information worksheet, you can use 3-D references to display the same information on this worksheet and the Pmt function to calculate the monthly payment.

The range G5:G7 summarizes the closing costs, which include the loan origination fee (2% of the loan principal) and the loan points (which range from 1% to 3% of the loan principal) based upon the loan term. In addition, customers who currently have or plan to open an investment account with EFS receive a 1% discount on the loan points. The total closing cost is the sum of the origination fee and the points. These values can be calculated from the loan information displayed in cells B4 and B6 of the Payment Schedule worksheet, and cell F4 of the Customer Information worksheet, which displays TRUE if the customer has opened or will open an investment account and FALSE if the customer does not have an account.

Preparing an Application for Distribution

When you create a custom application, you should test its functionality before you distribute it. However, before testing the application, you should prepare the application for distribution. In the EFS application, the Instructions worksheet provides menu options for opening the data entry form, generating and displaying the payment schedule, and displaying the Truth-in-Lending disclosure.

Create Code to Activate the Instructions Worksheet

STEP 3 All data entry is through the form; therefore, all the worksheets need to have protection set to prevent accidental data entry within the worksheet. The Payment Schedule worksheet will contain the loan amortization schedule. However, you want to create an easy way for a user to go back to the Instructions worksheet. Therefore, you will add a button that when clicked will display the Instructions worksheet again.

> **To create a statement that will open a worksheet, complete the following steps:**
>
> 1. Add an On Click event to a CommandButton.
> 2. Enter the code *Worksheets("NameOfWorksheet").Activate* and press Enter. The Activate method will activate or display the worksheet specified.

Add Formulas to the Disclosure Worksheet

STEP 4 The Disclosures worksheet summarizes the amount to be financed, the total finance charges, the total payments, the interest rate, the term, and the dates the first and last payments are due. You can create formulas that refer to values stored in other worksheets to display on this summary worksheet. In addition, you can insert functions to perform other summary calculations:

- CUMIPMT function: calculates the cumulative interest, which represents the total finance charges on the loan.
- PMT function: calculates the monthly payment, including principal and interest.
- DATE function: determines the last payment date, when nesting YEAR, MONTH, and DAY functions and their respective arguments.

Users have two methods of navigating the application interface: using the buttons to open and display the various application components or using the sheet tabs. Although the sheet tabs can be hidden, many Excel users prefer the sheet tabs to navigate through a workbook. The sheet tabs display the worksheets; to make changes to the loan scenario or customer information, users need to use the buttons on the Instructions worksheet. After you make the final changes to each worksheet, you can set worksheet protection and then test the worksheet.

TIP: HIDING EXCEL WINDOW ELEMENTS

When you create your own applications, you can create a more streamlined appearance by hiding the Formula Bar and row and column headings on an unprotected worksheet. To do this, click the File tab, and click Options. Click Advanced, and deselect the Show formula bar and the Show row and column headers check boxes. Click OK, and protect the appropriate worksheets.

Quick Concepts

7. Why is a counter variable needed when using code to create a list on a worksheet? **p. 112**

8. What statement would ensure the intThisRow variable starts on row 15? What would be the last line of code within a loop to make sure the variable starts on the next blank row in the worksheet? **p. 112**

Hands-On Exercises

Skills covered: Prepare the Worksheet and Obtain Input • Write Code to Create a List • Understand Other Sections on the Payment Schedule Worksheet • Create Code to Activate the Instructions Worksheet • Add Formulas to the Disclosure Worksheet

3 Loan Payment Schedule and Disclosure Worksheets

You will write the code behind the View the Loan Payment Schedule button to populate and view the loan payment schedule. You will also add a button to the Payment Schedule worksheet to return to the Instruction worksheet. In addition, you add formulas to provide summary data about the loan on the Truth-in-Lending worksheet.

STEP 1 ›› PREPARE THE WORKSHEET AND OBTAIN INPUT

You will write the initial code for the cmdCreateSchedule button. When the user clicks the button, the VBA code will unprotect the Payment Schedule worksheet so that the worksheet can be altered. The code will clear the existing range containing the loan payment schedule, declare variables, and perform some calculations. Refer to Figure 2.17 as you complete Step 1.

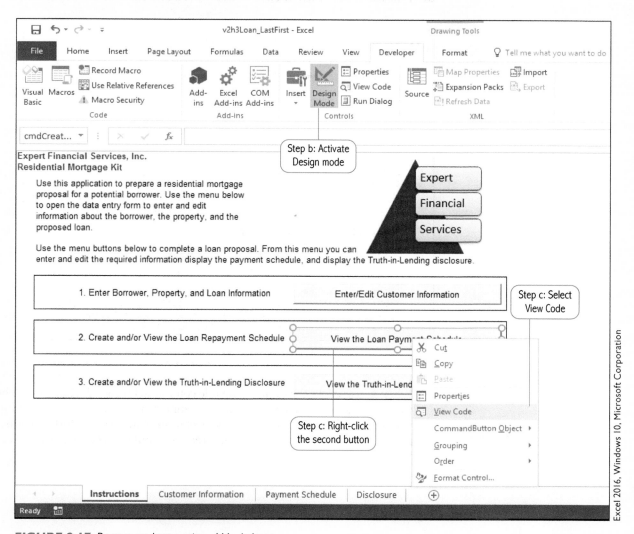

FIGURE 2.17 Button on Instructions Worksheet

a. Open the *v2h2Loan_LastFirst* macro-enabled workbook if you closed it at the end of Hands-On Exercise 2 and save it as **v2h3Loan_LastFirst**, changing h2 to h3.

b. Click the **Instructions sheet tab**, ensure the **Developer tab** is displayed, and then click **Design Mode** in the Controls group to enable Design mode.

> **TROUBLESHOOTING:** The Instructions worksheet should still be unprotected. If not, right-click the Instructions sheet tab and select Unprotect Sheet.

c. Right-click the **View the Loan Payment Schedule command button** and select **View Code**.

VBA creates the Private Sub cmdCreateSchedule_Click() and End Sub lines.

> **TROUBLESHOOTING:** If you click View Code in the Controls group on the Developer tab, the VB Editor shows existing code. It does not create a sub procedure for the button. If this happens, close the VB Editor, right-click the button, and select View Code.

d. Type the code shown in Code Window 2.12 and click **Save** on the toolbar.

```
Private Sub cmdCreateSchedule_Click()

    'Disable worksheet protection
    Worksheets("Payment Schedule").Unprotect

    'Clear any previous schedules
    Worksheets("Payment Schedule").Range("A10:G369").Clear

    'Declare variables for input and calculated values
    Dim curPrincipal As Currency
    Dim dblRate As Double
    Dim intTerm As Integer
    Dim curPpmt As Currency
    Dim curIpmt As Currency

    'Current row number for entering data in the list
    Dim intCurrentRow As Integer

    'Counter variable to control loop iterations
    Dim intCounter As Integer

    'Obtain worksheet values to calculate and store other values
    intTerm = Worksheets("Payment Schedule").Range("B6") * 12
    curPrincipal = Worksheets("Payment Schedule").Range("B4")
    dblRate = Worksheets("Payment Schedule").Range("B5") / 12
```

CODE WINDOW 2.12

When a user clicks the Create Schedule command button, the Payment Schedule worksheet is unprotected so that it can clear a range of data. The procedure declares variables, and uses data on the worksheet to store in variables intPayments, curPrincipal, and dblRate. You will add to the cmdCreateSchedule procedure in the next step.

Your next task is to complete the code for the cmdCreateSchedule button. You will use the For…Next repetition structure to iterate enough times to enter data in a list on the Payment Schedule worksheet. Refer to Figure 2.18 as you complete Step 2.

Residential Mortgage Kit

Principal:	$	150,000
Rate:		5.50%
Term:		30
Payment:		$851.68

Closing Costs	
Origination Fee:	$3,000.00
Points:	$4,500.00
Total Fees:	$7,500.00

Payment Number	Principal	Interest	Cumulative Principal	Cumulative Interest	Total Paid	Balance
1	$164.18	$687.50	$164.18	$687.50	$851.68	$149,835.82
2	$164.94	$686.75	$329.12	$1,374.25	$1,703.37	$149,670.88
3	$165.69	$685.99	$494.81	$2,060.24	$2,555.05	$149,505.19
4	$166.45	$685.23	$661.26	$2,745.47	$3,406.73	$149,338.74
5	$167.21	$684.47	$828.47	$3,429.94	$4,258.41	$149,171.53
6	$167.98	$683.70	$996.45	$4,113.64	$5,110.09	$149,003.55
7	$168.75	$682.93	$1,165.20	$4,796.57	$5,961.77	$148,834.80
8	$169.52		$1,334.72	$5,478.73	$6,813.45	$148,665.28
9	$170.30		$1,505.02	$6,160.11	$7,665.13	$148,494.98
10	$171.08	$680.60	$1,676.10	$6,840.71	$8,516.81	$148,323.90
11	$171.87	$679.82	$1,847.97	$7,520.53	$9,368.50	$148,152.03
12	$172.65	$679.03	$2,020.62	$8,199.56	$10,220.18	$147,979.38
13	$173.44	$678.24	$2,194.06	$8,877.80	$11,071.86	$147,805.94
14	$174.24	$677.44	$2,368.30	$9,555.24	$11,923.54	$147,631.70
15	$175.04	$676.65	$2,543.34	$10,231.89	$12,775.23	$147,456.66
16	$175.84	$675.84	$2,719.18	$10,907.73	$13,626.91	$147,280.82
17	$176.65	$675.04	$2,895.83	$11,582.77	$14,478.60	$147,104.17
18	$177.46	$674.23	$3,073.29	$12,257.00	$15,330.29	$146,926.71
19	$178.27	$673.41	$3,251.56	$12,930.41	$16,181.97	$146,748.44
20	$179.09	$672.60	$3,430.65	$13,603.01	$17,033.66	$146,569.35

Step c: View the Loan Payment Schedule

◀ ▶ | Instructions | Customer Information | **Payment Schedule** | Disclosure | ⊕

Ready

Excel 2016, Windows 10, Microsoft Corporation

FIGURE 2.18 Payment Schedule Created from VBA Procedure

a. Make sure the insertion point is on the blank line after the *dblRate = Worksheets*... statement that you just typed. Press **Enter** and type the code shown in Code Window 2.13.

```
'Specify starting row number for the list
intCurrentRow = 10

'Loop through each monthly payment to calculate & display values
For intCounter = 1 To intTerm
    'Enter current payment number in Column A of current row
    Worksheets("Payment Schedule").Range("A" & intCurrentRow) = intCounter

    'Calculate monthly payment and enter it in Column B of current row
    curPpmt = PPmt(dblRate, intCounter, intTerm, -curPrincipal)
    Worksheets("Payment Schedule").Range("B" & intCurrentRow) = curPpmt

    'Calculate current interest and enter it in Column C of current row
    curIpmt = IPmt(dblRate, intCounter, intTerm, -curPrincipal)
    Worksheets("Payment Schedule").Range("C" & intCurrentRow) = curIpmt

    'Calculate the cumulative interest and cumulative principal
    'Enter values in Columns D and E of current row
    Worksheets("Payment Schedule").Range("D" & intCurrentRow) = curPpmt _
        + Val(Worksheets("Payment Schedule").Range("D" & intCurrentRow - 1))
    Worksheets("Payment Schedule").Range("E" & intCurrentRow) = curIpmt _
        + Val(Worksheets("Payment Schedule").Range("E" & intCurrentRow - 1))

    'Calculate the total paid to date from Columns D and E of current row
    'Enter total paid in Column F of current row
    Worksheets("Payment Schedule").Range("F" & intCurrentRow) = _
    Worksheets("Payment Schedule").Range("D" & intCurrentRow) + _
    Worksheets("Payment Schedule").Range("E" & intCurrentRow)

    'Calculate the outstanding balance and enter it in Column G of current row
    Worksheets("Payment Schedule").Range("G" & intCurrentRow) = _
    curPrincipal - Val(Worksheets("Payment Schedule").Range("D" & intCurrentRow))

    'Increment the row number for the next row in the worksheet
    intCurrentRow = intCurrentRow + 1
Next

'Enable worksheet protection
Worksheets("Payment Schedule").Protect
Worksheets("Payment Schedule").Activate
```

CODE WINDOW 2.13

The procedure you started in Step 1 sets the intTerm variable equal to the value in the intPayments variable that was obtained from a calculation from cell B6. The first statement sets the intCurrentRow value to 10 so that the procedure will start entering data on row 10 of the worksheet.

The repetition statement loops through each monthly payment (based on the intCounter variable's value) to calculate and display values on the respective row. During each iteration, the loop places data on the next available row in the worksheet. Finally, the procedure protects the Payment Schedule worksheet again and then activates it because the Click event occurred on the Instructions worksheet.

b. Save the code, close the VB Editor, and then click **Design Mode** in the Controls group to deactivate Design mode.

c. Click the **View the Loan Payment Schedule button**. Save the workbook.

TROUBLESHOOTING: If a Compiler Error message box or a Debugging window displays, review each line of code to determine where the error exists. Fix the error, save the code, and then click the Create Schedule command button again to execute the sub procedure.

You want users to be able to go back quickly to the Instructions worksheet after viewing the results in the Payment Schedule worksheet. Therefore, you need to insert a button with VBA code on the Payment Schedule worksheet to make the Instructions worksheet active again. Refer to Figure 2.19 as you complete Step 3.

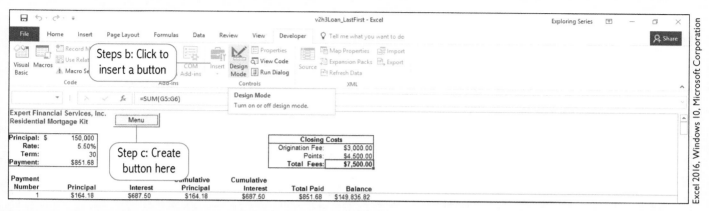

FIGURE 2.19 Menu Button on Payment Schedule Worksheet

a. Right-click the **Payment Schedule sheet tab** and select **Unprotect Sheet**.

b. Click **Insert** in the Controls group on the Developer tab and click **Command Button (ActiveX Control)**.

c. Drag to create a command button to the right of the Expert Financial Services heading in the top-left corner.

d. Click **Properties** in the Controls group, type **cmdReturn** in the Name property box, and then type **Menu** in the Caption property box. Adjust the height and width to be similar to the button you created on the Customer Information worksheet in Hands-On Exercise 1. Close the Properties window.

e. Right-click the **Menu button** and select **View Code**.

VBA creates the Private Sub cmdReturn_Click() and End Sub lines.

f. Press **Enter**, press **Tab**, type **Worksheets("Instructions").Activate**, and then press **Enter**.

g. Save and close VBA. Click **Design Mode** in the Controls group to deactivate it.

h. Right-click the **Payment Schedule sheet tab**, select **Protect Sheet**, and then click **OK** in the Protect Sheet dialog box.

After inserting the command button and coding it, you protect the worksheet again.

i. Click the **Menu button** you just created on the Payment Schedule worksheet to return to the Instructions worksheet. Save the workbook.

The Disclosure worksheet needs formulas that get data from other worksheets and perform calculations, such as the cumulative interest payment and the last payment date. In addition, you need to insert a command button on the Disclosure worksheet to return to the Instructions worksheet again. Refer to Figure 2.20 as you complete Step 4.

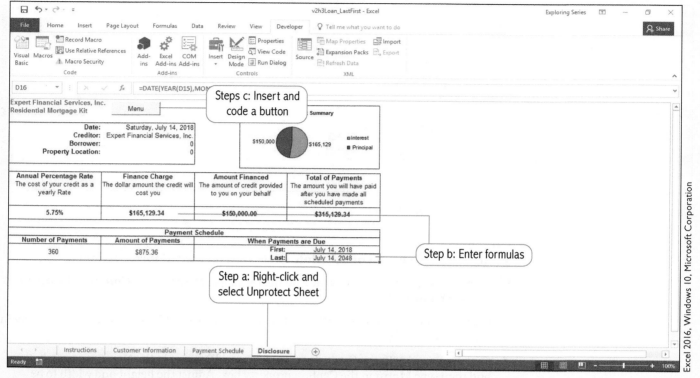

FIGURE 2.20 Disclosure Worksheet Data

a. Right-click the **Disclosure sheet tab** and select **Unprotect Sheet**.

b. Use the Go To feature to go to the respective cells, and then enter the following formulas in the worksheet:

- Cell B4: **=NOW()**
- Cell B6: **='Customer Information'!$B$4**
- Cell B7: **='Customer Information'!$B$13**
- Cell A11: **='Customer Information'!$F$8**
- Cell A15: **='Customer Information'!F10*12**
- Cell B11: **=-CUMIPMT(A11/12,A15,C11,1,A15,0)**

Make sure you type the minus sign in cell B11 after the equal sign so that the result will be converted to a positive number.

> **TROUBLESHOOTING:** The cell will display #NUM! error here because cell A11 currently contains 0. The error message will disappear when you enter real values later.

- Cell B15: **=PMT('Customer Information'!F8/12, 'Customer Information'!F10*12, -'Customer Information'!F6)**
- Cell C11: **='Customer Information'!F6**
- Cell D11: **=B11+C11**
- Cell D15: **=B4+15**
- Cell D16: **=DATE(YEAR(D15),MONTH(D15)+A15,DAY(D15))**

Cells B6 and B7 display zeroes because the cells referenced by the formulas do not contain any values yet. After you add information about the borrower and the property, these cells will display the name of the borrower and the location of the property.

c. Repeat Step 3b–g to insert a command button on the Disclosure worksheet.

d. Right-click the **Disclosure sheet tab**, select **Protect Sheet**, and then click **OK** in the Protect Sheet dialog box.

After inserting the command button and coding it, you need to protect the worksheet again.

e. Click the **Menu button** you just created on the Disclosure worksheet to return to the Instructions worksheet.

f. Click the **View the Truth-in-Lending Disclosure button** to ensure it works, and click the **Menu button** in the Disclosure worksheet to return to the Instructions worksheet.

g. Click each button on each worksheet to test the functionality of each button again. If errors exist, view the code, identify the error, save the code, and then click the buttons again.

h. Make sure each worksheet is protected.

i. Save and close the workbook. Based on your instructor's directions, submit v2h3Loan_LastFirst.

Chapter Objectives Review

After reading this chapter, you have accomplished the following objectives:

1. Create forms.

- To create a form in VBA, click Insert on the menu bar and select UserForm.
- Set the Form Properties: After creating a form, specific properties can be set.

2. Add controls to forms.

- The Toolbox contains controls that you can add to a form. Each control provides specific functionality.
- Name the Controls: Name the controls after inserting them on a form.
- Insert Label and TextBox controls: Label and TextBox controls provide descriptions and data entry, respectively.
- Insert Frame Control: Insert a frame control when you plan to add multiple controls on a form.
- Insert ListBox, CheckBox, and CommandButton controls: Users can select items from a list, select one or more options, and click to execute code, respectively.

3. Adjust specialized properties.

- Set the Enabled, TabStop, and TabIndex properties: The Enabled property determines if a control can receive focus. Focus is the ability for a control to be able to be interacted with by the user. The TabStop property determines whether or not a control can receive focus when the user presses Tab. The TabIndex property determines the order in which a control receives focus.
- Use bound and unbound controls: Use a bound control to connect the control to a data source, such as a range in a worksheet. The ControlSource and RowSource properties can be used to specify the location of the data.
- Set properties for the loan application form: It is a good practice to list the names of the controls, their properties, and the desired settings before creating a form.

4. Insert controls on a worksheet.

- You can use the Developer tab in Excel to insert controls directly on a worksheet.
- Use Design mode to insert and design the controls. Disable Design mode when you are ready to use the controls.
- Use Properties in the Control group on the Developer tab to adjust the properties of controls on a worksheet.

5. Add a procedure to a control.

- Right-click a control and select View Code to display the Code window. VBA will create the procedure header and End statement for that control.
- Use object hierarchy: The object hierarchy is used to specify the level of objects.
- Manipulate object properties, methods, and events: Use the Properties window to set the settings for a control's properties. After typing the period, VBA will prompt with suggested methods that apply for that control.

- Show, hide, close, and unload forms: Use the Show method to show a form or a worksheet, the Hide method to hide a form or worksheet but keep it in memory, the Close method to close a form or a worksheet, and the Unload method to close a form or a worksheet and unload it from memory.

6. Create and call a function procedure.

- A function is a procedure that contains code that can be called from any procedure and returns a single value.
- Create the main procedure with the calling statement: Any procedure can call a function that is created within the same workbook. From within the main procedure, create a statement that calls or invokes the function. You can pass variables to the function that the function can then manipulate.
- Create the function procedure: The function can receive variables passed from the main procedure. The parameters must be the same data type and number of parameters. When the function completes its task, it returns a value back to the calling statement and returns control back to the calling statement.
- Process the returned value from the function: The function returns a value. The calling statement then assigns that value to a variable or does some other action with the variable, such as displaying it onscreen.

7. Create a list in a worksheet.

- You can use VBA code to create a list within a worksheet where data is entered on individual rows.
- Prepare the worksheet and obtain input: The VBA code often unprotects a worksheet so that data can be entered to create the list. Variables are declared, and statements perform any necessary calculations.
- Write code to create a list: Use a repetition structure, such as a For...Next loop to iterate enough times to add data to create the list in a worksheet. The statement before the loop primes the loop by specifying the starting row number with a variable. The body of the loop must include specific column letters that will concatenate with the current row number to populate the list. The last statement of the loop increments the row counter so that data will be entered on the next row during the next iteration of the loop.
- Understand other sections of the payment schedule worksheet: To complete the worksheet, you need to perform calculations to summarize closing costs.

8. Prepare an application for distribution.

- Create code to active the Instructions worksheet: Right-click a button to write the code behind it.
- Add formulas to the Disclosure worksheet: Complete any formulas needed in the workbook.
- Protect worksheets where users should not change data directly.

Key Terms Matching

Match the key terms with their definitions. Write the key term letter by the appropriate numbered definition.

a. Bound control
b. Calling procedure
c. Caption property
d. CheckBox control
e. CommandButton control
f. Control
g. ControlSource property
h. Enabled property
i. Frame control
j. Label control

k. ListBox control
l. Name property
m. Object
n. RowSource property
o. TabIndex property
p. TabStop property
q. TextAlign property
r. TextBox control
s. Toolbox
t. Unbound control

1. _____ A text string, such as frmClient, that identifies an object; this attribute may be used in VBA code to manipulate the object. **p. 79**

2. _____ A control that enables the user to select one or more options at the same time. **p. 84**

3. _____ A window that contains the standard controls that can be added to a form. **p. 80**

4. _____ A property with a value of True or False that determines whether a control can receive focus and respond to the user. **p. 85**

5. _____ A control that is connected to a data source in the host application. **p. 85**

6. _____ A property that defines the cell to which a control is bound. **p. 85**

7. _____ A property that specifies items in an Excel worksheet range that will appear in a list box or combo box at run time. **p. 86**

8. _____ A control that is not connected to a data source in the host application. **p. 85**

9. _____ A procedure that contains a statements which calls a function **p. 102**

10. _____ A property that specifies the horizontal alignment of a caption appearing in a label. **p. 82**

11. _____ An object that displays a border around selected controls on a form. **p. 82**

12. _____ The property of an object or control that displays onscreen, such as the text that appears onscreen for a form's title bar. **p. 79**

13. _____ A property that has a value of True or False that determines whether a control receives focus when the Tab key is pressed. **p.85**

14. _____ An element, such as a worksheet cell, within a host application. **p. 78**

15. _____ An object, such as a text box, that enables interaction with the user. **p. 80**

16. _____ An object that displays text onscreen, usually to describe other controls that do not have captions. **p. 82**

17. _____ A property that determines the order in which a control receives the focus. **p. 85**

18. _____ An object that when clicked by the user, triggers VBA code to complete an algorithm. **p. 84**

19. _____ An object that enables the user to type data on a form. **p. 82**

20. _____ An object that displays a list of items from which the user may select. **p. 83**

Multiple Choice

1. What are the steps to creating a user form in Excel?

    (a) Click the Developer tab, click Insert in the Controls group, and then select Form.

    (b) Click the Developer tab, click Visual Basic in the Controls group, click Insert on the VBA menu, and then select UserForm.

    (c) Click the Insert tab, click Visual Basic in the Charts group, click Insert on the VBA menu, and then select Form.

    (d) Click the Insert tab, click Reports in the Visual Basic group, click Insert on the VBA menu, and then select UserForm.

2. Which statement correctly makes cell E5 the active cell in the Salary worksheet?

    (a) Worksheet(Salary).Cell(E5)

    (b) Worksheets("Salary").Range("E5")

    (c) Cell("E5").Worksheet("Salary")

    (d) Cell(E5).Worksheet(Salary)

3. What property displays text onscreen for a Label control?

    (a) Name

    (b) ControlSource

    (c) TextAlign

    (d) Caption

4. Which of the following statements is the correct code to unload a form named frmStats?

    (a) frmStats.Unload

    (b) Unload.frmStats

    (c) Unload frmStats

    (d) frmStats Unload

5. What type of control is used to organize other controls on a form?

    (a) Frame control

    (b) ComboBox control

    (c) TextBox control

    (d) BorderStyle control

6. Which statement correctly displays a worksheet named Payments within a workbook named Finances?

    (a) Workbook.Payments.Display

    (b) Finances.Payments.Display

    (c) Payments.Finances.Show

    (d) Workbooks("Finances").Worksheets("Payments").Activate

7. Which statement clears existing text within the txtCity text box?

    (a) txtCity.Clear

    (b) txtCity = 0

    (c) txtCity.Text = " "

    (d) txtCity.Text(Clear)

8. Which of the following statements is NOT true about a function calling statement?

    (a) The return value may be assigned to a variable.

    (b) The calling statement starts with the name of the function.

    (c) The returned value may be displayed as output on screen.

    (d) The calling statement passes variables to the function to process.

9. Study the following function that calculates net pay.

    Function NetPay(GrossPay, FederalTaxes, StateTaxes, LocalTaxes)

        NetPay = GrossPay – (FederalTaxes + StateTaxes + LocalTaxes)

    End Function

    Given the values curGrossPay = 800, curFedTaxes = 75, curStateTaxes = 20, and curLocalTaxes = 10, what is the value returned by the function?

    (a) 855

    (b) 905

    (c) 105

    (d) 695

10. Which of the following statements would correctly add an item to the list box lstTest?

    (a) lstTest.AddItem = "10"

    (b) lstTest.Add = 10

    (c) lstTest.AddItem (10)

    (d) lstTest.Add.Item = 10

Practice Exercises

1 Neighborhood Bake Sale

Each year your neighborhood hosts a bake sale. The proceeds earned are donated to the local animal shelter. Currently all sales are handwritten and then transferred to an Excel spreadsheet. As a recent college graduate, you have offered to enhance the spreadsheet with user forms, to eliminate the need to handwrite entries. The current spreadsheet contains price information and sales data. You have already added a worksheet to serve as a starting point and you will now automate the calculation of earnings, as well as create a user form. Refer to Figure 2.21 as you complete this exercise.

FIGURE 2.21 Community Bake Sale

a. Open the macro-enabled workbook *v2p1BakeSale* and save it as **v2p1BakeSale_LastFirst**. Click each worksheet tab to see what work has been done and what work you will do.

b. Click the **Developer tab** and click **Visual Basic** in the Code group. Click **Insert** on the VBA menu bar, select **UserForm**, display the Properties window, and then set these form properties:

- Name: **frmTransaction**
- Caption: **Community Bake Sale**
- BackColor: &H00C0FFFF&
- Height: **182**
- Width: **168**

c. Click the form to display the Toolbox, click **Label** in the Toolbox, and then create four labels and set their properties as the following:

- Name: **lblItem**
- Caption: **Item**
- BackColor: &H00C0FFFF&
- Height: **12**
- Left: **6**
- Top: **6**
- Width: **24**
- Name: **lblQuantity**
- Caption: **Quantity**
- BackColor: &H00C0FFFF&
- Height: **12**
- Left: **6**

- Top: **54**
- Width: **36**
- Name: **lblRound**
- Caption: **Round Up**
- BackColor: &H00C0FFFF&
- Height: **12**
- Left: **90**
- Top: **60**
- Width: **42**
- Name: **lblTotal**
- Caption: **Total**
- BackColor: &H00C0FFFF&
- Height: **12**
- Left: **6**
- Top: **96**
- Width: **42**

d. Insert other controls as shown in Figure 2.21 and set their properties as indicated in Table 2.7.

TABLE 2.7	Controls and Properties	
Control	**Property**	**Setting**
ListBox	Name	lstItem
	Height	42
	Left	30
	RowSource	Items
	Top	6
	Width	116
TextBox	Name	txtQuantity
	Left	48
	Top	54
	Width	18
TextBox	Name	txtTotal
	Left	48
	TabIndex	1
	Top	90
	Width	60
SpinButton	Name	spnQuantity
	Left	66
	Top	54
	Width	12
CheckBox	Name	chkRound
	Left	132
	Top	60
	Width	12
CommandButton	Name	cmdTotal
	Caption	Total
	Left	6
	Top	126
	Width	138

Pearson Education, Inc.

e. Right-click the spnQuantity Spin control and select View Code. Place the insertion point after the statement **Private Sub spnQuantity_Change()** and type the statement **txtQuantity.value = spnQuantity.value**.

This statement uses the SpinButton created earlier as a control source for the txtQuantity text box.

f. Right-click the **cmdTotal button**, select **View Code**, and then enter the code shown in Code Window 2.14.

The code locates the item price based on the selection in the list box. It then calculates the total based on the option to round the price up to the nearest dollar for an additional donation and places the formatted output in the txtTotal text box and places the full entry on the data worksheet.

```vba
Private Sub cmdTotal_Click()

    'Declarations
    Dim strItem As String
    Dim curPrice As Currency

    strItem = lstItem

    'Opens Price List worksheet and sets cell A2 active
    Worksheets("Price List").Select
    Cells(2, 1).Select

    'Use Find dialog box to find the sale item and select corresponding price
    Cells.Find(What:=strItem, After:=ActiveCell, LookIn:=xlFormulas, _
        LookAt:=xlWhole, SearchOrder:=xlByColumns, SearchDirection:=xlNext, _
        MatchCase:=False, SearchFormat:=False).Activate
        ActiveCell.Offset(0, 1).Select
    curPrice = ActiveCell.Value

    'Use an IF statement to determine total based on extra donation
    If chkRound = "True" Then
        txtTotal = Format(Round(curPrice * txtQuantity, 0), "currency")
    Else
        txtTotal = Format(curPrice * txtQuantity, "Currency")
    End If

    'Insert a row in the Data worksheet
    Worksheets("Data").Range("A2").EntireRow.Insert

    'Places transactions on data worksheet in the newly inserted row
    Worksheets("Data").Range("A2") = Date
    Worksheets("Data").Range("B2") = lstItem
    Worksheets("Data").Range("C2") = CDbl(txtQuantity)
    Worksheets("Data").Range("D2") = CDbl(txtTotal)

    'Sets the columns in the table to autofit
    Worksheets("Data").Columns("A:D").AutoFit

End Sub
```

CODE WINDOW 2.14

g. Click **Save**, exit the VB Editor, and then ensure the Home worksheet active.

h. Ensure Design Mode is active, right-click the **Price List button**, and then select **View Code**.

i. Press **Enter**, press **Tab**, and then type the statement **Worksheets("Price List").Activate**.

j. Exit the VB Editor and ensure Design Mode is still active. Right-click the **Phone Entry button** and select **View Code**.

k. Press **Enter**, press **Tab**, and then type the statement **MsgBox "To place a phone entry have customers call 1-800-222-2222", vbInformation, "Order by phone"**

l. Exit the VB Editor and ensure Design Mode is still active. Right-click the **Enter Order button**, and select **View Code**.

m. Press **Enter**, press **Tab**, and then type the statement **frmTransaction.Show**.

n. Exit the VB Editor. Disable Design Mode and then test each button and the frmTransaction form.

o. Save and close the workbook. Based on your instructor's directions, submit v2p1BakeSale_LastFirst.

2 Monthly Investment Schedule

Janelle Mayer is a financial consultant. She works with people who are considering investment opportunities. Because of your extensive work with Excel and interest in VBA coding, you volunteered to help create an application in which Janelle can enter data for a potential investment, click a button, and then display a summary of results and a list of month-by-month data to show how much interest is made. Refer to Figure 2.22 as you complete this exercise.

	A	B	C	D	E	F
1	**Summary Area**			*Due to rounding, these values may be different from the list ending value by a few cents.		
2	APR	6%				
3	No. of Years	4				
4	No. of Pmts per Year	12				
5	Deposit per Period	$100.00				
6	Start of 1st Period	1/1/2018				
7	Start of Last Period	12/1/2021				
8	Maturity Date	1/1/2022				
9	Maturity Value*	$5,436.83		Cross-Check*	$5,436.83	
10						
11	Period Start Date	Beginning Value	Beg-of-Period Invest	Interest Earned	Ending Value	
12	1/1/2016		$100.00	$0.50	$100.50	
13	2/1/2016	$100.50	$100.00	$1.00	$201.50	
14	3/1/2016	$201.50	$100.00	$1.51	$303.01	
15	4/1/2016	$303.01	$100.00	$2.02	$405.03	
16	5/1/2016	$405.03	$100.00	$2.53	$507.56	
17	6/1/2016	$507.56	$100.00	$3.04	$610.60	
18	7/1/2016	$610.60	$100.00	$3.55	$714.15	
19	8/1/2016	$714.15	$100.00	$4.07	$818.22	
20	9/1/2016	$818.22	$100.00	$4.59	$922.81	
21	10/1/2016	$922.81	$100.00	$5.11	$1,027.92	
22	11/1/2016	$1,027.92	$100.00	$5.64	$1,133.56	
23	12/1/2016	$1,133.56	$100.00	$6.17	$1,239.73	

Inputs   **Investment**   (+)

FIGURE 2.22 Monthly Investment Schedule

a. Open the macro-enabled workbook *v2p2Invest* and save it as **v2p2Invest_LastFirst**.

b. Click the **Developer tab**, enable **Design Mode**, click **Insert** in the Controls group, click **Command Button (ActiveX Control)**, and then draw a command button in the **range A10:A11** on the Inputs sheet. Click **Properties** in the Controls group, type **cmdDisplayResults** in the Name property box, type **Display the Results** in the Caption property box, change the **Height property** to **26.25**, change the **Width property** to **145.5**, and then close the Properties window.

c. Right-click the **Display the Results command button** and select **View Code**. Type the variable declarations shown in Code Window 2.15.

These variables will store data the user enters in the Inputs worksheet, calculations to display in the Investment worksheet, and variables needed for the VBA code. You will continue adding to the procedure in the next step.

```vba
Private Sub cmdDisplayResults_Click()

    'Declare variables for input from worksheet cells
    Dim dblAPR As Double
    Dim intYears As Integer
    Dim dblAmountInvest As Double
    Dim dteStartDate As Date

    'Declare variables for calculated output
    Dim dteLastPeriod As Date
    Dim dteMaturityDate As Date
    Dim dblFutureValue As Double

    'Declare variables for calculations and loop
    Dim intCounter As Integer
    Dim dteCurrentDate As Date
    Dim dblBegBalance As Double
    Dim dblBalance As Double
    Dim dblInterest As Double
    Dim intPrevRow As Integer
    Dim intStartRow As Integer
```

CODE WINDOW 2.15

d. Position the insertion point two blank lines below the code you just typed and type the code shown in Code Window 2.16. You will continue adding to the procedure in the next step.

```vba
'Clear any previous schedules
Worksheets("Investment").Unprotect
Worksheets("Investment").Range("A12:E373").Clear

'Get inputs from worksheets
dblAPR = Worksheets("Inputs").Range("B4")
intYears = Worksheets("Inputs").Range("B5")
dblAmountInvest = Worksheets("Inputs").Range("B6")
dteStartDate = Worksheets("Inputs").Range("B7")
dteLastPeriod = Worksheets("Investment").Range("B7")

'Calculate and verify maturity date (should be equal to B8 in Investments)
dteMaturityDate = Application.WorksheetFunction.EDate(dteStartDate, intYears * 12)

'Calculate and display first period's interest and balance
dblInterest = dblAmountInvest * dblAPR / 12
dblBalance = dblAmountInvest + dblInterest
Worksheets("Investment").Range("A12") = Format(dteStartDate, "Short Date")
Worksheets("Investment").Range("C12") = Format(dblAmountInvest, "$##,##0.00")
Worksheets("Investment").Range("D12") = Format(dblInterest, "$##,##0.00")
Worksheets("Investment").Range("E12") = Format(dblBalance, "$#,##0.00")
```

CODE WINDOW 2.16

This first block of code unprotects the Investment worksheet, clears existing data.

The second block of code obtains values from the Inputs and Investment worksheets and stores the values in the variables you declared.

The third block of code uses the Excel EDate function to determine the ending or maturity date of the investment.

The final block of code calculates the interest and balance for the first investment period and then displays formatted results in the first row (row 12).

e. Position the insertion point two blank lines below the code you just typed and type the code shown in Code Window 2.17.

This code uses the intStartRow variable to designate row 13 as the row to start the rest of the table. Prior to the loop, the code populated the first month's data. The loop takes over starting with the second investment period because it must identify the previous month's balance and add this month's investment to calculate the interest earned.

The code then formats and displays output for the current month during each iteration of the loop, and then increments the intStartRow variable so that the next iteration of the loop places data on the next available row in the worksheet.

After the loop terminates, the code provides a cross-check to determine if the future value is almost identical (excluding a little rounding in cents) with what is produced by the Excel FV function and with the final ending investment value produced by the loop.

Finally, the procedure protects the Investment worksheet and displays it to the user.

```
'Initialize row to start the loop
intStartRow = 13

'Loop through each monthly period to calculate and display values
For intCounter = 1 To (intYears * 12 - 1)
    intPrevRow = intStartRow - 1

    'Calculate beginning balance, balance after deposit, and interest
    dteCurrentDate = Application.WorksheetFunction.EDate(dteStartDate, intCounter)
    dblBegBalance = Val(Worksheets("Investment").Range("E" & intPrevRow))
    dblBalance = dblBegBalance + dblAmountInvest
    dblInterest = dblBalance * dblAPR / 12

    'Display formatted values in the list
    Worksheets("Investment").Range("A" & intStartRow) = _
            Format(dteCurrentDate, "Short Date")
    Worksheets("Investment").Range("B" & intStartRow) = _
            Format(dblBegBalance, "$##,##0.00")
    Worksheets("Investment").Range("C" & intStartRow) = _
            Format(dblAmountInvest, "$##,##0.00")
    Worksheets("Investment").Range("D" & intStartRow) = _
            Format(dblInterest, "$##,##0.00")
    Worksheets("Investment").Range("E" & intStartRow) = _
            Format(dblBalance + dblInterest, "$##,##0.00")

    'Increment the row number
    intStartRow = intStartRow + 1
Next

'Calculate and display a cross check to compare with last cell in list
dblFutureValue = FV(dblAPR / 12, intYears * 12, -dblAmountInvest, , 1)
Worksheets("Investment").Range("E9") = Format(dblFutureValue, "$##,##0.00")

'Finalize worksheet
Worksheets("Investment").Protect
Worksheets("Investment").Activate

End Sub
```

CODE WINDOW 2.17

f. Save and close the VB Editor. Turn off Design Mode on the Developer tab.

g. Click the **Inputs sheet tab** and select the **range B4:B7**. Click the **Home tab**, click **Format**, and then click **Format Cells**. Click the **Protection tab**, deselect the **Locked check box**, and then click **OK**.

h. Right-click the **Inputs sheet tab**, select **Protect Sheet**, and then click **OK** in the Protect Sheet dialog box.

i. Type **6**, **4**, **100**, and **1/1/2018** in the respective input cells in the Inputs worksheet. Ensure Design Mode is deactivated and click the **Display the Results button**. After the VBA code executes, the Investment worksheet is active and displays the data. Scroll through the list to review the monthly start date, beginning balance, investment, interest earned, and ending balance.

j. Save and close the workbook. Based on your instructor's directions, submit v2p2Invest_LastFirst.

Mid-Level Exercises

1 Test Scores

You are a teaching assistant for one of your professors, Dr. Patti Rosequist. You created a small gradebook with student IDs, first names, and three test scores to create a prototype application that you can modify for other classes. Dr. Rosequist would like a program that prompts her for a student's ID and test number and then displays the student's name, test score, and letter grade. You will use VBA to create an easy-to-use form within Excel. In addition, you need to create a command button that Dr. Rosequist can click to open the form. Refer to Figure 2.23 as you complete this exercise.

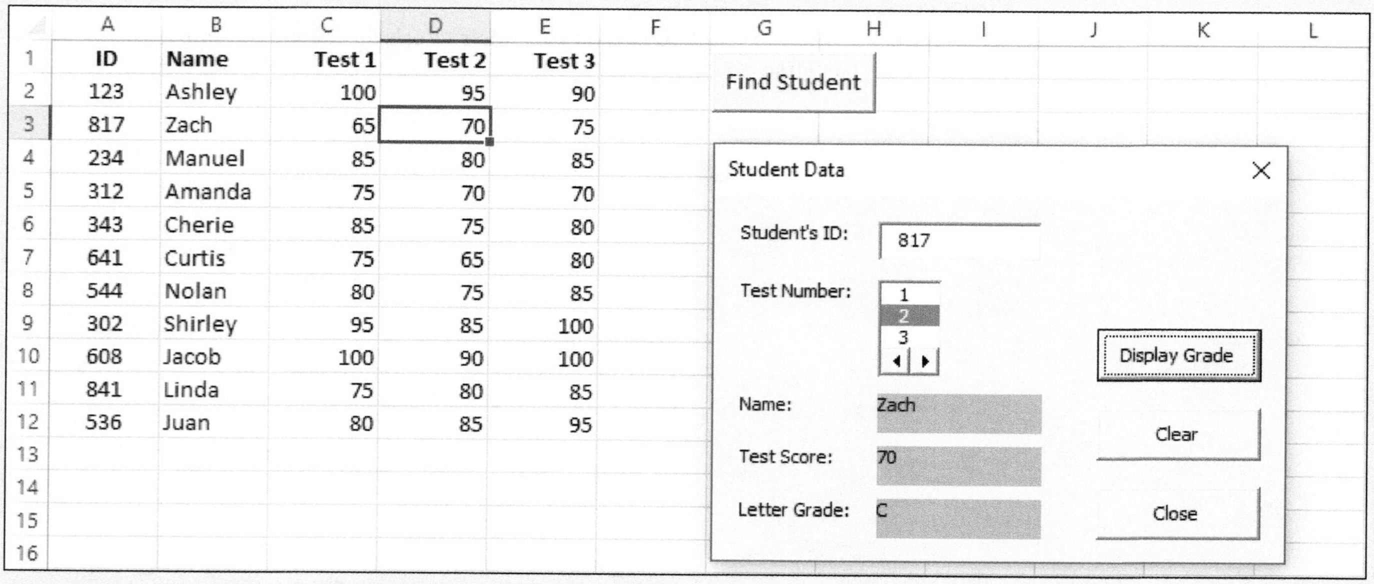

	A	B	C	D	E	F	G	H	I	J	K	L
1	ID	Name	Test 1	Test 2	Test 3		Find Student					
2	123	Ashley	100	95	90							
3	817	Zach	65	70	75							
4	234	Manuel	85	80	85							
5	312	Amanda	75	70	70							
6	343	Cherie	85	75	80							
7	641	Curtis	75	65	80							
8	544	Nolan	80	75	85							
9	302	Shirley	95	85	100							
10	608	Jacob	100	90	100							
11	841	Linda	75	80	85							
12	536	Juan	80	85	95							
13												
14												
15												
16												

Student Data

Student's ID: 817

Test Number: 1 / 2 / 3

Display Grade

Name: Zach

Test Score: 70

Letter Grade: C

Clear

Close

FIGURE 2.23 Gradebook with Student IDs

a. Open the macro-enabled workbook *v2m1Grades* and save it as **v2m1Grades_LastFirst**.

b. Use VBA to create a form named **frmStudent** with the labels, text boxes, list box, and command buttons shown in Figure 2.23. Set these properties for the controls:
  • Name: Use standard prefixes and descriptive names.
  • Caption: Use captions as shown in the figure.
  • Left: Align common controls on the left side.
  • BackColor: Use a light blue background color for the output labels as shown.

c. Adjust the widths, heights, and vertical spacing as needed to ensure balance and consistency.

d. Write the VBA procedure for the **Clear button** to do the following:
  • Clear the text box where the user types a student's ID.
  • Set the list box value to −1 (to avoid selecting a test number by default)
  • Clear the three output labels, such as lblName = " ".
  • Set the focus back to the input text box, such as txtID.SetFocus.

e. Write the VBA procedure for the **Close button** to hide the form.

f. Write the VBA procedure for the **Display Grade button**:
  • Declare integer variables for the ID, test number, and test score. Declare a string variable for the student's name.
  • Assign the values in the form's text box and list box to appropriate variables. Convert the list box selected test number to a value before assigning it to a variable.

- Create a function call to a GetName function in which you pass the ID variable. The returned value should be the student's name, which you assign to the string variable you declared.
- Use a Select Case statement that uses the selected test number to move the active cell to the right on the same row by the correct number of columns. Each Case statement uses the ActiveCell.Offset method to offset the active cell on the same row and over the appropriate number of columns (1 through 3, respectively), such as ActiveCell.Offset(0, 1).Select.
- Store the active cell's respective test score in a variable using ActiveCell.Value, such as intScore = ActiveCell.Value.
- Display the string variable and test score variable contents in respective output labels within the form.
- Create a function call to a GetGrade function in which you pass the test score variable and then display the respective returned letter grade in an output label on the form.

g. Create a **GetName function** shown in Code Window 2.18 to go to cell A1, find the ID and make that the active cell, select the current student's name, and assign the text string to the GetName function name so that it will be returned to the calling statement.

```
Function GetName(intID)

    'Make cell A1 active
    Application.Goto Reference:="R1C1"

    'Use the Find dialog box to locate ID within the list
    Cells.Find(What:=intID, After:=ActiveCell, LookIn:=xlFormulas, LookAt:= _
        xlWhole, SearchOrder:=xlByColumns, SearchDirection:=xlNext, MatchCase:=False _
        , SearchFormat:=False).Activate

    'Get student's name for respective ID
    ActiveCell.Offset(0, 1).Select
    GetName = ActiveCell.Value

End Function
```

CODE WINDOW 2.18

h. Create a **GetGrade function** that receives the integer test score from the calling statement and uses a Select Case statement block to do the following:
- If the score is greater than or equal to 90, assign an A to the function name. The code should look similar to this:
  Case Is >= 90
  GetGrade = "A"
- If the score is greater than or equal to 80, assign a B to the function name.
- If the score is greater than or equal to 70, assign a C to the function name.
- If the score is greater than or equal to 60, assign a D to the function name.
- For all other scores, assign an F to the function name.

DISCOVERY
i. Change the Object from **General** to **UserForm** at the top of the code window and select the **Initialize procedure**. Delete any other empty procedures that might be created as you get to this one. This procedure will populate the list box and set the focus when the form first loads each time.
- Enter three lines of code to populate the list box with 1, 2, and 3. For example, to populate the list box with the first item, the code looks like this: lstTest.AddItem ("1")
- Set the focus to the first text box in the form.

j. Save and close the VB Editor. Enable Design mode. Create a **Find Student button** and write the code so that when a user clicks it, the Student Data form displays.

k. Deactivate Design mode. Click the **Find Student button** you created on the worksheet, type **343** in the text box, select **3** in the list box, and then click the **Display Grade button** on the form (see Figure 2.23). Clear the form and try out several other combinations to ensure the program selects the right data.

l. Test the **Close button** to make sure it works.

m. Save and close the workbook. Based on your instructor's directions, submit v2m1Grades_LastFirst.

2 Financial Functions

You want to compare the results of Excel financial functions with the results of VBA financial functions. You will use a workbook that contains two worksheets. You will write the code for three command buttons on the Inputs worksheet that, when clicked, will execute respective procedures. Each procedure will call functions that can be used by multiple procedures that get user input via input boxes. The results will display on the Output worksheet, along with the results from direct financial functions in that worksheet.

DISCOVERY

a. Open the macro-enabled workbook *v2m2Finance* and save it as **v2m2Finance_LastFirst**.

b. Enter the following finance functions on the Output worksheet:

- PV function in **cell B8**. Use cell references in column B as the three arguments.
- FV function in **cell E9**. Use cell references in column E as the four arguments. Make sure the result is a positive value.
- RATE function with formula to convert to APR in **cell H8**. Use cell references in column H as the three arguments.

c. Select the Input worksheet. Display the VB Editor, change the Object to **(General)** and change the Procedure to **(Declarations)**. Type **Option Explicit** and declare the following variables: **dblPV, dblAPR, dblYears, dblRate, dblNPER, dblPMT**, and **dblFV**. You declare these at this level so that they are available throughout all procedures.

d. Create these four functions with each function displaying an input box asking for the appropriate data and storing it in the function name. Make sure the functions are Public, not Private, so that the functions can be accessed from any given module or procedure.

- **GetAPR function.** Display the prompt **Enter the annual rate, such as 0.06 instead of 6%:**. The input box title bar should display **Rate**. The data entered by the user should be converted to a value and then saved to the function name so that the value gets returned back to the calling statement in the main procedure. To complete the function type: **GetAPR = Val(InputBox("Enter the annual rate, such as 0.06 instead of 6%: ", _"Rate"))**
- **GetYears function.** Display the prompt **Enter the number of years for the annuity:**. The input box title bar should display **Term in Years**. The data entered by the user should be converted to a value and then saved to the function name so that the value gets returned back to the calling statement in the main procedure.
- **GetPMT function.** Request the monthly payment with an appropriate prompt and title for the input box. Convert the value, and then save it to the function name.
- **GetPV function.** Request the present value of the annuity with an appropriate prompt and title for the input box. Convert the value and save it to the function name.

e. Create the procedure for the **cmdPresentValue button** with these requirements. Refer to Code Window 2.19 to complete this procedure.

- Include function calls for the APR, years, and monthly payment, and then store each returning value in the appropriate variable. The calling statements do not pass any variables to the functions you created.
- Calculate the periodic rate, the NPER, and the present value. Store each calculated result in the respective variable.
- Unprotect the Output worksheet.

- Display the results in cells B2 through B7 for the APR, rate, years, NPER, payment, and present value. Format the percentages and monetary values appropriately within the VBA code.
- Protect the Output worksheet again and activate the Output worksheet.

```
Private Sub cmdPresentValue_Click()

    'Function calls to get and assign values
    dblAPR = GetAPR()
    dblYears = GetYears()
    dblPMT = GetPMT()

    'Calculations
    dblRate = dblAPR / 12
    dblNPER = dblYears * 12
    dblPV = PV(dblRate, dblNPER, -dblPMT)

    'Display output
    Worksheets("Output").Unprotect
    Worksheets("Output").Range("B2") = Format(dblAPR, "#0.00#%")
    Worksheets("Output").Range("B3") = Format(dblRate, "#0.00#%")
    Worksheets("Output").Range("B4") = dblYears
    Worksheets("Output").Range("B5") = dblNPER
    Worksheets("Output").Range("B6") = Format(dblPMT, "$###,##0.00")
    Worksheets("Output").Range("B7") = Format(dblPV, "$###,##0.00")

    'Protect and activate the worksheet
    Worksheets("Output").Protect
    Worksheets("Output").Activate

End Sub
```

CODE WINDOW 2.19

f. Create the procedure for the **cmdFutureValue button** with these requirements:
   - Include function calls for the APR, years, monthly payment, and present value, and then store each returning value in the appropriate variable. The calling statements do not pass any variables to the functions you created.
   - Calculate the periodic rate, the NPER, and the future value. Store each calculated result in the respective variable. To complete the task, type the code:
     dblFV = -FV(dblRate, dblNPER, dblPMT, dblPV)
   - Unprotect the Output worksheet. Display the results in cells E2 through E8 for the APR, rate, years, NPER, payment, present value, and future value. Format the percentages and monetary values appropriately within the VBA code.
   - Protect the Output worksheet again, and activate the Output worksheet.

g. Create the procedure for the **cmdAPR button** with these requirements:
   - Include function calls for the years, monthly payment, and present value, and then store each returning value in the appropriate variable. The calling statements do not pass any variables to the functions you created.
   - Calculate the NPER, the periodic rate, and the APR. Store each calculated result in the respective variable. To calculate the periodic rate, type the code:
     dblRate = Rate(dblNPER, dblPMT, -dblPV)
   - Unprotect the Output worksheet. Display the results in cells H3 through H7 for the present value, years, NPER, payment, and APR. Format the percentages and monetary values appropriately within the VBA code.
   - Protect the Output worksheet again, and then activate the Output worksheet.

h. Save the code and close the VB Editor.

i. Protect the Input worksheet in Excel (not VBA code).

j. Click the **Present Value button** on the Input worksheet and type these values when prompted: **0.05** (APR), **15** (years), and **125.35** (payment). Click the **Go Back button** on the Output worksheet.

k. Click the **Future Value button** on the Input worksheet and type these values when prompted: **0.075** (APR), **25** (years), **125.50** (payment), and **50000** (present value). Click the **Go Back button** on the Output worksheet.

l. Click the **APR button** on the Input worksheet and type these values when prompted to test your work: **20** (years), **965.02** (payment), and **100000** (present value). Click the **Go Back button** on the Output worksheet.

m. Save and close the workbook. Based on your instructor's directions, submit v2m2Finance_LastFirst.

Beyond the Classroom

Valentine's Day Dance

GENERAL CASE

Victoria Johnson is a party organizer for a student organization that is sponsoring a Valentine's Day Ball at your university. She has identified income and expenses and started an Excel workbook. However, she does not want people to enter data directly in the worksheet. As the IT developer for the student organization, you volunteer to create forms and write VBA code that provide prompts for users to enter information and store it in the protected worksheet. Open the macro-enabled workbook *v2b1Dance* and save it as **v2b1Dance_LastFirst**. Open *v2b1Dance.docx* in Word to read more details about the program, what buttons are needed, what event procedures are needed, and so on. Use this document to guide you as you design the form and create VBA procedures in the workbook.

The Instructions worksheet should have four buttons. The first button displays an input box to ask the user for the number of attendees, the second button displays a form to enter income sources, the third button displays a form to enter expenses, and the fourth button displays the results on the protected worksheet. The Budget worksheet contains some formulas, but clicking the OK button on the Expenses form performs two calculations.

Save and close the workbook. Based on your instructor's directions, submit v2b1Dance_LastFirst.

Studio Equipment Loan

DISASTER RECOVERY ✚

You work for a company that sells studio audio equipment. Most customers make a down payment and obtain a short-term loan to pay off the balance for the equipment they purchase. To help them determine how much their monthly payment will be and to see the portion of each payment that goes toward the principal and the interest, you developed a workbook that contains a list of inputs and a place for the monthly payment information. Open the macro-enabled workbook *v2b2Equipment* and save it as **v2b2Equipment_LastFirst**.

You created a VBA form to accept input and then to store the values obtained in the top-left corner of the worksheet. However, the form does not populate the list box correctly, and several financial functions are producing incorrect results. Furthermore, the output is often incorrect or not formatted correctly. Review the VBA code carefully and make all necessary corrections. Save and close the workbook. Based on your instructor's directions, submit v2b2Equipment_LastFirst.

Capstone Exercise

You have been hired as the statistician for your college baseball team. Currently, all stats are recorded by hand and entered manually into Excel. You have decided to automate the process using VBA and user forms in Excel.

Create navigation

You want to use VBA to automate the navigation buttons at the top of the Home worksheet. When clicked, the batting page should display the batting worksheet. The starting and relief pitching buttons should open the Pitching worksheet. The Summary button should open the Summary worksheet. As your last task, you would like to create home buttons on each worksheet to allow the user to return to the Home worksheet.

a. Open the macro-enabled workbook *v2c1StatTracker* and save it as **v2c1StatTracker_LastFirst**.

b. Create a sub procedure for the Batting button Click event. When clicked, the button should display the Batting worksheet.

c. Adapt the code used in Step b for each of the remaining navigation buttons.

d. Insert an ActiveX Control Command button underneath the data table on the Pitching worksheet.
   • Give the command button an appropriate name.
   • Type **Home** as the Caption Property.

e. Create a sub procedure for the Home button Click event. When clicked, the button should display the Home worksheet.

f. Add Home buttons to the remaining worksheets by adapting steps d-e.

g. Save the VBA code.

Enter the number of pitchers

You want to click the Enter Pitching Stats button on the Home worksheet to display an input box to enter the number of pitchers to track. The result should store the value in a publicly declared variable that is accessible from all procedures.

a. Open the VB Editor and insert a new module. Type the **Option Explicit** statement at the top of the General Declarations section of the code window for the Home worksheet. Create a public integer variable to store the number of players.

b. Create a sub procedure for the Enter Pitching Stats button Click event.
   • Display an input box to ask the user how many pitchers played in the current game. Include an appropriate title for the input box title bar.
   • Assign the value entered by the user to the appropriate public variable you declared in Step b.
   • Save the VBA code.

Design Input Form

You want to enter pitching statistics using an input form. You will create a user form for pitching statistics that will allow the user to input information for both starting and relief pitchers.

a. Create a user form named **frmPitching**, type **Pitching Statistics** in the caption property, set **175** for the Height property, and then set **312** for the Width property.

b. Set the BackColor property to **light green (&H00C0FFC0&)**.

c. Create and format a label with the caption: **Name**. Enter **12** for the Left property, **12** for the Height property, and **6** for the Top property.

d. Insert a text box to the right of the Name label. Assign the name **txtName**. Enter **90** for the Left property, **16** for the Height property, and **6** for the Top property.

e. Insert a Frame control below the Name label and text box. Assign the following properties:
   • Enter an appropriate name for the frame.
   • Enter the caption **Pitching Statistics**.
   • Enter **12** for the Left property.
   • Enter **90** for the Height property.
   • Enter **276** for the Width property.
   • Enter **42** for the Top property.

f. Create and format four labels for Innings pitched, Strike outs, Runs, and Position. Assign the properties as follows:
   • Innings pitched – Name **lblInnings**, Height **12**, Left **6**, Top **12**, Width **60**
   • Runs - Name **lblRuns**, Height **12**, Left **6**, Top **36**, Width **60**
   • Strike outs – Name **lblStrikeOuts**, Height **12**, Left **150**, Top **12**, Width **42**
   • Position – Name **lblPosition**, Height **12**, Left **150**, Top **36**, Width **36**

g. Insert four text boxes to the right of the labels created in the prior step. Assign descriptive names and the properties as follows:
   • txtInnings - Height **16**, Left **84**, Top **12**, Width **54**
   • txtRuns - Height **16**, Left **84**, Top **36**, Width **54**
   • txtStrikeOuts - Height **16**, Left **198**, Top **12**, Width **66**
   • txtPosition – Height **16**, Left **198**, Top **36**, width **66**
   • Insert a command button in the bottom-left corner of the frame named **cmdERA**. Set the Caption property to **Calculate ERA** and the BackColor to **green (&H0000C000&)**.

h. Insert a command button in the top-right corner of the form named **cmdSave**. Set the Caption property to **Save** and the BackColor to **green (&H0000C000&)**.

i. Set the TabIndex property for the text boxes and command button in proper sequence with the txtName control with a value of **0** and the cmdSave control with a value of **6**.

j. Save the VBA code.

Code the Form's Initialize Method

The form will display several times during execution, once for each pitcher. To ensure the form is cleared of previously entered data, you need to create an Initialize method for the frmPitching form.

a. Display the code window for the **frmPitching** form and select the **UserForm object** and the **Initialize method**.

b. Type statements to clear each text box on the form, such as txtName.Text = "", substituting the actual text box names you assigned.

c. Type a statement to set the focus back to the txtName text box on the form.

d. Save the VBA code.

Code the Calculate ERA button

When the frmPitching form is displayed and the Calculate ERA button is clicked, the pitcher's ERA (earned run average) should be displayed in a message box. ERA is calculated by multiplying the runs allowed by 9 and dividing by the total innings pitched. You will use the values entered in the txtInnings and txtRuns to complete the calculations.

a. Display the frmPitching form in the VB Editor.

b. Add an On Click event to the Calculate ERA button (cmdERA).

c. Type the statement **MsgBox ("Pitcher " & Me.txtName & "'s ERA is " & Format(Me.txtRuns * 9 / Me.txtInnings, "Standard"))**

d. Save the VBA code.

Code the Form's Save Button

When the form displays, the user enters data into the text boxes and then clicks the Save button. You need to write the sub procedure to obtain the data in the text boxes, and then display formatted output on the Pitching worksheet.

a. Create a sub procedure for the Save button.

b. Enter a statement that inserts a new row starting in Row 2 on the Pitching worksheet.

c. Enter a statement that places the current date in **cell A2** of the Pitching worksheet.

d. Enter a statement that places txtName in **cell B2**, txtPosition in **cell C2**, intInnings in **cell D2**, txtStrikeOuts in **cell E2**, and txtRuns in **cell F2**.

e. Enter a statement that sets **columns A:F** in the pitching worksheet to AutoFit.

f. Type the statement **Unload frmPitching** to unload the form from memory. You do not want to simply hide the form or it will preserve the previously entered data.

g. Save the VBA code.

Code the Enter Pitching Stats Button

To complete the code for the Pitching Stats button, you need to add a For ... Next loop to display the frmPitching form for each pitcher that played in the current game.

a. Open the code for the cmdPitchingStats button in the VB Editor.

b. Write a For...Next loop to iterate as many times as the number of pitchers. The first statement in the body of the loop should load the frmPitching form, and the second statement should show the form. No other statements should be in the body of the loop. The form's Save button's sub procedure takes over when the user clicks Save each time.

c. Save the VBA code. Close the VB Editor.

Code the Enter Batting Stats Button

Your next task is to code the Batting Stats button. The button functions similarly to the pitching stats button; therefore, you will copy and modify the code from the prior steps to code the button.

a. Open and copy the code for the Enter Pitching Stats button in the VB Editor.

b. Create a new On Click event for the Enter Batting Stats button.

c. Paste the code in the code window and make the following edits.

Prior Code	Edited Code
intNumPlayers = InputBox("Please enter the number of pitchers", "Game Stats")	intNumPlayers = InputBox("Please enter the number of batters", "Game Stats")
Load frmPitching frmPitching.Show	Load frmBatting frmBatting.show

d. Save the VBA code. Close the VB Editor.

Code the Get Help Button

Your last task to complete the worksheet, is to code the Get Help button. The button should display the tech support email address (help@PerformanceStats.com) in a message box.

a. Add an On Click procedure to the Get Help button.

b. Enter a statement to display a message box with the following message: **For tech support please email help@PerformanceStats.com**.

c. Save the VBA code. Close the VB Editor.

Test the Buttons

You test the buttons to ensure the application works.

a. Click the **Home sheet tab**. Click the **Enter Pitching Stats** button, type **2**, and then click **OK**.

b. Enter **Exploring Series**, **5 innings pitched**, **3 strike outs**, **1 run**, and **SP** as the position.

c. Press **Save**. Enter **your name**, **3 innings pitched**, **1 strike outs**, **1 run**, and **RP as the position**.

d. Click **Calculate ERA**, click **OK**, and then click **Save**.

e. Click the **Enter Batting Stats button**, type **1**, and then click **OK**.

f. Enter **Exploring Series**, **2 Games**, **3 AB**, **1 run**, **2 Hits**, **1 HR**, and **1 RBI**. Click **Save**.

g. Click the **Get Help button**, and then click **OK**.

h. Review the Pitching, Batting, and Summary worksheets to view the results.

i. Save and close the workbook. Based on your instructor's directions, submit v2c1StatTracker_LastFirst.

Access and VBA

- You will use VBA to perform calculations in Access.
- You will use VBA to work with recordsets.
- You will use VBA to automate forms in Access.
- You will handle errors using VBA.

OBJECTIVES & SKILLS: After you read this chapter, you will be able to:

CASE STUDY | Croton Sporting Goods

Croton Sporting Goods is a locally owned sporting goods store that specializes in outdoor adventure sports. After 20 years of business, Randy Barnes, the owner of Croton, has decided to update his business processes by incorporating a Microsoft Access database into his company's everyday business functions. The current database manages customers, inventory, suppliers, and transactions.

Randy has added you to his management team as an IT intern. As part of your job responsibilities, you will add new features to the database including data validation, data entry, shortcuts, and the ability to search all records easily based on multiple search criteria. After researching the requests, you have decided to use VBA to accomplish your goals.

Customizing Access with VBA

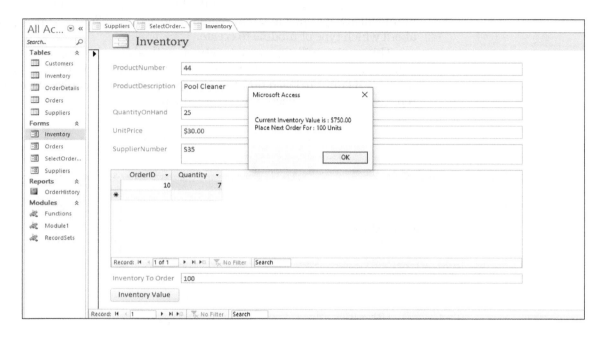

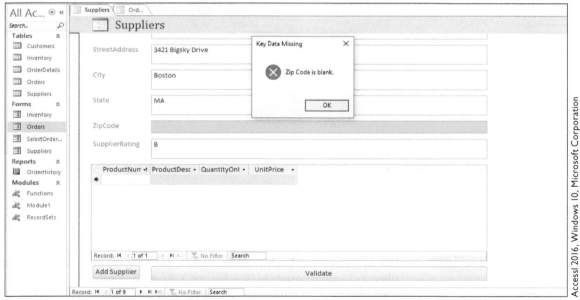

FIGURE 3.1 Croton Sporting Goods Database

Starting File	Files to be submitted
v3h3Croton	**v3h2Croton_LastFirst_*CurrentDate*** **v3h3Croton_LastFirst**

VBA in Access

When working in database design, the first steps require the creation of objects such as tables or reports. Once these objects are created, Access includes some basic macro actions that can add additional functionality in the way the objects interact. Although these included actions can be manipulated using the Access Macro Builder, they are only a small portion of what can be achieved using VBA. By using VBA in Access, you will gain the ability to perform tasks that could not be accomplished any other way. As you work with VBA in Access, you will need to open the Visual Basic Editor (VB Editor) as shown in Figure 3.2. Because the VB Editor is a separate program from Access, the program will always open in a new window. Once the VB Editor is open, you may be unsure about which type of module to create.

This section will explore a variety of methods for creating code and modules so that you can determine how to create the correct procedure in the correct module. You will use the VB Editor to learn how to create procedures in modules, write code for forms and reports, work with objects, and create functions.

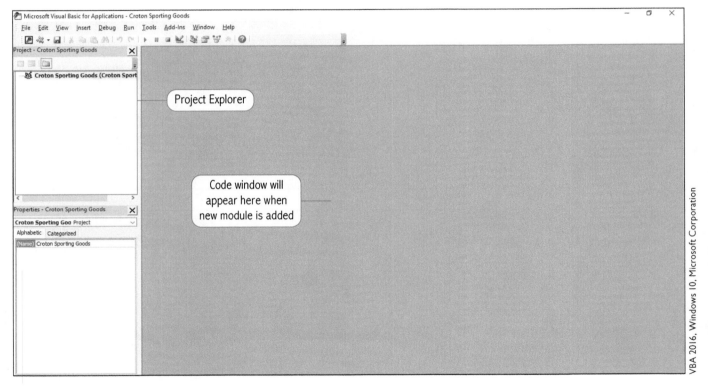

FIGURE 3.2 VB Editor

Writing Code in Modules

 When you create VBA code in Access, you can create the code using one of three modules: a standard module (see Figure 3.3), a class module, or an Access object module. A standard module stores procedures that are available to any event in the application and an Access object module stores procedures that are available to a specific form or report. Class modules are advanced programs that are used to create custom objects similar to the preexisting objects that are included in Microsoft Office. You can create a class module to group related actions into one location.

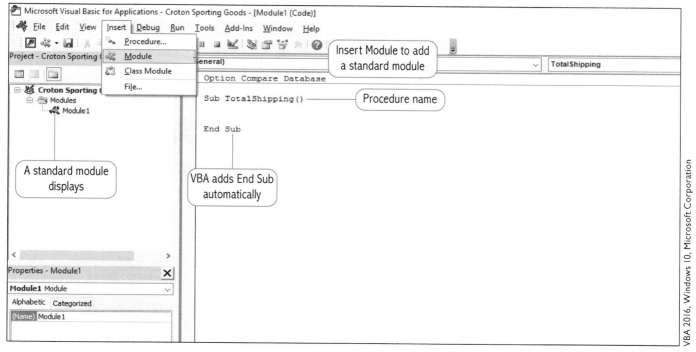

FIGURE 3.3 Creating a Standard Module

To Insert a Standard Module, complete the following steps:

1. Open Access and press Alt+F11 to open the VB Editor.
2. Click Insert on the menu bar and select Module. The VB Editor appears with the statement Option Compare Database at the top of the Code window; Module1 appears in the Project Explorer on the left.
3. Type Sub followed by the name of the procedure, such as Sub TotalShipping (). Note that the Sub name cannot contain spaces. The editor will add End Sub automatically after you press Enter, as shown in Figure 3.3. Continue typing the rest of the code until the procedure is completed.

To Insert a Class Module, complete the following steps:

1. Click Insert on the menu bar and select Class Module. The Code window appears with the statement Option Compare Database at the top; Class1 displays in the Project Explorer on the left.
2. Type Public Sub followed by the name of the procedure, such as Public Sub AddVendor(). The editor will add End Sub automatically after you press Enter, as shown in Figure 3.4.
3. Type the rest of the code until the procedure is completed.

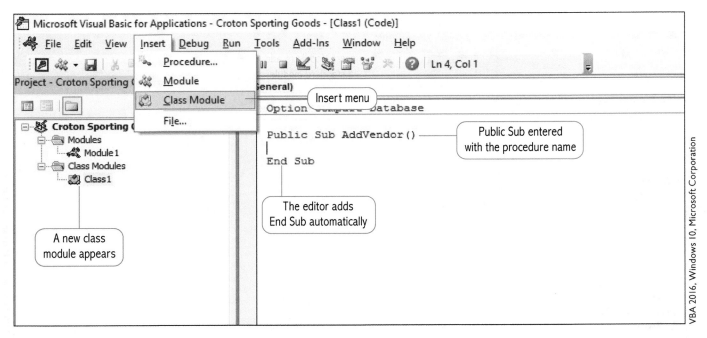

FIGURE 3.4 Creating a Class Module

> ### To create an Access object module, complete the following steps:
>
> 1. Open an Access form or report in Design view and insert an event procedure into an event property. Access will automatically open the VB Editor and insert the respective object module. VBA begins the procedure by adding Private Sub followed by the name of the procedure based on the event, such as Private Sub Form_Current(). The editor will add End Sub automatically.
> 2. Type the remaining code between the Sub and End Sub statements until the procedure is completed.

TIP: SHORTCUTS TO THE VB EDITOR
You can open the VB Editor by pressing Alt+F11. Another way to open the VB Editor is to double-click a module or a class module in the Navigation Pane. When you double-click a module in the Navigation Pane, the VB Editor opens that module so you can view or edit the code immediately. Note the modules will not appear until they have been initially saved.

Writing Code for Forms and Reports

 Forms and reports are two pivotal objects that appear within Access databases. Reports provide clean business-oriented and -formatted information. Forms provide the ability to review and enter information into the database without the need to access a data table. Access contains many tools to enable the customization of forms and reports; however, you can use VBA to add functionality that can surpass what is achievable with built-in features.

To create VBA code for a form or a report, complete the following steps:

1. Open the object in Design view and on the Form Design Tools tab, on the Design tab, click Property Sheet in the Tools group.
2. Select an event on the Event tab (e.g., On Load) and click Build on the right side of the property cell. The Choose Builder dialog box, as shown in Figure 3.5, appears with three options—Macro Builder, Expression Builder, and Code Builder.
3. Select the Code Builder and click OK to open the VB Editor.

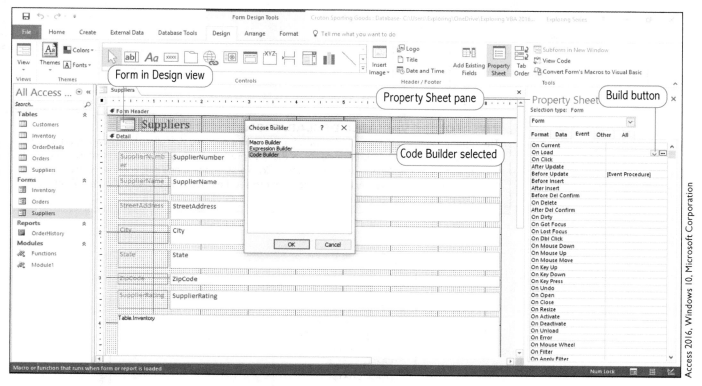

FIGURE 3.5 Opening the VB Editor from Inside a Form

When the VB Editor opens, a new object module is created to store the VBA code for the selected form. Notice the Private Sub statement is automatically inserted into the Code window by the editor along with the End Sub statement. The Option Compare Database and Option Explicit declarations also appear at the top of the code by default. The ***Option Compare Database*** statement is used in a module to declare that string comparisons are not case sensitive when data is compared. The ***Option Explicit*** statement is used in a module to require that all variables be declared before they are used. This is a best practice that is often used by programmers and can be set as a default setting in the VB Editor options menu.

At this point, you (the programmer) probably have a reason for wanting to add a procedure to the On Load event of the form. For example, you may want to remind the user where the supplier of a warehouse item is located. Add the remaining code to your procedure, as shown in Figure 3.6, and then save the code. When you close the VB Editor, the original Access form is available.

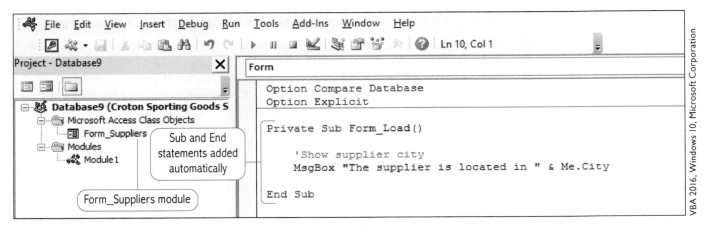

FIGURE 3.6 VB Editor Opened from a Form

TIP: REQUIRE VARIABLE DECLARATION

The Option Explicit statement at the top of a procedure requires that all variables be declared before they are used in a statement. Because this is the best practice used by most programmers, you should set this feature as the default. In the VB Editor, click Tools on the menu bar, and then select Options. Click the Require Variable Declaration check box to set the option, as shown in Figure 3.7, and then click OK to close the dialog box.

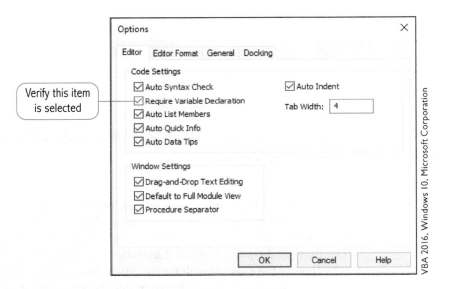

FIGURE 3.7 Set Require Variable Declaration to Yes

Working with Objects

 STEP 3 ▶▶ VBA works with the objects in the various ***object libraries*** that are available in the applications that support VBA. You can use objects in the object libraries along with their resources to accomplish the programming tasks. These object libraries include Access and Excel, which are the two most popular applications that support VBA. Word, PowerPoint, and Outlook can also be automated using VBA.

In addition to the Office applications, you can also set references to other object libraries, such as Adobe Acrobat, Skype, and Yahoo! Messenger, if the programs are installed on your system. All of these libraries require you to set a reference in the VB Editor.

To set references to other object libraries, complete the following steps:

1. Click Tools on the menu bar, click References.
2. Select the check boxes for the references (or libraries) that you need in the References dialog box, as shown in Figure 3.8.
3. Click OK when finished. By default, some of the references you need may already be selected. Knowing which references to select will take practice and some trial and error.

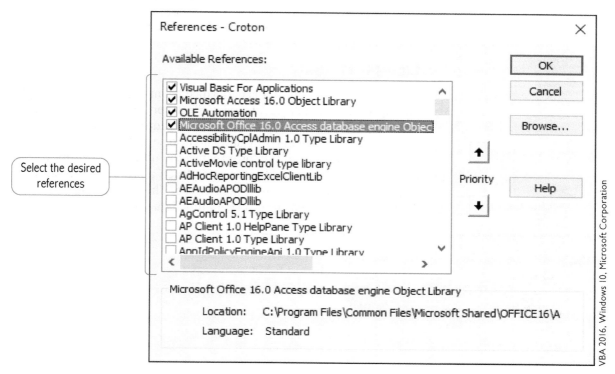

FIGURE 3.8 Select the Object Libraries

Set Properties

A property is a physical attribute of an object. When working with forms, you will notice they each have a size, a type of border, a back color, and various bound and unbound controls. All of these represent properties of the form except for the bound and unbound controls, which are objects themselves. As a rule, any form property you can change in Design view can also be changed using VBA code. If you can change the back color property of a label or textbox to Text 2, Lighter 80%, you can also change the same property using VBA. When using VBA to designate a color, you must use the numerical equivalent. For example, if you create a form based on the Office Theme, you can set the back color to yellow in VBA using the RGB number 255,255,0. As shown in Code Window 3.1, the Forms.Section property is used to modify the details section BackColor of a form.

Change the background color of a form using VBA

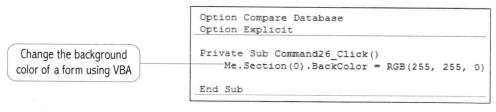

```
Option Compare Database
Option Explicit

Private Sub Command26_Click()
        Me.Section(0).BackColor = RGB(255, 255, 0)

End Sub
```

CODE WINDOW 3.1

Use Methods

A method is an action that is performed by an object. A few examples of form methods are .Open, .Close, .RefreshAll, and .GoToRecord. You can accomplish all of these actions manually in Form view by using the Ribbon and the Record Navigation bar. Many actions that you can perform in Form view can also be performed automatically using VBA code. For example, to refresh the form to give the user the most up-to-date information, you could create a command button and attach a procedure, as shown in Figure 3.9. The VBA code to refresh a form is Me.Refresh. This uses the Refresh method to update the data in the form based on the originating data source.

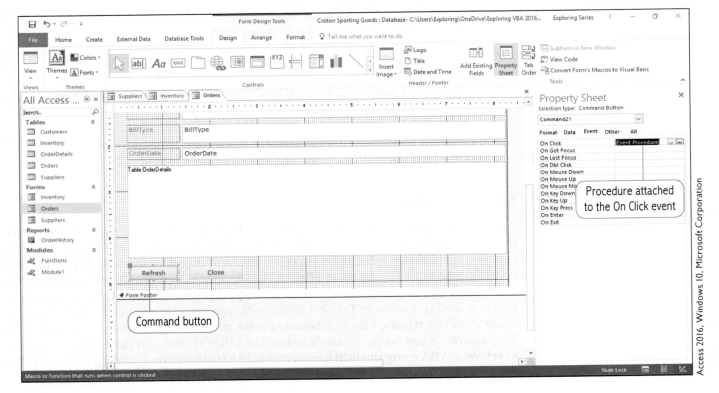

FIGURE 3.9 Refresh a Form

At first, you may find it difficult to differentiate between methods and properties. You may want to change a property or use a method only to discover that VBA reports an error. VBA provides some visual help when adding code to a procedure using the Me prefix. Me refers to the current instance of the object you are in. When you type the Me keyword and then type a period, the editor will provide a list of available items and indicate which items are properties and which are methods using a unique icon. This list is helpful, because you do not have to memorize all the properties and methods on a form or report. If you are still unsure and use a property or method improperly, VBA will correct you. As a rule, methods are more difficult to use and master.

Set Events

An event is triggered when a user takes an action. For example, users can take the following actions when working in a form: change a record, open a form, close a form, and filter the records in a form. The corresponding events that are triggered are shown in Table 3.1.

TABLE 3.1 Event Examples		
User Action	**How Access Responds**	**Event Triggered**
Change and save a record in a form	Saves the record	Before Update
Click a button to open a form	Opens the form	On Click
Click the Close button to close a form	Closes the form	On Close
Find records in a form with certain criteria	Filters the record source	On Filter

Events are extremely useful to programmers because they can interrupt user actions and verify that the user really wants to take the action they requested. The first example in Table 3.1, change and save a record in a form, may need confirmation from the user. Did the user intentionally change the data? Adding a message that asks, "Do you want to save your changes?" helps eliminate inadvertent changes. You can intercept the save process with the Before Update event and then ask the user to confirm; this gives the user a chance to discard the changes. The message would appear to the user as shown in Figure 3.10.

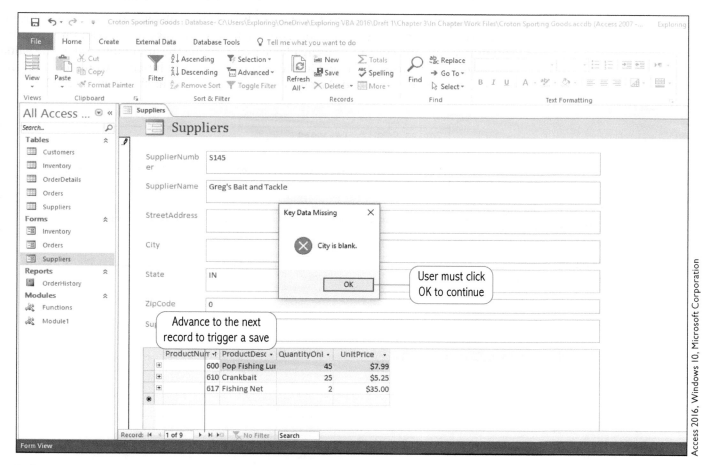

FIGURE 3.10 Using the Before Update Event

Creating Functions

 As discussed earlier, a function is a procedure that performs an action and returns a value. Many functions are predefined in VBA and ready to use. To use a predefined function, simply add the function to your procedure and insert the required arguments; when the procedure runs, the function will assign the value to the function name.

When no preexisting function will fit your needs, you can author calculations directly into procedures; however, a custom function allows cleaner design. To create a custom function, open a module, and then type a statement into the Code window with the format:

Function NameOfFunction(Argument As Data Type) As Data Type
End Function

The VB Editor automatically adds the statement End Function after you press Enter. An *argument* is the value that the procedure passes to the function; arguments can be assigned a specific data type. The data type at the end of the first statement refers to the type of data the function returns to the procedure. Add the remaining lines of code to complete the function, save, and then test the function. When a procedure encounters a function, the procedure takes the following steps:

1. The procedure runs and encounters the function.
2. The procedure calls the function and passes one or more values to it.
3. The function receives the values and processes them according to the function code.
4. The function returns a different value (with possibly a different data type) to the calling procedure by assigning the result to the function name.

For example, you could create a custom function to calculate the amount of inventory to order from a product vendor. The function would take the maximum inventory quantity minus the current units available to determine the amount to order. The value could then be returned to a field in the current form. The function would contain the lines of code as shown in Code Window 3.2, with the result as shown in Figure 3.11.

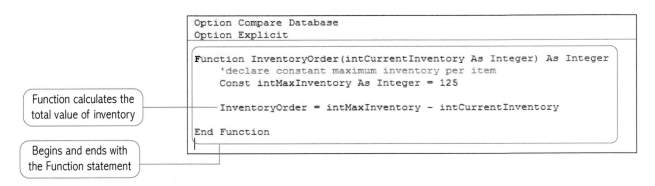

CODE WINDOW 3.2

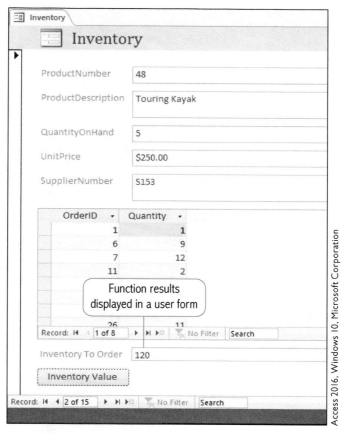

FIGURE 3.11 Function Calculation Displayed in Form

1. What is the difference between a standard module, class module, and a function? *p. 144*

2. What does the statement Option Explicit mean and when is it used? *p. 147*

3. What is a Before Update event and how is it best utilized? *p. 151*

Hands-On Exercises

1 VBA in Access

After reviewing the current needs of the database, you have decided to add a welcome message box indicating the current date and company name, as well as add data validation to identify and highlight required fields that are missing data in the Suppliers form. Your last step will be to create a custom function to allow for automatic calculation of inventory value.

STEP 1 ›› WRITE CODE IN MODULES

You need to open the VB Editor and verify that the Require Variable Declaration check box is set to Yes. You also will write a simple procedure to practice creating and running a procedure. Refer to Figure 3.12 as you complete Step 1.

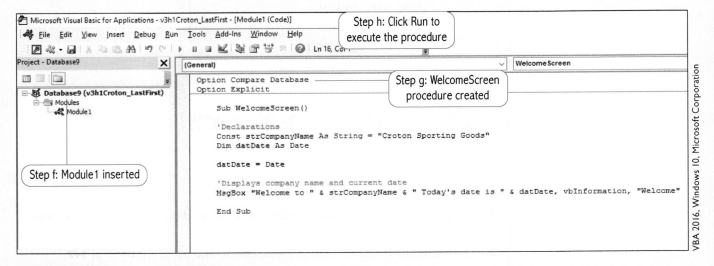

FIGURE 3.12 Creating a New Module

a. Start Access. Open *v3h1Croton,* click **Enable Content**, and save it as **v3h1Croton_LastFirst.accdb**.

> **TROUBLESHOOTING:** If you make any major mistakes in this exercise, you can close the file, open *v3h1Croton* again, and start this exercise over.

b. Click the **Database Tools tab** and click **Visual Basic** in the Macro group.

The VB Editor opens.

c. Click **Tools** on the menu bar and select **Options.**

The Options dialog box opens.

d. Ensure the **Require Variable Declaration check box** is selected.

This option requires that all variables be declared prior to being introduced.

e. Click **OK** to close the Options dialog box.

f. Click **Insert** on the menu bar and select **Module.**

g. Place the insertion point on **Ln4, Col1**, press **Tab,** and then create a new procedure by typing the code shown in Code Window 3.3.

```
Option Compare Database
Option Explicit

    Sub WelcomeScreen()

    'Declarations
    Const strCompanyName As String = "Croton Sporting Goods"
    Dim datDate As Date

    datDate = Date

    'Displays company name and current date
    MsgBox "Welcome to " & strCompanyName & " Today's date is " & datDate, vbInformation, "Welcome"

    End Sub
```

CODE WINDOW 3.3

h. Click **Run Sub/UserForm** on the toolbar with the insertion point inside the WelcomeScreen procedure.

The welcome screen and current date are now displayed.

i. Click **OK** to close the dialog box. Click **Save** on the toolbar and click **OK** in the Save As dialog box to save the new module as **Module1**. Close the VB Editor.

STEP 2 ›› **WRITE CODE TO TEST FOR KEY DATA IN A FORM**

You would like to create a procedure to check for missing city information in the supplier's form before it is saved. If the city, state, or zip code data is missing, your code will display a message box warning the user. Refer to Figures 3.13 and 3.14 as you complete Step 2.

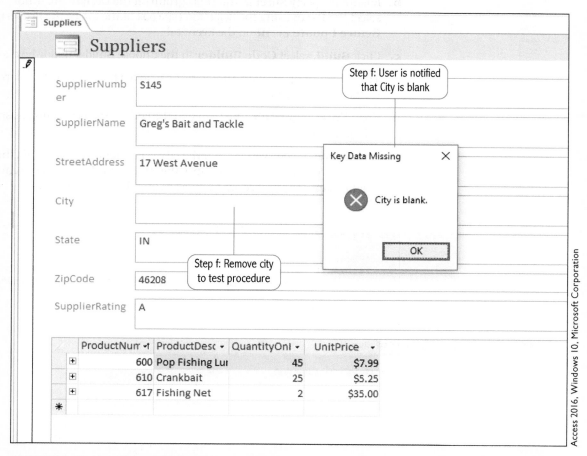

FIGURE 3.13 Use VBA to Validate Data on a Form

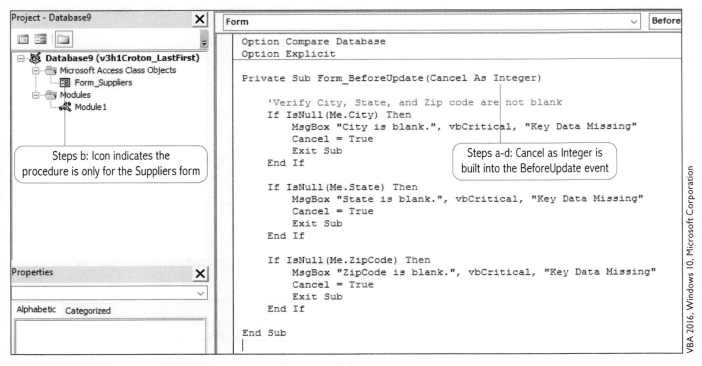

FIGURE 3.14 Procedure to Validate Data

a. Open the Suppliers form in Design view from the Navigation Pane.

b. Ensure Property Sheet in the Tools group on the Design tab. If not already selected, select the **Form** using the Selection type box at the top of the Property Sheet. Click the **Before Update event** on the Event tab.

c. Click **Build**, select **Code Builder** in the Choose Builder dialog box, and then click **OK**.

The VB Editor opens with Suppliers form added to the Project Explorer. A new procedure is started in the Code window.

d. Press **Enter**, press **Tab**, and then add the code to the procedure, as shown in the Code Window 3.4.

This section of code verifies that the city is not blank. If it is blank, the user is notified and the record cannot be saved, because the statement Cancel = True cancels the update. Exit Sub stops the procedure from executing the rest of the code.

```
Private Sub Form_BeforeUpdate(Cancel As Integer)

    'Verify City, State, and Zip code are not blank
    If IsNull(Me.City) Then
        MsgBox "City is blank.", vbCritical, "Key Data Missing"
        Cancel = True
        Exit Sub
    End If

End Sub
```

CODE WINDOW 3.4

e. Save the procedure and minimize the VB Editor. Display the Suppliers form in Form view.

f. Delete the City in the first record of the Suppliers form. Press **Tab** until the focus reaches the State. Continue to press **Tab** until the message box appears. When the message appears, click **OK** and press **Esc** to restore the city.

g. Return to the VB Editor. Place the insertion point at the end of the existing code. Press **Enter** and add the additional code to the Form_BeforeUpdate procedure, as shown in Code Window 3.5.

This section of code verifies that the State and ZipCode are not blank. If either field is blank, the user is notified and the record cannot be saved, because the statement Cancel = True cancels the update.

```
If IsNull(Me.State) Then
    MsgBox "State is blank.", vbCritical, "Key Data Missing"
    Cancel = True
    Exit Sub
End If

If IsNull(Me.ZipCode) Then
    MsgBox "ZipCode is blank.", vbCritical, "Key Data Missing"
    Cancel = True
    Exit Sub
End If
```

CODE WINDOW 3.5

h. Save the procedure and minimize the VB Editor.

i. Delete the State in the first record of the Suppliers form. Press **Tab** until the focus reaches the ZipCode. Press **Tab** twice. When the message appears, click **OK** and press **Esc** to restore the State.

j. Delete the ZipCode in the first record of the Suppliers form. Press **Tab** until the focus reaches the Supplier Rating. Press **Tab** again. When the message appears, click **OK** and press **Esc** to restore the ZipCode.

> **TROUBLESHOOTING:** If you receive a run-time error, return to the VB Editor and match your code against the completed code in Figure 3.14.

k. Save the changes to the Suppliers form.

You decide to add additional style to the validation by highlighting key fields with missing data. You will use a command button to trigger the validation. Refer to Figure 3.15 as you complete Step 3.

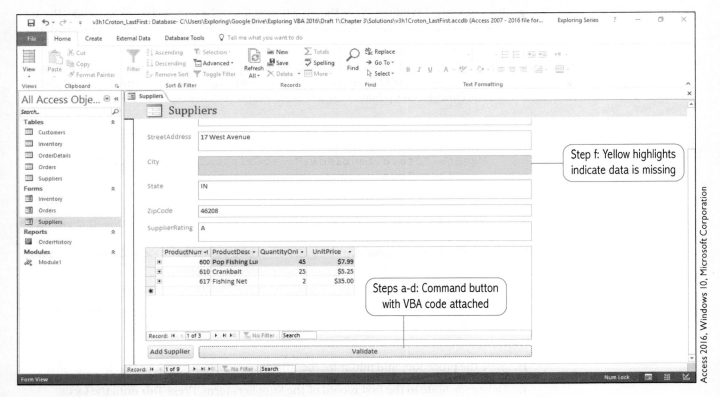

FIGURE 3.15 Use VBA to Alert User About Missing Data

a. Display the Suppliers form in Design View and ensure the Property Sheet is displayed.

b. Scroll down, select the **Validate button**, and then click the **All tab** in the Property Sheet. Modify the Name property to display **cmdValidate**.

c. Click the **Event tab** in the Property Sheet, click the **On Click event**, and then click **Build**. Select **Code Builder** in the Choose Builder dialog box and click **OK**.

The VB Editor opens and a new procedure, Sub cmdValidate_Click(), is added to the Code window above the Form_BeforeUpdate procedure.

d. Press **Enter**, press **Tab**, and then type the code shown in Code Window 3.6 into the Sub cmdValidate_Click() procedure.

This section of code verifies that the City is not blank. If the city textbox is blank, the field is highlighted in yellow (RGB code 255,255,0) to alert the user; if it does contain information, the BackColor property will be set to white (RGB code 255,255,255).

```
Private Sub cmdValidate_Click()

    'Validate key data by highlighting fields with missing data.
    If IsNull(Me.City) Then
        Me.City.BackColor = RGB(255, 255, 0)
    Else
        Me.City.BackColor = RGB(255, 255, 255)
    End If

End Sub
```

CODE WINDOW 3.6

e. Save the procedure, and then minimize the VB Editor. Display the Suppliers form in Form view.

f. Delete the City in the first record of the Suppliers form. Click the **Validate button**.

The background color of the City field is highlighted in yellow, alerting you that the City field is blank.

g. Retype the city name (Indianapolis) in the City field and click the **Validate button**. Note the box color changes back to white. Return to the VB Editor and add additional code to the cmdValidate_Click() procedure, as shown in Code Window 3.7.

This section of code verifies that the State and ZipCode are not blank. If either is, the user is alerted with a yellow background, the same as in the City field. This code also returns the background color to white if the information is entered into the fields.

```
If IsNull(Me.State) Then
    Me.State.BackColor = RGB(255, 255, 0)
Else
    Me.State.BackColor = RGB(255, 255, 255)
End If

If IsNull(Me.ZipCode) Then
    Me.ZipCode.BackColor = RGB(255, 255, 0)
Else
    Me.ZipCode.BackColor = RGB(255, 255, 255)
End If
```

CODE WINDOW 3.7

h. Save the procedure and minimize the VB Editor.

i. Delete the State in the first record of the Suppliers form. Click the **Validate button**.

The State field is highlighted with a yellow background.

j. Press **Esc** to restore the deleted State. Delete the ZipCode in the first record of the Suppliers form. Click the **Validate button**.

The ZipCode field is highlighted with a yellow background.

k. Retype the deleted ZipCode (46208) and click **Validate**. Note the yellow color returns to white. Close the VB Editor and save the changes to the Suppliers form. Close the form.

After adding validation to the Suppliers form, you have decided to add functionality to the Inventory form. You would like to create a custom function that will determine the amount of product to order based on the maximum desired amount in stock of 125 per item. When called, not only will it return the quantity to order from the vendor, but it will also calculate the total value of inventory in the warehouse. Refer to Figure 3.16 as you complete Step 4.

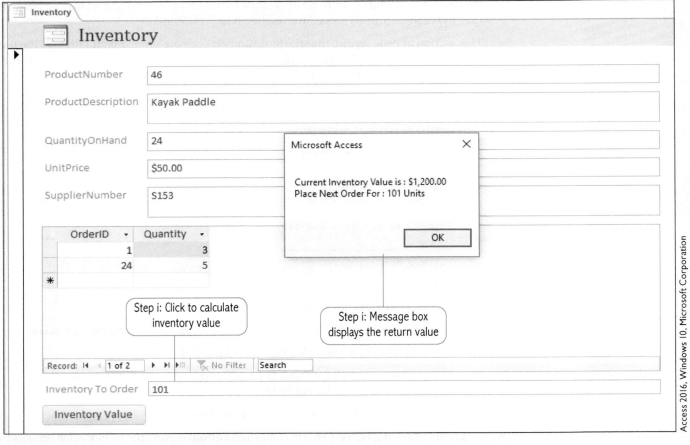

FIGURE 3.16 Function Calculates Units to Order

a. Display the Database Tools tab, and in the Macro group, click **Visual Basic**.

b. Click **Insert** on the menu bar and select **Module**.

Module2 appears in the Project Explorer.

c. Type the code as shown in Code Window 3.8 into the Code window:

This code creates a function that calculates the total amount of product to order by finding the difference between the current stock in the warehouse and the declared constant maximum inventory of 125 units.

```
Function InventoryOrder(intCurrentInventory As Integer) As Integer

    'Declarations
    Const intMaxInventory As Integer = 125

    InventoryOrder = intMaxInventory - intCurrentInventory

End Function
```

CODE WINDOW 3.8

d. Save the module with the name **Functions** and press **Alt+F11** to exit the VB Editor.

Now you will add a function to the InventoryToOrder text box on the bottom of the form, as well as to the Inventory Value button to call the function and display a message box that displays the total inventory value as well as the quantity to order.

e. Open the Inventory form in Design View, and click the **InventoryToOrder text box** located at the bottom of the form. Type the following function into the text box: **=Inventory Order([QuantityOnHand])**.

This uses the function created in Step c to return the amount of inventory to order. Because a text box was used, this will display for every record that is displayed and does not need to be activated with a button.

> **TROUBLESHOOTING:** If you experience difficulties entering the function directly into the text box, you can also enter the function as the Control Source in the Property Sheet.

f. Click the **Format tab** on the Property Sheet and select **General Number** from the Format menu.

g. Select the **Inventory Value button** in the Inventory form. Click **On Click event** in the Event tab. Click the **Build button**, select **Code Builder** in the Choose Builder dialog box, and then click **OK**.

h. Place the insertion point at **Ln5, Col1**, press **Enter**, and then press **Tab**. Add the code shown in Code Window 3.9.

Code Window 3.9 references the textbox that calls the InventoryOrder function and adds the value to a message box if the quantity on hand is less than the maximum quantity of 125. It then displays the value of the amount in the warehouse based on the quantity on hand and the unit price.

```
Private Sub cmdTotalInventoryValue_Click()

    'Displays quantity to order and inventory value text box
    If Me.InventoryToOrder = 0 Then
        MsgBox ("Current Inventory Value is : " & Format(Me.QuantityOnHand * Me.UnitPrice, "Currency"))
    Else
        MsgBox ("Current Inventory Value is : " & Format( _
        Me.QuantityOnHand * Me.UnitPrice, "Currency") & " " & vbNewLine & _
        "Place Next Order For : " & Me.InventoryToOrder & " " & "Units")
    End If

End Sub
```

CODE WINDOW 3.9

i. Save the procedure and minimize the VB Editor.

j. Return to the Inventory form, and switch to Form view. Click **Next Record** in the Navigation bar of the form and click the **Inventory Value button**.

The total value of the inventory is now displayed.

k. Click **OK** to close the dialog box. Save and Close the Inventory form.

l. Exit the VB Editor. Keep the database open if you plan to continue with Hands-On Exercise 2. If not, close the database, and then exit Access.

Working with Recordsets

A *recordset* is a set of records selected from a table or query loaded in the random access memory of your computer. A recordset is similar to a table or a query; the same data source would be represented in all three cases. For example, if you were working with a database that contained supplier data, the same results would be achieved with any of the three methods shown in Table 3.2.

TABLE 3.2 Table Data Achieved with Three Methods

Method	Results
Open Suppliers table	All columns and all records are displayed
Create a query based on the Suppliers table	All columns and all records are displayed (as long as all columns are added to the design grid)
Create a Recordset using VBA based on the Suppliers table	All columns and all records are stored in memory (as long as all columns are selected in the OpenRecordset statement)

The Suppliers table would display all the columns and all the records in Datasheet view, but could then be filtered into groups and sorted based on multiple criteria. A query based on the Suppliers table could limit the number of columns (by selecting a subset of fields); the query could also limit the number of records by entering criteria on one or more fields. A recordset could limit the number of columns and fields, evaluate each record in the recordset individually, and then take action based on the logic of the procedure.

The benefit of the recordset is the versatility of working with records and data programmatically. Although you can manipulate records and data using an action query, only recordsets enable you to update records using decision structures.

In this section, you will learn how to manipulate recordsets using DAO (Data Access Objects) and ADO (ActiveX Data Objects).

Using DAO to Access Data

DAO (Data Access Objects) refers to an object library specifically created to work with Access databases. The DAO object library was first released in 1992 along with Access 1.0. Needless to say, it has evolved and improved with all the versions of Access released since, including Access 2016. Although newer database object libraries have been created, DAO remains the object library of choice for many Access developers.

Create Recordsets

STEP 1 ⟩⟩ As stated earlier, a recordset is a set of records in memory. To create the recordset, you first write a procedure using VBA that extracts data from one or more tables in an Access database and then places the results in memory. Once the recordset has been placed in memory, you can then logically examine the records and make decisions and changes based on your own criteria.

To create a recordset in DAO, you must first explicitly connect to a database, usually the database that is currently open. Next, you create a recordset object based on a table, a query, or an SQL statement. Then, you can loop through the records in the recordset and count the total number of records, count only the records that meet certain criteria, or modify field data of all records that meet certain criteria.

An outline for a procedure that creates a DAO recordset is shown in Figure 3.17.

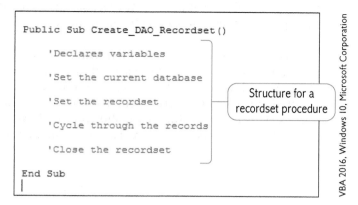

FIGURE 3.17 Module Contains the Outline for a Recordset

Find Records in a Recordset

STEP 2 ›› To create a recordset and search for records that meet certain criteria, you must first identify the table or query that contains the initial recordset. For example, if you need to find all the suppliers who live in Indiana, you could create a recordset based on the Suppliers table. After the recordset has been set, you could use the **MoveNext** method to advance through the records of the recordset. Stopping at each record, you could test the supplier's State to see if it equals IN. If a supplier resides in IN, the procedure would then take the appropriate action to update one or more field values in the matching records. Figure 3.18 shows a sample procedure that creates a DAO recordset and then advances through the records looking for suppliers who live in IN.

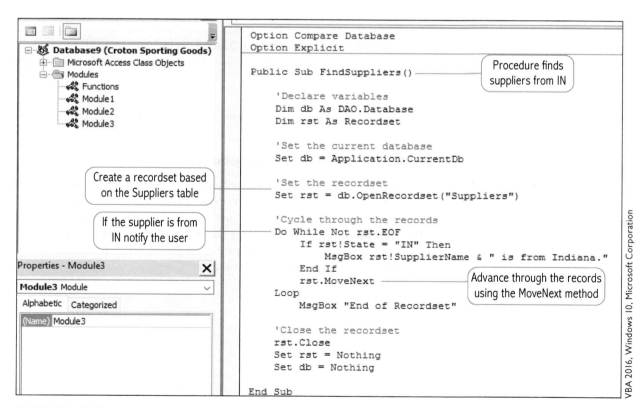

FIGURE 3.18 Recordset Searches for Records from IN

The line of code Set rst = db.OpenRecordset("Suppliers"), establishes the recordset using the OpenRecordset method of the db object. Our example opens the Suppliers table and sets the rst object equal to it. At this point, the recordset object (rst) exists in memory. The procedure can now cycle through the records looking for a match to the code's criteria.

The Do Loop is used in combination with the MoveNext method to cycle through the Supplier records. The While clause is used to end the loop when the End of File (EOF) is reached. As each new record is visited, the state value is compared to IN. If it matches, then a predefined action is performed. In our example, the user is notified that a supplier is from IN. This Do Loop statement, shown in Code Window 3.10, is often used when working with recordsets; you will repeat these statements for almost every recordset you create.

```
'Cycle through the records
Do While Not rst.EOF
    If rst!State = "IN" Then
        MsgBox rst!SupplierName & " is from Indiana."
    End If
    rst.MoveNext
Loop
    MsgBox "End of Recordset"
```

CODE WINDOW 3.10

Finally, the recordset object rst is closed and set to nothing. The database object db is also set to nothing. Closing the recordset and setting it to nothing frees the computer memory being used by VBA so that it is available for other procedures and applications. Your computer could become sluggish if you open several large recordsets without closing them because they tie up memory resources.

TIP: WORKING WITH RECORDSET FIELDS
When you create a recordset procedure in VBA, you refer to the fields in the recordset using the rst! prefix. When you create a recordset object, refer to the field names as rst!SupplierName, rst!SupplierRating, and rst!SupplierAddress. If you omit the object rst or the ! delimiter, the fields will not be recognized by VBA.

Update Records in a Recordset

To update the field values in a recordset, you must first open the recordset for edits, make the change, and then close the recordset to further edits. This process repeats for each record you need to edit. The two methods you need to accomplish a recordset edit are **Edit** and **Update**. Edit enables the change to happen and Update saves the changes and completes the edit process. See Figure 3.19 for a sample procedure that updates the supplier rating for suppliers based in Indiana.

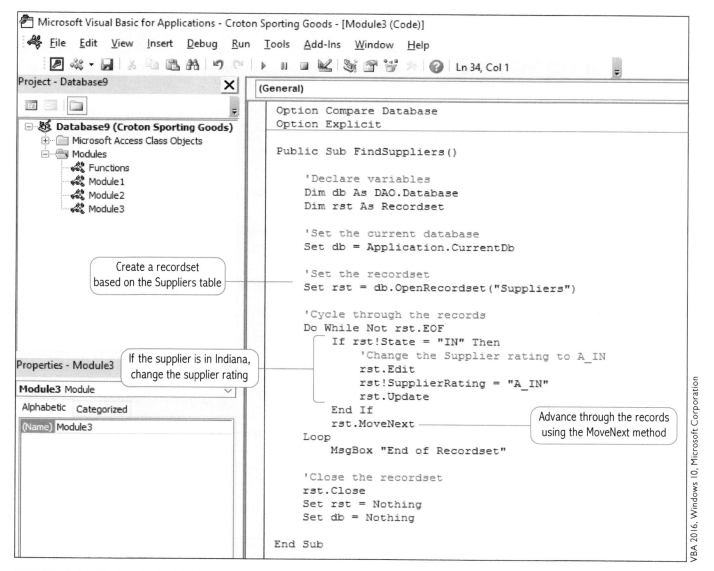

FIGURE 3.19 Update the Field Values in a Recordset

Because VBA updates to a recordset are not easily reversible, you should back up your database before you run an update procedure. The first time you create an update procedure, you must be prepared for errors and unexpected results. Always check the results by opening the affected table(s); if there are problems, revert to the backup version of the database.

Delete Records in a Recordset

STEP 4 Sometimes, you may need to delete records from a table. Instead of scanning the records in the table and then pausing to delete the records that you want to remove, you can create a VBA procedure to cycle through the records and delete only the records that meet your predefined criteria. Using VBA to perform this action is much more efficient. Figure 3.20 shows a sample procedure that deletes all suppliers from the Suppliers table who have an Inactive rating.

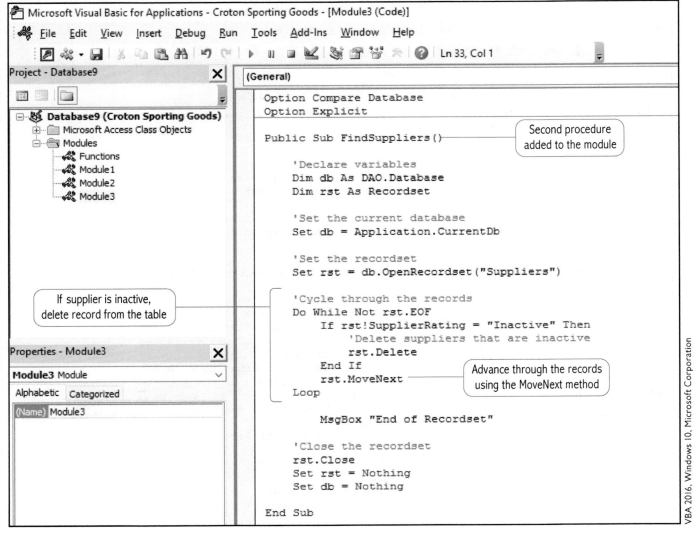

FIGURE 3.20 Delete Records from a Recordset

The key lines of code that enable you to delete records from a recordset are shown in Code Window 3.11. The Delete method actually provides the delete as the Do Loop cycles through the records in the table.

```
'Cycle through the records
Do While Not rst.EOF
    If rst!SupplierRating = "Inactive" Then
        'Delete suppliers that are inactive
        rst.Delete
    End If
    rst.MoveNext
Loop

    MsgBox "End of Recordset"
```

CODE WINDOW 3.11

Insert Records in a Recordset

STEP 5 Sometimes, you may want to insert records into a table. You can create a VBA procedure to insert a record when a certain event takes place in your database. For example, if a customer enters data into an application form for processing, you may want to insert the data into another table only after the application is approved. See Figure 3.21 for a sample procedure that inserts a record into the Suppliers table.

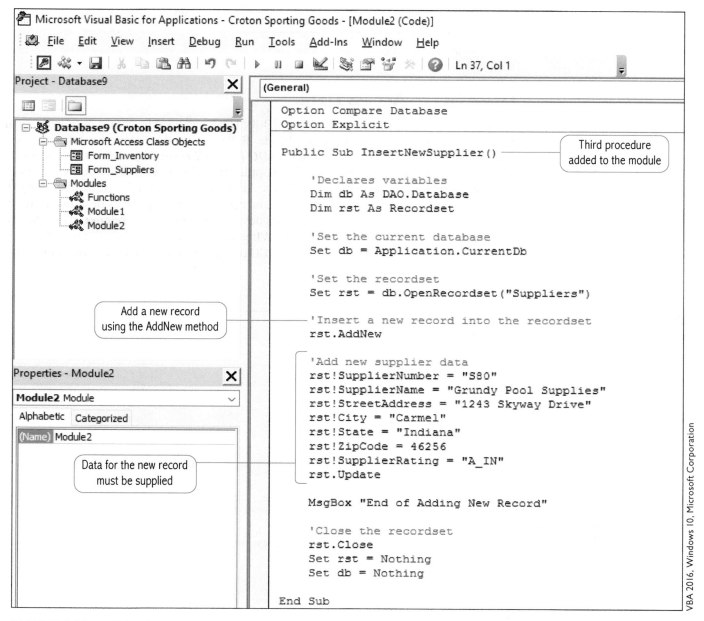

FIGURE 3.21 Add New Records to a Recordset

The key lines of code that enable you to insert a record into a recordset are shown in Code Window 3.12. The AddNew method actually provides the permission for the procedure to insert a new record into the recordset. The Update method completes the insertion of the new data into the recordset.

```
'Insert a new record into the recordset
rst.AddNew

'Add new supplier data
rst!SupplierNumber = "S80"
rst!SupplierName = "Grundy Pool Supplies"
rst!StreetAddress = "1243 Skyway Drive"
rst!City = "Carmel"
rst!State = "Indiana"
rst!ZipCode = 46256
rst!SupplierRating = "A_IN"
rst.Update
```

CODE WINDOW 3.12

Use ADO to Access Data

Prior to the release of Microsoft Access 2000, DAO was used to obtain data from local Access databases and Remote Data Objects. RDO was used to access larger databases such as SQL. Microsoft introduced ADO, **ADO (ActiveX Data Objects)** as a replacement for the older DAO and RDO. RDO has lost popularity to the newer ADO, but there are still many who opt for DAO in certain situations. ADO was designed with the functionality to connect to a wide range of external data sources. Although DAO was designed to work with your local Access database, ADO was designed to connect to relational databases, ISAM data sources, disk files, and so on. Whereas DAO uses the db = CurrentDb statement to connect to the current database, ADO uses the CurrentProject.Connection argument, as shown in Figure 3.22.

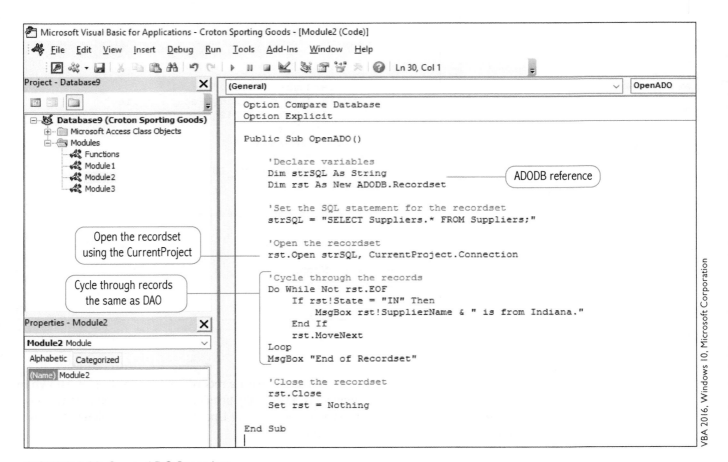

FIGURE 3.22 Create ADO Recordset

In ADO (as in DAO), it is important to declare database variables with the object library prefix. For example, when declaring the rst variable, use *Dim rst As ADODB. Recordset*. After the variable is declared, you can open the recordset using the rst.Open statement. Cycle through the records in the recordset using the Do Loop (the same as the DAO recordset).

Before you can use the ADO object library, you must create a link to the library by clicking Tools on the menu bar, and then selecting References. Figure 3.23 shows the References dialog box for an Access database, including a link to the ADO library.

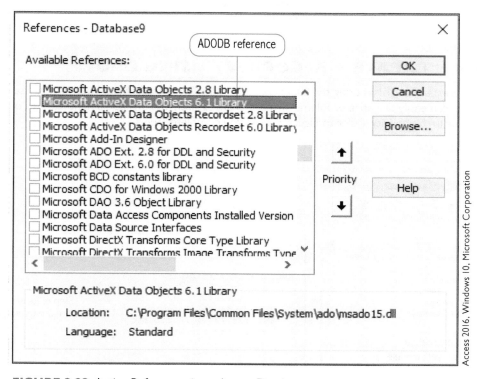

FIGURE 3.23 Active References in an Access Database

TIP: MAKE A COPY BEFORE CHANGING REFERENCES
Changing the references in a database can cause serious problems. Always make a copy of your database before changing references. If anything goes wrong, you can revert to the original database. Even if your database contains no VBA code, the built-in functions that are probably in use in various places will stop working if you disconnect one of the references.

Quick Concepts

4. What is DAO, and how is it used? ***p. 162***

5. What is a recordset, and how does it compare to a query? ***p. 162***

6. What is ADO, and how is it used? ***p. 168***

Hands-On Exercises

Skills covered: Create Recordsets • Find Records in a Recordset • Update Records in a Recordset • Delete Records in a Recordset • Insert Records in a Recordset

2 Working with Recordsets

Randy would like you to add the ability to locate, review, update, and if necessary delete selected records within the company's database. You have decided to use VBA to create recordsets to reach his goal.

STEP I ›› CREATE A RECORDSET USING DAO

You need to create a recordset using the Suppliers table in the Croton database. You will make sure to add comments for each section so you can easily diagnose problems or make changes later. You will add additional lines of code as you complete the remaining steps in this activity. Refer to Figure 3.24 as you complete Step 1.

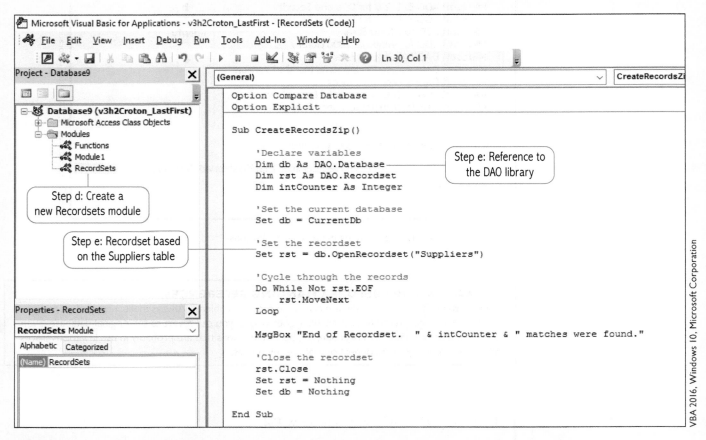

FIGURE 3.24 Create a New Recordset

    a. Open the *v3h1Croton_LastFirst*, and save it as **v3h2Croton_LastFirst** changing h1 to h2.

TROUBLESHOOTING: If the Security Warning toolbar displays, click Enable Content.

---

b. Click the **Database Tools tab** and click **Visual Basic** in the Macro group.

The VB Editor opens.

c. Click **Insert** on the menu bar and select **Module**.

The Option Compare Database and Option Explicit statements appear at the top of the Code window.

d. Click **Save** on the toolbar, type **RecordSets** in the **Save As dialog box** as the module name, and then click **OK**.

The RecordSets module appears in the Project Explorer.

e. Type the lines of code shown in Code Window 3.13.

```
Sub CreateRecordsZip()

    'Declare variables
    Dim db As DAO.Database
    Dim rst As DAO.Recordset
    Dim intCounter As Integer

    'Set the current database
    Set db = CurrentDb

    'Set the recordset
    Set rst = db.OpenRecordset("Suppliers")

    'Cycle through the records
    Do While Not rst.EOF
        rst.MoveNext
    Loop

    MsgBox "End of Recordset.  " & intCounter & " matches were found."

    'Close the recordset
    rst.Close
    Set rst = Nothing
    Set db = Nothing

End Sub
```

CODE WINDOW 3.13

f. Click **Run Sub/Userform** on the toolbar, with the insertion point inside the CreateRecordsZip procedure. Click **OK** when the message appears.

The procedure runs, and returns zero records found. This occurs because there is no criterion specified for the recordset. In the next step, you will specify a zip code to locate and count within the record set.

g. Save the RecordSets module.

You need to revise the Suppliers recordset to find records with a certain zip code. Because this step does not alter the data, you do not have to save a backup of the database. You will display the count of matching records using the MsgBox function. Refer to Figure 3.25 as you complete Step 2.

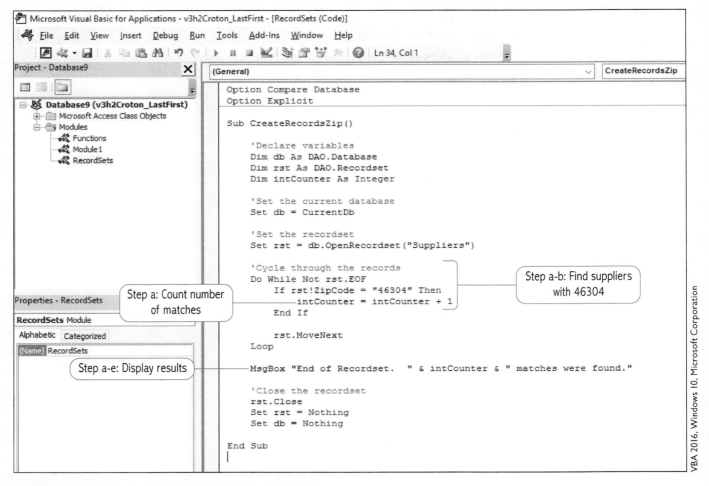

FIGURE 3.25 Recordset Procedure to Test the Zip Code

a. Place the insertion point on **Ln 18, Col 25.** Press **Enter**, press **Tab**, and then type the three lines of code shown in Code Window 3.14 into the procedure.

This code will add one to the counter if the ZipCode is 46304.

```
'Cycle through the records
Do While Not rst.EOF
    If rst!ZipCode = "46304" Then
        intCounter = intCounter + 1
    End If

    rst.MoveNext
Loop

MsgBox "End of Recordset.  " & intCounter & " matches were found."
```

CODE WINDOW 3.14

b. Place the insertion point inside the CreateRecordsZip procedure and click **Run Sub/ Userform** on the toolbar. Click **OK**.

Now when this procedure runs it will count the one occurrence of zip code 46304.

c. Press **Alt+F11** to exit the VB Editor. Open the Suppliers table and click the **filter arrow** for the ZipCode data. Deselect all zip codes except 46304 and click **OK**.

Note there is one occurrence of 46304 in the database. The VBA code entered in Step d will automate this process.

d. Press **Alt+F11** to return to the VB Editor. Locate the ZipCode 46304 in the code.

As shown in Code Window 3.15, alter the zip code to the new location 46208 and rerun the sub to verify its functionality.

The procedure identifies the new criteria and returns a count of 3 occurrences.

```
'Cycle through the records
Do While Not rst.EOF
If rst!ZipCode = "46208" Then
    intCounter = intCounter + 1
End If
|
```

CODE WINDOW 3.15

e. Click **OK** and minimize the VB Editor. Open the Suppliers table and filter the table for zip code 46208. Verify there are three suppliers within the 46208 zip code. Close the table without saving.

> **TROUBLESHOOTING:** If the VB Editor reports an error, stop the procedure and press F8 to step into the code. Continue to press F8 until a portion of the code is highlighted in yellow. This is the erroneous code. Check your work against Code Window 3.15; then make the appropriate corrections.

Due to the frequency of shipments from your Indiana supplier, it has been suggested you modify all Indiana zip codes to add -9999 to each corresponding code to conform to the post office's more specific ZIP+4 notation, and then display the number of matching records using the MsgBox function. Because this step alters the data, you save a backup copy of the database. Refer to Figure 3.26 as you complete Step 3.

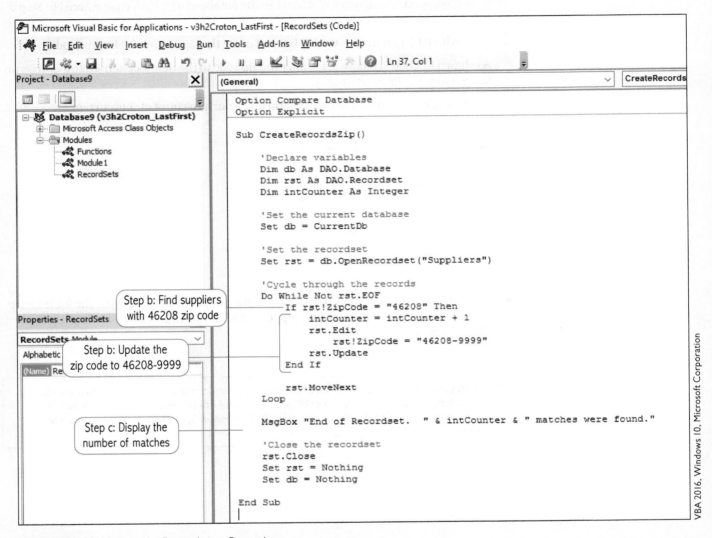

FIGURE 3.26 Update the Records in a Recordset

a. Click the **File tab**, click **Save As**, and then click **Save Database As**. Click **Back Up Database** and click **Save As**. Accept the default file name (e.g., *v3h2Croton_LastFirst_ CurrentDate*), and click **Save**.

The following steps will alter the data within the database. To safeguard against data loss when you are crafting the updated code, you created a backup of the database. Verify that the original *v3h2Croton_LastFirst* database is still open.

b. Ensure the VB Editor is open and place the insertion point at **Ln20, Col36**. Press **Enter** and revise the procedure by adding three lines of code, as shown in Code Window 3.16.

```
'Cycle through the records
Do While Not rst.EOF
    If rst!ZipCode = "46208" Then
        intCounter = intCounter + 1
        rst.Edit
            rst!ZipCode = "46208-9999"
        rst.Update
    End If
```

CODE WINDOW 3.16

c. Run the procedure.

The procedure runs and then displays the number of supplier records that were affected.

d. Minimize the VB Editor. Open the Suppliers table, and filter the table for zip code 46208-9999. Verify that the table contains three records with the new zip code. Close the table without saving.

e. Return to the VB Editor and save the module.

STEP 4 ⟫ DELETE RECORDS IN A RECORDSET

You need to create a new procedure that identifies inactive suppliers and removes them from the database. You will first display the matching records using the message box function. Next, you will delete the records of inactive suppliers. Refer to Figure 3.27 as you complete Step 4.

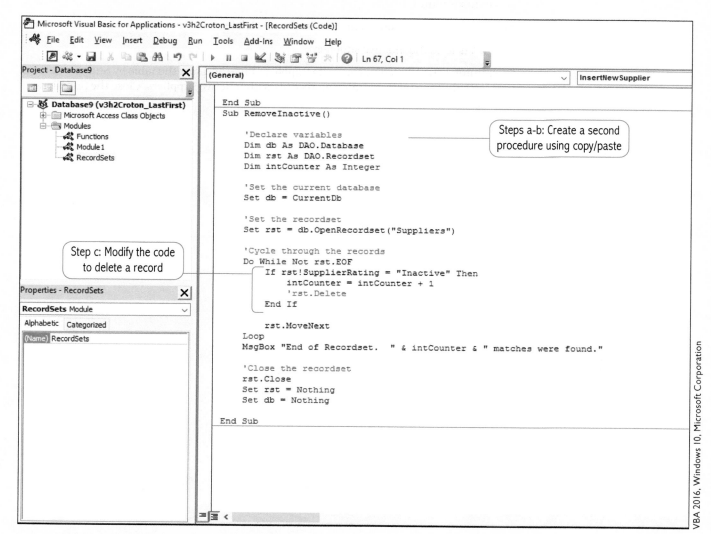

FIGURE 3.27 Delete Records from a Recordset

a. Copy the entire CreateRecordsZip procedure **(Ln 4, Col 1** through **Ln 35, Col 1)** excluding Option Compare Database and Option Explicit, and paste it below the End Sub statement starting at line 36.

b. Change the name of Sub CreateRecordsZip to **Sub RemoveInactive**.

c. Modify the procedure by changing the *Do While Not* section of the code, as noted in Code Window 3.17. (Note that some lines need to be deleted.)

```
'Cycle through the records
Do While Not rst.EOF
    If rst!SupplierRating = "Inactive" Then
        intCounter = intCounter + 1
        'rst.Delete
    End If

    rst.MoveNext
Loop
MsgBox "End of Recordset.  " & intCounter & " matches were found."
```

CODE WINDOW 3.17

d. Run the procedure.

The procedure runs, and then displays the End of Recordset message noting that one match is found.

e. Remove the comment (') in front of the rst.Delete statement. Run the procedure again.

VBA deletes the inactive supplier.

f. Minimize the VB Editor. Open the Suppliers table and sort the table by SupplierRating. Verify that the table contains no records with inactive suppliers. Close the Suppliers table.

g. Return to the VB Editor and save the module.

You need to create a new procedure that inserts a new supplier into the Suppliers table. You will supply the key field data in the procedure and insert the data into the table. You will verify that the record was added by opening the table. Refer to Figure 3.28 as you complete Step 5.

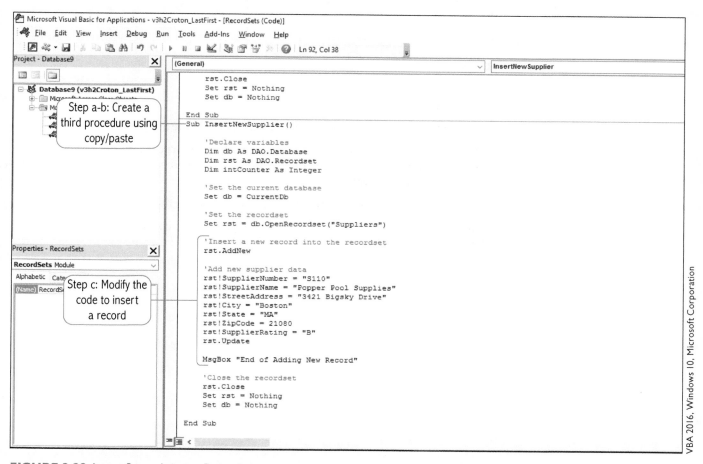

FIGURE 3.28 Insert Records into a Recordset

a. Copy the entire CreateRecordsZip procedure **(Ln 4, Col 1** through **Ln 35, Col 1)** and paste it below the last End Sub statement in the Code window starting at line 66.

b. Change the name CreateRecordsZip to **InsertNewSupplier**.

c. Modify the procedure by removing the *'Cycle through the records* section of the code and adding the Insert section as noted below in Code Window 3.18. (Note that some lines will need to be deleted.)

```
'Insert a new record into the recordset
rst.AddNew

'Add new supplier data
rst!SupplierNumber = "S110"
rst!SupplierName = "Popper Pool Supplies"
rst!StreetAddress = "3421 Bigsky Drive"
rst!City = "Boston"
rst!State = "MA"
rst!ZipCode = 21080
rst!SupplierRating = "B"
rst.Update

MsgBox "End of Adding New Record"
```

CODE WINDOW 3.18

d. Run the procedure.

The procedure runs and inserts the new supplier into the Suppliers table.

e. Minimize the VB Editor. Open the Suppliers table, and sort the table by descending SupplierNumber. Verify that the table contains the new record. Close the Suppliers table, and do not save the sort.

f. Return to the VB Editor, save the module, and then close the VB Editor.

g. Save the database. Keep the database open if you plan to continue with Hands-On Exercise 3. If not, close the database, and exit Access.

Forms, Reports, and Errors in VBA

Enhancing the functionality of forms and reports is one of the most common uses of VBA. By themselves, Access forms and reports work well most of the time. However, sometimes, you may need the programming power of VBA to add functionality to a form or report. When a user opens a form and begins to enter data, VBA can monitor the data entry process and warn the user when invalid data is entered. VBA can also increase the versatility of a report by allowing the user to choose from a list of parameters. For example, a user may want to see a report based on the previous fiscal year as opposed to the current fiscal year. VBA can help accomplish this.

When you add VBA code to your application, you should include error trapping in your procedures. Errors are a common occurrence whenever you add VBA code to a database; *error trapping* is the process of intercepting and handling errors at runtime. Errors are part of any software application and it is important to account for them. As a VBA programmer, your job is to test and find the logical and syntax errors before the code runs; once the code runs, you must also account for runtime errors. These runtime errors can be addressed with VBA's error trapping techniques. The VB Editor also enables error debugging as part of the built-in tools; these tools enable you to pinpoint the cause of an error and hopefully help you find a solution.

In this section, you will learn how to enhance forms and reports using VBA. You will also learn how to handle runtime errors that appear in VBA code.

Using VBA to Add Events to Forms

Almost all of the VBA code added to a form is triggered by an event (refer to Table 3.1 for examples). Common events include On Open, On Click, On Enter, On Exit, Before Update, and After Update. As you learned earlier, events occur when a user takes action. In order for the On Open event to be triggered, the user must open a form. All of the available events are found on the Event tab on the Property Sheet, as shown in Figure 3.29.

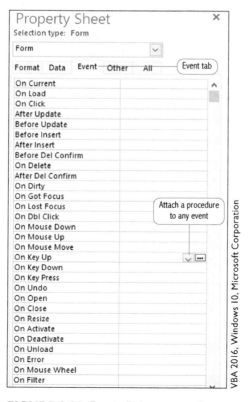

FIGURE 3.29 Events Relevant to a Form

A form or report has one set of events, and each object on a form or report has another set of events. Many events overlap between a form and the objects on a form. For example, a form and a text box on a form both have the On Click event. They also both contain the Before Update and After Update events. However, although a form contains the On Current event, a text box does not. *On Current* is the event that is triggered by a record being loaded into a form. A text box is needed to display the data in a record, but it is not responsible for loading the data. *After Update* is an event that is triggered after a record is saved.

A text box can trigger the On Enter event, but a form does not. *On Enter* refers to the act of placing the insertion point in a text box (using the mouse or pressing Tab or Enter). However, a form is opened rather than entered.

Add an Event Procedure to a Form

STEP 1 »» While you are editing a record in a form, the pencil appears in the record selector on the left. When the pencil disappears, the record has been saved. A user may miss the pencil (or the pencil may be missing if the record selector is turned off). To notify the user when a record is being changed, you could add a hidden message to the top of the form and then make the message visible while a user is changing a record (see Figure 3.30). After the record is saved, the message could be hidden again.

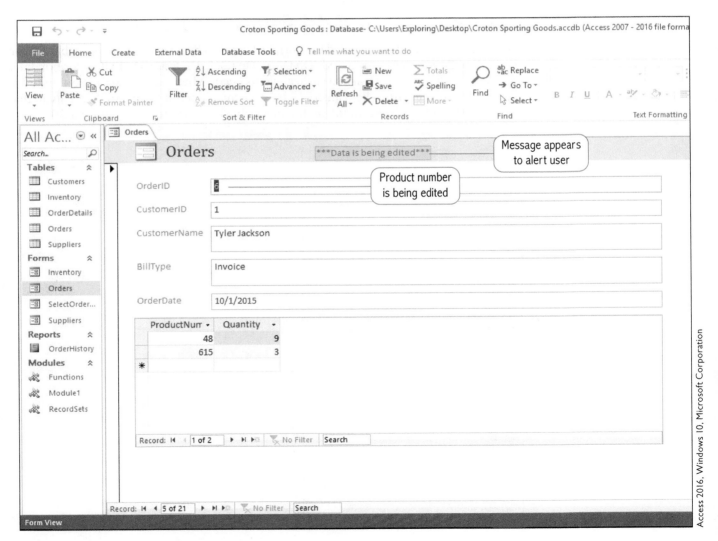

FIGURE 3.30 Display a Message While Editing a Record

To add a hidden message as shown in Figure 3.30, complete the following steps:

1. Add a label control to a form in the desired location.
2. Display the form in Design view and create an event procedure using the Code Builder for the On Dirty property. The ***On Dirty*** property is used to discover if a record has been edited since its last save.
3. Display the VB Editor and set visibility to true for the label created in Step 1.
4. Create a second event for the AfterUpdate property.
5. Set visibility to False in the VB Editor.

The two event procedures will then control whether the label is visible in Form view. The procedures would only contain one line of code each (in addition to the Sub and End Sub statements). The two procedures are shown in Figure 3.31.

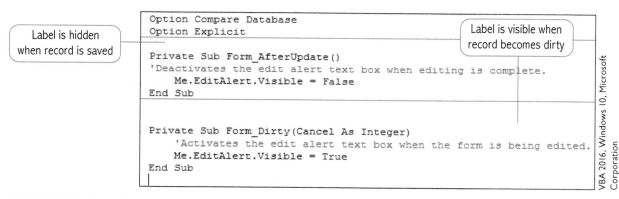

Label is hidden when record is saved

Label is visible when record becomes dirty

```
Option Compare Database
Option Explicit

Private Sub Form_AfterUpdate()
'Deactivates the edit alert text box when editing is complete.
    Me.EditAlert.Visible = False
End Sub


Private Sub Form_Dirty(Cancel As Integer)
    'Activates the edit alert text box when the form is being edited.
    Me.EditAlert.Visible = True
End Sub
```

VBA 2016, Windows 10, Microsoft Corporation

FIGURE 3.31 Event Procedures to Hide/Unhide a Label

Validate Data Before an Update

The Before Update event can be used to intercept the saving of a record if any key fields are blank or if any fields contain data outside the acceptable boundaries. ***Before Update*** is triggered before a record is saved. Notifying a user that fields are blank or that data is outside normal boundaries can greatly improve the reliability of the data. Retrieving the data later, running reports, and analyzing data with queries will be much more effective if the data is reliable.

To create a procedure that will validate a record before saving it, complete the following steps:

1. Start an event procedure attached to the Before Update event.
2. Add a comment in the Code window that explains what each statement is validating.
3. Add the appropriate conditional statements. Add one section for each type of validation; each section should contain a comment, a conditional statement (If...Then), and a message to the user if the condition is violated. If a condition is violated, cancel the update and exit the procedure.

For example, if you were working with the Inventory form, you could verify that the following conditions were not violated:

- Quantity on hand is between 0 and 125
- Unit Price must be greater than 0

If a condition is not met, cancel the update and exit from the procedure; this will give the user a chance to correct the first problem before notifying him or her of the next issue. See Figure 3.32 for a sample Before Update procedure that checks the two conditions mentioned earlier. The alert message when data is entered outside of the acceptable range is shown in Figure 3.33.

TIP: ADD A PROCEDURE TO AN EVENT

To quickly add a procedure to an event, double-click the event name. [Event Procedure] appears in the event property box. Next, click Build, and you are immediately taken to the VB Editor.

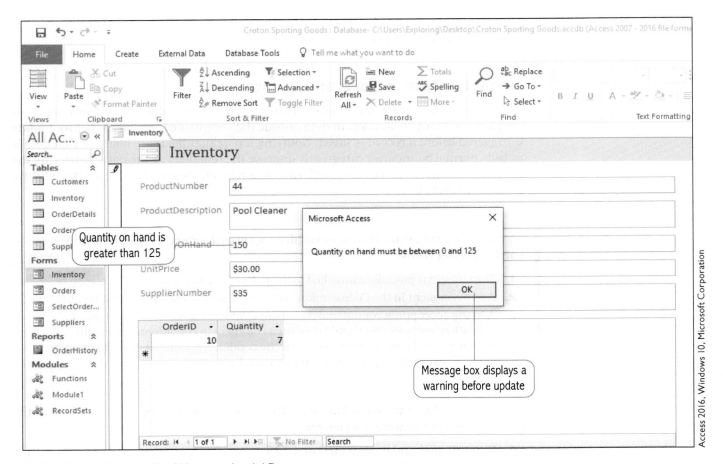

```
Private Sub Form_BeforeUpdate(Cancel As Integer)
    'Quantity on hand must be between 0 and 125
    If Not (Me.QuantityOnHand >= 0 And Me.QuantityOnHand <= 125) Then
        'Stop the save
        Cancel = True
        MsgBox "Quantity on hand must be between 0 and 125"
        Exit Sub
    End If

    If Not (Me.UnitPrice > 0) Then
        'Stop the save
        Cancel = True
        MsgBox "Unit price must be greater than $0.00"
        Exit Sub
    End If
End Sub
```

Validate Quantity on hand

Validate Unit price

VBA 2016, Windows 10, Microsoft Corporation

FIGURE 3.32 Before Update Procedure to Validate Data

FIGURE 3.33 Message Box Warning – Invalid Data

Adding VBA to Reports

Sometimes, you may want to modify the layout of a report before the report prints. For example, a report that contains multiple sections may have one or more sections that you want to hide, even though they contain data. Access does not have an option for hiding a section at runtime. You can use VBA to test if a section matches a certain criteria and tell Access how to respond when the condition is met. One option is to tell Access simply to hide the matching sections and show all other sections. The procedure would be similar to the code in Figure 3.34.

```
Private Sub ReportHeader_Print(Cancel As Integer, PrintCount As Integer)

    'Decision statement to determine header visibility
    If Me.State <> "IN" Then
        Me.GroupHeader0.Visible = False
        Me.Detail.Visible = False
    Else
        Me.GroupHeader0.Visible = True
        Me.Detail.Visible = True
    End If

End Sub
```

If the State is not IN the header is hidden

VBA 2016, Windows 10, Microsoft Corporation

FIGURE 3.34 Procedure to Hide One Section of a Report

Create Report Events

Report events are similar to form events; however, once a report runs, most of the events happen in succession with very little intervention by the user. When you run a report, the On Open, On Load, and On Activate events trigger in succession. A user cannot change the order of events; the order is predefined by Access. An explanation of these three events is listed in Table 3.3.

TABLE 3.3	Explanation of Common Report Events
Event	**Explanation**
On Open	This event is triggered when the report is opened but before the first record is displayed. If there are no records, you can add Cancel = True to the procedure to cancel the opening of the report.
On Load	This event occurs when the report is opened and its record(s) are displayed. Here, you can set the values of controls or do calculations with records displayed on the report.
On Activate	This event occurs when the window of your report becomes the active window.

Set the Record Source Based on Form Properties

STEP 3 A report is more versatile if you let the user set one or more parameters before you open it. Setting parameters can be done using a blank form that contains no record source. The form would contain all the parameters that affect the report and a method for selecting the parameters. For example, if an order history report contained a list of OrderIDs, a combo box containing all the OrderIDs could be created. The user could select an order before running the inventory report. Figure 3.35 shows a sample parameter form with an OrderID combo box and a button to view the order history report.

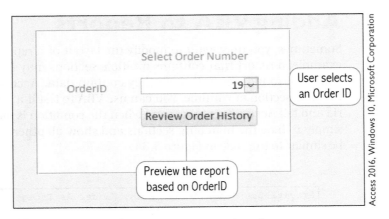

FIGURE 3.35 Create a Parameter Form for a Report

When the report opens, a procedure (triggered by the On Open event) looks at the selected parameter (e.g., OrderID 19) and then creates the record source, as shown in Figure 3.36. Because the On Open event is triggered before the report contains any records, the record source can be created using the selected supplier. Next, the On Load event is triggered and the record source has been set. The report is displayed for Order ID 19 only, as shown in Figure 3.37.

```
Private Sub Report_Open(Cancel As Integer)

    'Declare variables
    Dim strRs As String
    Dim intOrderHistory As Integer

    'Get the orderID from the select order history form
    intOrderHistory = Forms![SelectOrderID]![cboOrderHistory]

    'Set the record source
    strRs = "SELECT [Orders].* FROM [Orders] WHERE OrderID =" & intOrderHistory
    Me.RecordSource = strRs

Exit Sub
```

Combo box reference on the parameter form

SQL statement becomes the record source

FIGURE 3.36 Procedure for an On Open Event of a Report

FIGURE 3.37 Order History Report for OrderID 19

Handling Errors in VBA

STEP 4 Two types of errors exist in VBA—handled and unhandled. If you create procedures and functions without error handling, when VBA reports an error message, the code will stop working and the user will be presented with a confusing list of options. However, if you create a procedure with a built-in error handling routine, you can intercept errors and tell VBA to display a friendly message to the user, with options that make sense.

As an example, the procedure in Figure 3.36 illustrates how to assign the record source to a report after the user selects a supplier. If the user did not choose a supplier—and the combo box was left blank on the parameter form—the report would produce an error, as shown in Figure 3.38. Some users might understand the problem immediately and know how to fix it, but the message contains perplexing choices: Continue, End, Debug, and Help. Continue is unavailable, and clicking Debug or Help may cause additional confusion. Clicking End would be the only choice that would enable the user to select another region, and then try again.

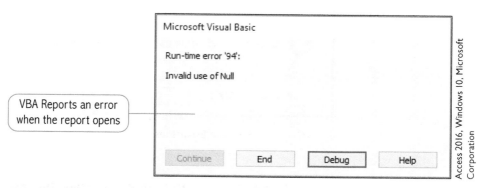

FIGURE 3.38 Unhandled Error Message in VBA

Add an Error Handling Routine

Error messages generated from VBA can be quite confusing and frustrating to a novice user. To help relieve some of the ambiguity caused by error codes, you can produce a more user-friendly error message using an error routine. A typical error routine has been added to the procedure shown in Code Window 3.19. In this procedure, when an error occurs, the **On Error statement** directs the code to skip to a particular line in the procedure (usually at the bottom) where the appropriate message is displayed and any corrective action can be taken.

```
Private Sub Report_Open(Cancel As Integer)
On Error GoTo Error_Routine                    On Error
                                               statement added
    'Declare variables
    Dim strRs As String
    Dim intOrderHistory As Integer

    'Get the orderID from the select order history form
    intOrderHistory = Forms![SelectOrderID]![cboOrderHistory]

    'Set the record source
    strRs = "SELECT [Orders].* FROM [Orders] WHERE OrderID =" & intOrderHistory
    Me.RecordSource = strRs

Exit_Routine:
    Exit Sub                      Exit routine added

Error_Routine:                    Error routine added
    If Err.Number = 94 Then
        MsgBox "Select Order ID cannot be blank.", vbCritical, "An error has occured."
        Cancel = True
    Else
        MsgBox Err.Number & " " & Err.Description & vbCrLf & _
            "Contact your technical support staff.", vbCritical, "An error has occured."
    End If
    Resume Exit_Routine

End Sub
```

CODE WINDOW 3.19

When using an error routine in a procedure, and an error occurs, a custom message is displayed and the user only has the option to click OK (see Figure 3.39). This message replaces the confusing message shown previously in Figure 3.38. If another error occurs, the procedure will still display a revised message but not a custom message. If another error appears, a second custom error message could be added using the Else...If statement.

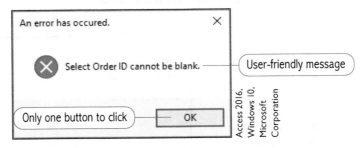

FIGURE 3.39 Custom Error Message

TIP: WHERE DO ERROR NUMBERS COME FROM?
Error numbers, such as 94, are generated by Microsoft Access. Error numbers range from 3 to 746 with gaps between some numbers. Errors can also fall between 31001 and 31037. Once an error number is known, you can use VBA's error handling techniques to trap the error and give the user a helpful message.

The **Resume Exit_Routine statement** directs the code to jump to the exit routine. The exit routine will then exit the procedure. If the Resume Exit_Routine statement did not exist, then the error routine would exit at the End Sub statement. The reason why the resume statement is used is to enable the procedure to execute a number of cleanup statements.

Test and Debug Code

In addition to error handling, programmers also need to debug code that is not working. Errors indicate that an obvious change is needed, but the lack of an error does not mean a procedure is working correctly. A VBA procedure must be tested thoroughly to verify it is working as expected. The more options and the more complex a procedure, the more difficult it will be to test the logic.

In addition to error messages, VBA also provides a tool to debug a procedure that is not working properly. When an error appears and it is not evident what is causing the error, you can use the debugger. The **VBA debugger** enables the programmer to momentarily suspend the execution of VBA code so that the following debug tasks can be done:

- Check the value of a variable in its current state.
- Enter VBA code in the Immediate window to view the results.
- Execute each line of code one line at a time.
- Continue execution of the code.
- Halt execution of the code.

To use the debugger, set a breakpoint by clicking in the left margin next to any line of executable code, as shown in Figure 3.40. When the procedure is triggered (e.g., when a report is opened in Print Preview), the debugger pauses at the breakpoint and waits for the user to take action. The current line appears highlighted in yellow, as shown in

Figure 3.41. To watch the procedure run one line at a time, press F8 or click Step Over on the Debug toolbar. To open the Debug toolbar, right-click any toolbar, and then select Debug from the list.

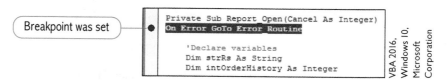

FIGURE 3.40 Set a Breakpoint in the Code Window

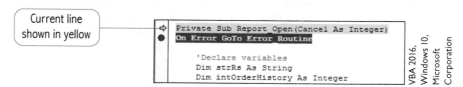

FIGURE 3.41 Debugger Stops at the First Breakpoint

As the debugger steps through each line of code, you can determine where the error(s) occur. Once you determine where the errors occur, you can stop the debugger and correct the code. To stop the debugger, click Reset on the Debug toolbar. After the code is fixed, remove the breakpoint by clicking the dot in the margin, and then run the procedure again.

Quick Concepts

7. What is the benefit of validating data before an update? **p. 181**

8. Why is error trapping important? **p. 184**

9. Why is it important to thoroughly check and debug code? **p. 186**

Hands-On Exercises

Skills covered: Add an Event Procedure to a Form • Validate Data Before an Update • Create Report Events • Set the Record Source Based on Form Properties • Add an Error Handling Routine • Test and Debug Code

3 Forms, Reports, and Errors in VBA

Your manager would like to add additional functionality to manage orders better. To accomplish this, you will use the existing Orders form. You will add code to the form to notify the user that a record is being modified; then you will add code to verify Billing Information. You also decide to add a user form to allow your manager to choose the order that is reported in the preexisting order history report. You will add an error routine so future users of the database will not have to deal with any unexpected errors later.

STEP 1 ▶▶ ADD AN EVENT PROCEDURE

You want to use a VBA procedure that displays text notification to alert the user that a record is being edited. Refer to Figure 3.42 as you complete Step 1.

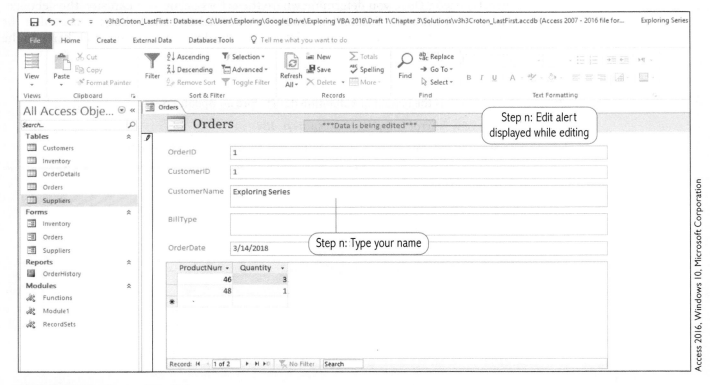

FIGURE 3.42 Custom Edit Alert

a. Open the *v3h2Croton_LastFirst* database if you closed it at the end of Hands-On Exercise 2 and save it as **v3h3Croton_LastFirst**, changing h2 to h3.

b. Open the **Orders Form** in Design View.

c. Add a text box to the top of the form that contains the following text: =“***Data is being edited***”. Delete the label that was created with the text box and format the box with a yellow fill color and red text, as shown in Figure 3.42. Continue using Figure 3.42 as a guide for color and format.

d. Select the newly created text box. Ensure the Property Sheet is displayed, click the **Other tab**, and then assign the name **txtEditAlert.**

e. Select **Form** in the Property Sheet and click the **Event tab**. Click the event **On Dirty**, click **Build**, and then click **Code Builder**.

This will open the VB Editor and create a new procedure that is activated when the file is being edited.

f. Place the insertion point on line 5, press **Tab**, and then press **Enter.** Type the comment **'Activates the edit alert text box when the form is being edited.**

g. Press **Enter** and enter the following code under the comment created in the prior step. **Me.txtEditAlert.Visible = True**

This sets the Visible property of the edit notice text box to true when the record is being edited.

h. Press **Alt+F11** to return to the form in Design view. Click **After Insert** on the Event tab of the Property Sheet, click **Build**, select **Code Builder** from the Choose Builder dialog box, and then click **OK**.

i. Place the insertion point on line 5, press **Tab**, and then press **Enter.** Next, type the following comment: **'Deactivates the edit alert text box when editing is complete.**

j. Press **Enter** and type **Me.txtEditAlert.Visible = True**.

This sets the Visible property of the edit notice text box to false after the record is updated.

k. Press **Alt+F11** to return to the form in Design view. Click **On Current** on the Event tab of the Property Sheet, click **Build**, select **Code Builder** from the Choose Builder dialog box, and click **OK**.

l. Press **Tab** and press **Enter**. Type **'Sets the current visibility to false.**

m. Press **Enter** and type **Me.txtEditAlert.Visible = False**.

This hides the text box until the On Dirty event is triggered.

n. Press **Alt+F11** to return to the form. Click the **Home tab**, click **View** in the Views group, and then select **Form view**. Save the form and type **your name** in place of the current customer name. Once the code is tested, replace your name with original customer name **Tyler Jackson**. Save but do not close the form.

You notice that the Bill Type is missing for the order listed on the orders form. You need to add a Before Update procedure to validate billing information. Refer to Figure 3.43 as you complete Step 2.

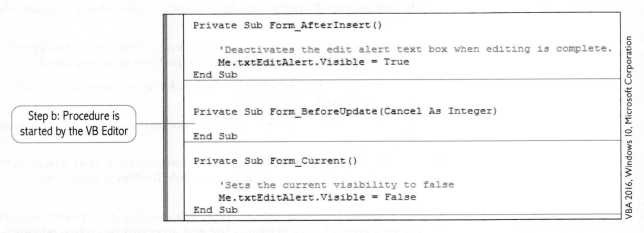

Step b: Procedure is started by the VB Editor

FIGURE 3.43 Before Update Procedure

a. Click the **Home tab**, click **View** in the Views group, and then select **Design View**.

b. Ensure the Property Sheet is visible. Select **Form** in the Selection type box at the top of the Property Sheet. Click the **Event tab**, click the **Before Update event,** and then click **Build**. Select Code Builder and click OK to open the VB Editor.

The VB Editor opens and a new subroutine is started in the code window, as shown in Figure 3.43.

c. Place the insertion point below **Private Sub Form_BeforeUpdate** and add the code as shown in Code Window 3.20.

```
Private Sub Form_BeforeUpdate(Cancel As Integer)

    If IsNull(Me.BillType) Then
        MsgBox "Bill type cannot be blank"
        Cancel = True
    Else
        'Do nothing
    End If
End Sub
```

CODE WINDOW 3.20

This section of code verifies that a billing type has been entered in the form. The user is notified and the record cannot be saved because of the statement Cancel = True.

d. Minimize the VB Editor, switch to Form view of the Orders form, type **9** in the CustomerID field, and then press **Tab** four times.

Note the responses from Step 1 trigger the Before Update event. Take note how the code responds to the missing data as well.

e. Press **OK** when the message box displays, type **1** in the CustomerID field, and then type **Credit** in the BillType field.

f. Maximize the VB Editor and save the procedure. Close the VB Editor and close the Orders form.

STEP 3 ›› SET A REPORT RECORD SOURCE BASED ON FORM PROPERTIES

Randy would like you to add functionality to the existing OrderHistory report to allow customized reports without the need for additional queries. You will use the existing report and the Orders table to create the SelectOrderID form to make it easy to select one order. Refer to Figures 3.44 and 3.45 as you complete Step 3.

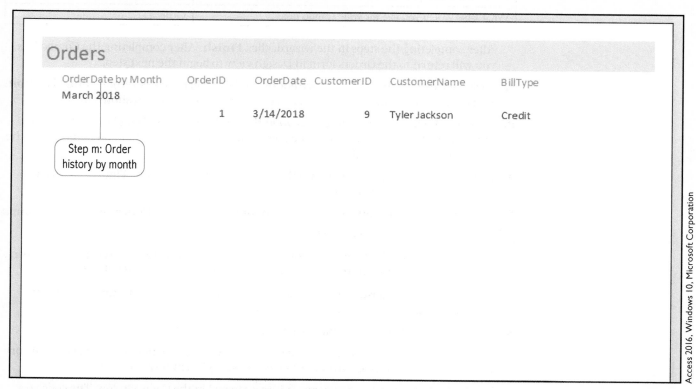

FIGURE 3.44 Report Results by Month

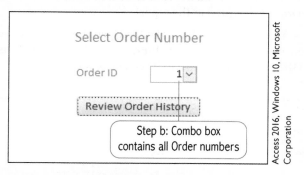

FIGURE 3.45 Select Order ID

a. Close all database objects. Click the **Create tab** and click **Form Design** in the Forms group.

   A blank form is displayed.

b. Click the **Combo Box control** in the gallery of the Controls group on the Design tab and click in the middle of the form.

Combo Box Wizard Question	Action
The wizard creates a combo box, which displays a list of values you can choose from. How do you want your combo box to get its values?	Select **Option 1** (*I want the combo box to get the values from another table or query.*)
Which table or query should provide the values for your combo box?	Select Table: **Orders**
Which fields contain the values you want included in your combo box?	Select **OrderID**
What sort order do you want for the items in your list box?	Skip
How wide would you like the columns in your combo box?	Keep default
What label would you like for your combo box?	OrderID

After completing the steps in the wizard, click **Finish**. After completing the Combo Box, you will return to the Orders form in Design view to begin the next step.

c. Click the **Design tab**, click the **More** button, and then click the **Rectangle control button**. Add a rectangle around the combo box created in the prior step, as shown in Figure 3.45.

d. Click the **Design tab** and click **Button** in the Controls group. Using Figure 3.45 as a guide, add a Command Button to the form. Click **Cancel** without making changes in the Command Button Wizard.

e. Click the **Design tab** and click **Label** in the Controls group. Using Figure 3.45 as a guide, add a label to the form.

f. Type **Select Order Number**. Click the **Format tab** and click **Center** in the Font group.

g. Save the form as **SelectOrderID**.

h. Display the SelectOrderID form in Design view. Click the **combo box**, and ensure the Property Sheet is open. Click the **All tab** and change the Name property to **cboOrderHistory**.

i. Click the **Command button**. Change the Name property to **cmdOrderHistory** and change the Caption property to **Review Order History**.

j. Click the **Event tab** and double-click the **On Click event**.

k. Click **Build** to open the VB Editor and type the following code under the cmdOrderHistory Private Sub. **DoCmd.OpenReport "OrderHistory", acViewPreview**

The VB Editor opens and a new procedure is started in the Code window. The code you enter will use the DoCmd statement to open the preexisting OrderHistory report when activated. You will add the code shown in Code Window 3.21 to enable the user to select the OrderID featured in the report.

l. Press **Alt+F11** to exit the VB Editor. Open the OrderHistory report in Design view and add a new procedure for the **On Open event**. Type the code as shown in Code Window 3.21 into the procedure and save the code and form object.

```
Private Sub Report_Open(Cancel As Integer)

    'Declare variables
    Dim strRs As String
    Dim intOrderHistory As Integer

    'Get the OrderID from the SelectOrderID form
    intOrderHistory = Forms![SelectOrderID]![cboOrderHistory]

    'Set the record source
    strRs = "Select [Orders].* FROM [Orders] WHERE OrderID =" & intOrderHistory
    Me.RecordSource = strRs

End Sub
```

CODE WINDOW 3.21

m. Minimize the VB Editor, display SelectOrderID form in Form view, select **order 1**, and click the **Review Order History button**.

The OrderHistory report is opened in Preview mode.

n. Close the report preview and save the form.

If the user attempts to run the Order History report without first selecting an OrderID from the combo box, an error will occur. You will add error handling to the VBA procedure to trap run-time errors. Refer to Figure 3.46 as you complete Step 4.

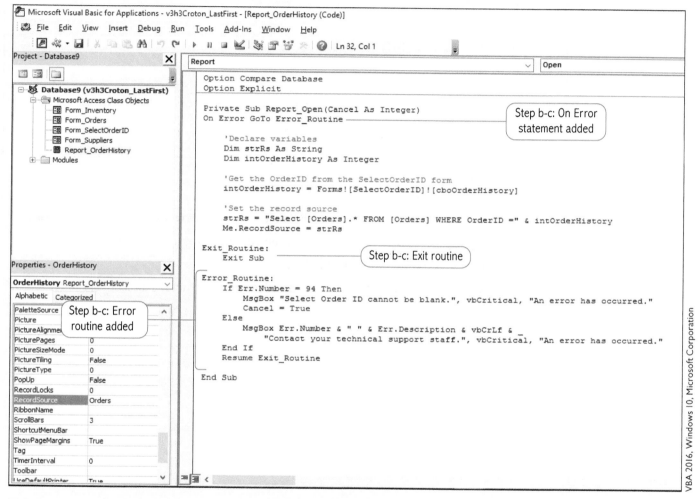

FIGURE 3.46 Error Routine Added to VBA Procedure

a. Return to the VB Editor and locate Report_Open procedure for the OrderHistory report.

b. Add the *On Error GoTo, Exit_Routine, and the Error_Routine* sections, as shown in Figure 3.46.

One line of code is added above the existing procedure; the rest of the code is added below the existing procedure.

c. Save the code.

d. Exit the VB Editor and ensure the SelectOrderID form is open in Form view. Delete the contents of the SelectOrderID combo box and click the **Review Order History button**.

A message box appears that says *Select Order ID cannot be blank.*

e. Click **OK** the message box to open the second message box and click **End.**

To clear the second message, an error routine must be added to the cmdOrderHistory_Click() procedure in the SelectOrderID form.

f. Open the VB Editor and revise the cmdOrderHistory_Click() procedure by adding the code shown in Code Window 3.22.

```
Private Sub cmdOrderHistory_Click()
On Error GoTo Error_Routine

    DoCmd.OpenReport "OrderHistory", acViewPreview

Exit_Routine:
    Exit Sub

Error_Routine:
    If Err.Number = 2501 Then
        'Do Nothing
    Else
        MsgBox Err.Number & " " & Err.Description & vbCrLf & _
            "Contact your technical support staff.", vbCritical, "An error has occurred."
    End If
    Resume Exit_Routine

End Sub
```

CODE WINDOW 3.22

g. Save the code and minimize the VB Editor. Click the **Review Order History button**.

Only the first message appears. The second message was intercepted by the error routine.

h. Close the VB Editor and close the form.

i. Close the database and exit Access. Based on your instructor's directions, submit the following:
v3h3Croton_LastFirst
v3h2_LastFirst_*CurrentDate*

Chapter Objectives Review

After reading this chapter, you have accomplished the following objectives:

1. **Write code in modules.**
   - When you create VBA code in Access, you can create the code using one of three modules: a standard module, a class module, or an Access object module.

2. **Write code for forms and reports.**
   - VBA can be used to add functionality to forms and reports.
   - VBA must be authored in the VB Editor.
   - To create VBA code for a form or a report, first open the object in Design view, and then click Property Sheet in the Tools group. Next, select an event on the Event tab, and then click Build on the right side of the property cell. The Choose Builder dialog box appears with three options—Macro Builder, Expression Builder, and Code Builder on the Event tab. Select the Code Builder, and then click OK.

3. **Work with objects.**
   - VBA works with the objects in the various object libraries that are available in the applications that support VBA. You can use objects in the object libraries along with their resources to accomplish the programming tasks. In addition to the Office applications, you can also set references to other object libraries such as Adobe Acrobat, Skype, and Yahoo! Messenger.
   - Set properties: A property is a physical attribute of an object that can be manipulated with VBA.
   - Use methods: A method is an action that is performed by an object, such as .Open, .Close, .RefreshAll.
   - Set events: An event occurs when a user triggers an action such as On Click, On Close, or On Filter.

4. **Create functions.**
   - A function is a procedure that performs an action and returns a value.
   - Many functions are predefined in VBA and ready to use.
   - When no preexisting function will fit your needs, you have the ability to author calculations directly into procedures; however, a custom function allows cleaner design.

5. **Use DAO to access data.**
   - Data Access Objects refers to an object library specifically created to work with Access databases.
   - Create recordsets: A recordset is a set of records stored in memory. DAO can be used to create a recordset.
   - Find records in a recordset: Once a table or query is identified, it can be searched to find records that fit specific criteria. These records can be saved as a recordset.
   - Update records in a recordset: Once a recordset is created, specific records can be isolated and updated.
   - Delete records in a recordset: Once a recordset is created, specific records can be deleted.
   - Insert records in a recordset: Once a recordset is created, VBA can be used to insert new records.
   - Use ADO to access data: ActiveX Data Objects was designed for connecting to a wide range of external data sources. In ADO (as in DAO), it is important to declare database variables with the object library prefix. Before you can use the ADO object library, you must create a link to the library by clicking Tools on the menu bar, and then selecting References.

6. **Use VBA to add events to forms.**
   - Enhancing the functionality of forms and reports is one of the most common uses of VBA.
   - Add an event procedure to a form: Almost all of the VBA code added to a form is triggered by an event. Common events include On Open, On Click, On Enter, On Exit, Before Update, and After Update.
   - Validate data before an update: When working with forms, the Before Update event can be used to validate data before it is saved.

7. **Add VBA to reports.**
   - Set report events: Report events are similar to form events; however, once a report runs, most of the events happen in succession with very little intervention by the user.
   - Set the record source based on form properties: A report is more versatile if you let the user set one or more parameters before you open it. This can be done using VBA.

8. **Handle errors in VBA.**
   - Add an error handling routine: Two types of errors exist in VBA—handled and unhandled. Error routines can be added to provide user-friendly error messages.
   - Test and debug code: If multiple errors occur, a Resume Exit Routine can direct the code to exit a procedure.

Key Terms Matching

Match the key terms with their definitions. Write the key term letter by the appropriate numbered definition.

a. ADO
b. After Update
c. Before Update
d. DAO
e. Edit
f. Error trapping
g. MoveNext
h. Object libraries
i. On Current

j. On Dirty
k. On Enter
l. On Error statement
m. Option Compare Database
n. Option Explicit
o. Resume Exit_Routine statement
p. Update
q. VBA debugger

1. _____ Statement used in a module to declare the default comparison method to use when string data is compared. **p. 147**

2. _____ Statement used in a module to require that all variables be declared before they are used. **p. 146**

3. _____ Contain the objects that are available in the application that supports VBA. **p. 148**

4. _____ Data Access Object refers to an object library specifically created to work with Access databases. **p. 162**

5. _____ Method used to advance through the records of a recordset. **p. 163**

6. _____ Method that enables you to change the data in a recordset. **p. 164**

7. _____ Method that enables you to save the changes in a recordset. **p. 164**

8. _____ ActiveX Data Objects designed for connecting to a wide range of external data sources. **p. 168**

9. _____ The process of intercepting and handling errors at run-time. **p. 179**

10. _____ The event that is triggered by a record being loaded into a form. **p. 180**

11. _____ An event triggered by placing the insertion point in a text box. **p. 180**

12. _____ An event triggered when a record is being edited. **p. 181**

13. _____ An event triggered after a record is saved. **p. 180**

14. _____ An event triggered before a record is saved. **p. 181**

15. _____ Directs the code to skip to a particular line in the procedure when an error occurs. **p. 185**

16. _____ Directs the code to jump to the exit line. **p. 186**

17. _____ Enables the programmer to suspend the execution of VBA code momentarily. **p. 186**

Multiple Choice

1. All of these types of modules are found in VBA *except*:
   - (a) Debug module.
   - (b) Class module.
   - (c) Standard module.
   - (d) Access object module.

2. Which of the following keystrokes will open the VBA Editor?
   - (a) Alt+F12
   - (b) F4
   - (c) Alt+F11
   - (d) Control+Shift+Enter

3. Which statement is incorrect?
   - (a) Object libraries are only used by Access and Excel.
   - (b) A property is an attribute of an object.
   - (c) A method executes an action on an object.
   - (d) An event is triggered by a user action.

4. Functions are created in:
   - (a) The Object Explorer.
   - (b) Procedures.
   - (c) Class modules.
   - (d) Standard modules.

5. DAO can be used to accomplish all of these *except*:
   - (a) Modify database objects.
   - (b) Connect to Excel spreadsheets.
   - (c) Create tables and queries.
   - (d) Add procedures to form events.

6. ADO is similar to DAO in which way?
   - (a) One is simply a newer version of the other.
   - (b) Both can easily access external data sources.
   - (c) Both can access database objects.
   - (d) Both were originally created by IBM.

7. A common reason to add VBA to a form is to:
   - (a) Display a different background color for different data entry tasks.
   - (b) Remind users which field comes next during data entry.
   - (c) Time a user as he or she enters data.
   - (d) Validate data as it is entered.

8. Which of the following events will be triggered if a form is being edited?
   - (a) On Click
   - (b) Before Update
   - (c) On Dirty
   - (d) On Current

9. The On Error GoTo statement is used to:
   - (a) Go to the line immediately after an error.
   - (b) Redirect the procedure to skip over code and execute the error routine.
   - (c) Start the debugger.
   - (d) Start over after the user clicks OK.

10. To update a record in a recordset, you use which VBA statement?
   - (a) rst.Update
   - (b) rst.Delete
   - (c) rst.MoveNext
   - (d) Set rst = Nothing

Practice Exercises

1 Wholesale Food Business

T&F Wholesalers exports its food products to customers in Germany, France, Brazil, the United Kingdom, and the United States. The owners of T&F would like to improve the efficiency of their data entry forms by adding a validation process. They would also like to add automatic entry for fields that are calculated based on other fields. Refer to Figure 3.47 as you complete this exercise.

```
Option Compare Database
Option Explicit

Private Sub OrderDate_Enter()
    'Set the order date = today
    If IsNull(Me.OrderDate) Then
        Me.OrderDate = Date
    End If
End Sub

Private Sub OrderDate_Exit(Cancel As Integer)
    'Set the expected ship date = order date plus 2 days
    If IsNull(Me.ExpectedShipDate) Then
        Me.ExpectedShipDate = Me.OrderDate + 2
    End If
End Sub

Private Sub Form_BeforeUpdate(Cancel As Integer)
    'Validate freight amount. Must be between 0 and 199.
    If Me.Freight >= 0 And Me.Freight <= 199 Then
        'do nothing
    Else
        MsgBox "Freight must be between $0 and $199", vbOKOnly, _
            "Invalid freight amount"
        Cancel = True
    End If
End Sub
```

VBA 2016, Windows 10, Microsoft Corporation

FIGURE 3.47 Form Module with Three Procedures

a. Open *v3p1Wholesale*. Save the database as **v3p1Wholesale_LastFirst**.
b. Open the Orders form in Design view. Click the **Order Date box**.
c. Ensure the Property Sheet is displayed. Click the **Event tab**, click the **On Enter event**, and then click **Build**. Select Code Builder and click OK.
d. Type the code from the *Sub OrderDate_Enter* section inside the procedure, as shown in Code Window 3.23.

```
Private Sub OrderDate_Enter()
    'Set the order date = today
    If IsNull(Me.OrderDate) Then
        Me.OrderDate = Date
    End If
End Sub
```

CODE WINDOW 3.23

e. Minimize the VB Editor and display the Orders form in Form view. Save the form.
f. Test the code using the first record. Press **Tab** until you reach the OrderDate, and verify that the code does nothing because an order date already exists. Then, delete the order date and test the code again by tabbing into the field to verify that today's date appears.

g. Switch to Design view. Verify that the OrderDate box is still selected. Click the **On Exit event**. Click **Build**, select **Code Builder**, and then click OK to open the VB Editor. Type the code from the *Private Sub OrderDate_Exit* section inside the procedure, as shown in Code Window 3.24. Save the code.

```
Private Sub OrderDate_Exit(Cancel As Integer)
    'Set the expected ship date = order date plus 2 days
    If IsNull(Me.ExpectedShipDate) Then
        Me.ExpectedShipDate = Me.OrderDate + 2
    End If
End Sub
```

CODE WINDOW 3.24

h. Minimize the VB Editor and open the Orders form in Form view. Test the code using the first record. Press **Tab** until you reach the ExpectedShipDate, then press **Tab** one more time to verify that the code does nothing because an expected ship date already exists. Then, delete the expected ship date and test the code again by pressing **Tab** until you are past the ExpectedShipDate field to verify the order date plus two days appears.

i. Switch to Design view and ensure the Property Sheet is displayed. Select the form using the Selection type box at the top of the Property Sheet. Double-click the **Before Update event** on the Event tab. Click **Build** to open the VB Editor. Type the code from the *Sub Form_BeforeUpdate* section inside the procedure, as shown in Code Window 3.25.

```
Private Sub Form_BeforeUpdate(Cancel As Integer)
    'Validate freight amount. Must be between 0 and 199.
    If Me.Freight >= 0 And Me.Freight <= 199 Then
        'do nothing
    Else
        MsgBox "Freight must be between $0 and $199", vbOKOnly, _
            "Invalid freight amount"
        Cancel = True
    End If
End Sub
```

CODE WINDOW 3.25

TROUBLESHOOTING: Your procedure may be at the top of the code window or under the other procedures. The order is not important.

---

j. Save the code, minimize the VB Editor, and then switch to Form view. Test the code using the first record. Type **200** into the Freight field and click **Next Record** to advance to the next record. Verify that the message *Freight must be between 0 and $199* appears and click **OK**. Press **Esc** to clear the data entry, then save and close the form.

k. Open the Products report in Design view. Ensure the Property Sheet is displayed and click the **Event tab**. Double-click the **On Open event**.

l. Click **Build** to open the VB Editor. Type the code shown in Code Window 3.26 inside the procedure. The code displays an Input Box that acquires the desired category used to filter the report.

```
Private Sub Report_Open(Cancel As Integer)
    'Declare variables
    Dim intCategory As Integer
    Dim strRS As String


    'Revise the record source -- filter by category
    If MsgBox("Do you want to filter the report by category?", vbYesNo, _
        "Input required") = vbYes Then
        'Filter by Category
        intCategory = InputBox("Enter category (1-8)")

        'Set the record source = the filtered Products table
        strRS = "SELECT Products.* FROM Products WHERE CategoryID =" & intCategory
        Me.RecordSource = strRS
    Else
        'Set the record source = the whole Products table
        Me.RecordSource = "Products"
    End If

End Sub
```

CODE WINDOW 3.26

m. Save the code and minimize the VB Editor. Test the code by opening the report in Print Preview. Verify that the messages appear and that there are no typographical errors. Click **Yes** and enter a **1** in the second message to verify that you can filter the report by one category. Click **OK** and close the report.

n. Save and close the database. Based on your instructor's directions, submit v3p1Wholesale_LastFirst.

You have been hired as a financial analyst for EBL Financial. Because of your background with VBA, you have been asked to add functionality to their current employee database. You will use VBA to calculate the monthly retirement contribution per employee, locate and edit errors in the database, and to add the ability to filter the Employees report by gender when run. Refer to Figure 3.48 as you complete this exercise.

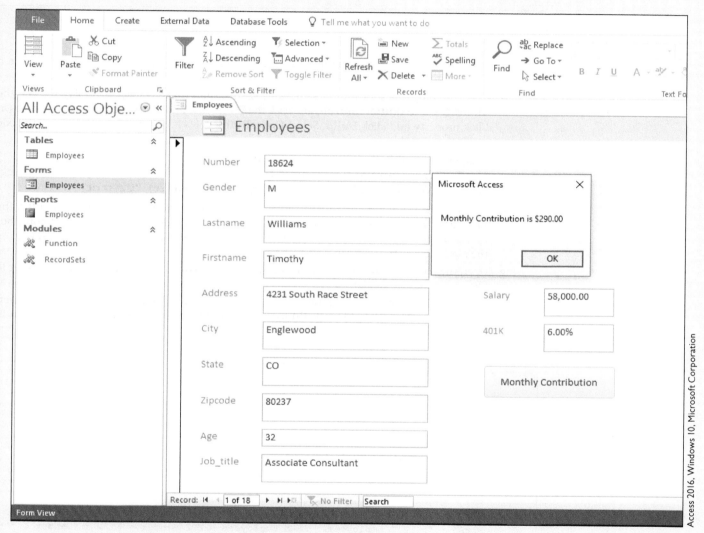

FIGURE 3.48 Custom Function Calculates Monthly Contribution

a. Open the *v3p2Retirement* database, click **Enable Content**, and then save it as **v3p2Retirement_LastFirst**.

b. Click the **Database Tools tab** and click **Visual Basic** to open the VB Editor.

c. Click **Insert** on the menu bar and select **Module**. Use the code shown in Code Window 3.27 and type the entire Public Function ContributionAmount into the Code window.

```
Public Function ContributionAmount(curSalary As Currency, sngPercentage As Single) As Currency

    'calculates total monthly investment
    ContributionAmount = curSalary / 12 * sngPercentage

End Function
```

CODE WINDOW 3.27

d. Save the module as **Function** and close the VB Editor. Next, you will call the function from a procedure inside the Employees form.

e. Open the Employees form in Design View. Ensure the Property Sheet is displayed, click the **Monthly Contribution button**, and click the **Event tab**. Choose **Event Procedure** for the On Click property and click **Build**. Select **Code Builder**, click **OK**, and type the following code inside the procedure:

'Displays Monthly Contribution amount
MsgBox ("Monthly Contribution is" & _
Format (ContributionAmount (Me.Salary, Me.Percentage), "Currency"))

f. Save the code, and minimize the VB Editor. Open the Employees form in Form view. Click the **Monthly Contribution button** for the first record. The employee's monthly 401K contribution is displayed in a message box. After reviewing the monthly contribution, click **OK** to close the message box, then save and close the form.

g. Open the Employees report. You will add a procedure to the report that will enable the user to filter employees by gender.

h. Switch to Design view. Ensure the Property Sheet is displayed and double-click the **On Open event** on the Event tab. Click **Build** to display the VB Editor. Type the procedure shown in Code Window 3.28.

```
Private Sub Report_Open(Cancel As Integer)

    'Declare variables
    Dim strGender As String
    Dim strRS As String

    'Revise the records source -- filter by gender
    If MsgBox("Do you want to filter the report by gender?", vbYesNo, _
            "Input required") = vbYes Then
        'Filter by Category
        strGender = InputBox("Enter gender (F, M.)")

        'Set the record source = the filtered employees table
        strRS = "SELECT Employees.* FROM Employees WHERE Gender = '" & strGender & "'"
        Me.RecordSource = strRS
    Else
        'Set the record source = the whole employees table
        Me.RecordSource = "Employees"
    End If

End Sub
```

CODE WINDOW 3.28

i. Save the code and minimize the VB Editor. Test the code by opening the report in Print Preview. Click **Yes** at the first message to verify that you can filter the report by gender and type **M** to show only males in the report. Close the report, and then save the changes if prompted.

j. Maximize the VB Editor and insert a new module named **RecordSet**. Type the code shown in Code Window 3.29 to create a procedure that locates and updates the spelling of **San Diego**, which currently appears as San Dieg in the database.

```
Option Compare Database
Option Explicit

Sub UpdateRecord()

    'Declare Variables
    Dim db As DAO.Database
    Dim rst As DAO.RecordSet
    Dim intCounter As Integer

    'Set Current Database
    Set db = CurrentDb

    'Set the recordset
    Set rst = db.OpenRecordset("Employees")

    'Cycle through the records
    Do While Not rst.EOF
        If rst!city = "San Dieg" Then
            intCounter = intCounter + 1
            rst.Edit
            rst!city = "San Diego"
            rst.Update
        End If
    rst.MoveNext
    Loop

    'Displays message based on number of records found
    If intCounter = 0 Then
        MsgBox " No records found"
    ElseIf intCounter = 1 Then
        MsgBox (intCounter & " Record Edited")
    Else
        MsgBox (intCounter & " Records Edited")
    End If

End Sub
```

CODE WINDOW 3.29

k. RunSub/UserForm on the toolbar to locate and update the spelling of San Diego.

l. Save the code, close the VB Editor. Close the database and exit Access. Based on your instructor's directions, submit v3p2Retirement_LastFirst.

Mid-Level Exercises

1 | Book Club

You have recently become a member of a community book club. The book club meets monthly at a local restaurant at which all food and beverages are covered by membership fees. Currently, all membership data is stored in an Access database. Based on your knowledge of VBA, you have offered to enhance the database by adding the ability to calculate dues and quickly remove inactive members.

a. Open *v3m1BookClub*. Save the database as **v3m1BookClub_LastFirst**. Enable the content.

b. Open the frmMemberInfo form in Design View, ensure the Property Sheet is open, and select the **Calculate Dues button**.

c. Create an **On Click** event. Place the insertion point on **Ln 5, Col**, press **Enter**, press **Tab**, and then type the code as displayed in Code Window 3.30. Save the code and exit the VB Editor.

```
Private Sub CalculateDues_Click()

    'Declarations
    Const curDues As Currency = 250
    Const sngLateFee As Single = 1.1

    Dim curAmountOwed As Currency

    'If statement to calculate fees
    If Me.MembershipFees = "Unpaid" Then
        curAmountOwed = curDues * sngLateFee
    Else
        curAmountOwed = 0
    End If

    'Display results
    MsgBox "Total amount owed is " & Format(curAmountOwed, "Currency")

End Sub
```

CODE WINDOW 3.30

d. Open the frmMemberInfo form in Form view and click the **Calculate Dues button**. The Total amount owed is $275.00, which is composed of the $250.00 membership fee and penalty. Click **OK** and close the form.

e. Open the VB Editor and insert a new module. Save the module as **DeleteInactive**.

f. Type the procedure into the code window as it is shown in Code Window 3.31. Note the **'rst.Delete** line is entered as a comment.

This code will locate all inactive members and returns a count of the records found. In a later step, you will remove the ' from the comment 'rst.Delete. Once removed, this will delete the inactive members and return a count on the records found.

```
Sub DeleteInactive()

    'Declarations
    Dim db As DAO.Database
    Dim rst As DAO.Recordset
    Dim intCounter As Integer

    'Set the current database
    Set db = CurrentDb

    'Set the recordset
    Set rst = db.OpenRecordset("tblMembers")

    'Cycle through the records
    Do While Not rst.EOF
    If rst!Status = "Inactive" Then
        intCounter = intCounter + 1
        rst.Delete
    End If
    rst.MoveNext
    Loop
    MsgBox "End of Recordset. " & intCounter & " matches were found."

    'Close the recordset
    rst.Close
    Set rst = Nothing
    Set db = Nothing

End Sub
```

CODE WINDOW 3.31

> **TROUBLESHOOTING:** Deleting records from a database cannot be undone. Be sure to make a backup before testing the DeleteInactive procedure.

g. Save the procedure and click **Run** in the VB Editor. Select **DeleteInactive** and click **Run**.

The code finds five inactive members but will not delete the inactive members until the ' is removed from the 'rst.Delete line.

h. Remove the ' from the **'rst.Delete** line, save the code, and then run the procedure. Click **OK** to close the message box, save the code, and then press **Alt+F11** to close the VB Editor.

i. Open the tblMembers table and verify that the five inactive members have been deleted.

j. Save and close all database objects. Close the database and exit Access. Based on your instructor's directions, submit v3m1BookClub_LastFirst.

2 Homeowner Association

You have recently been elected to the board of your neighborhood homeowner association (HOA) board. Your HOA reduces required annual dues by allowing residents to donate to the community. As part of your duties, you help raise funds for the community, as well as collect dues. Currently, all donations information is stored in a database. You have been asked to add customized reports to the database, as well as a method to calculate dues. Dues are $0.25 per square foot of the home. You have decided to use VBA to complete the tasks.

a. Open *v3m2HOA*. Save the database as **v3m2HOA_LastFirst** and enable the content.

b. Open the tblDonations table to view the donations to date. Close the table.

c. Open the Donations report in Design View and add an On Open event.

d. Type the code as it appears in Code Window 3.32.

```
Private Sub Report_Open(Cancel As Integer)

    'Declare variables
    Dim strPurpose As String
    Dim strRS As String


    'Revise the records source -- filter by category

        'Filter by Category
        strPurpose = InputBox("Please Select Tree Removal, Holiday Party, Lawn Care, or Landscaping")

        'Set the record source = the filtered products table
        strRS = "SELECT tblDonations.* FROM tblDonations WHERE Purpose = '" & strPurpose & "'"
        Me.RecordSource = strRS

End Sub
```

CODE WINDOW 3.32

e. Save the code and exit the VB Editor.

f. Open the report in Report View and enter **Tree Removal** when prompted to test your code.

g. Open the frmDashboard form in Design view and add an On Click event to the Information button that displays a message box with the following message: **Please contact board president Bill Adams for assistance.**

h. Add an On Click event to the Landscaping button and enter the following code:

Msgbox "Total donations for Landscaping are" & Format(DSum("Amount", "tblDonations", "Purpose = 'Landscaping'"), "Currency").

This statement displays a message box that calculates total dollars raised using the DSUM function. The DSUM function calculates a summary based on a specific criterion.

i. Adapt the code in Step h to add On Click events to the remaining donation buttons.

j. Add an On Click event to the HOA FEES button. Enter the code as it appears in Code Window 3.33.

```
Private Sub cmdFees_Click()
    'Declare variables
    Dim intSqft As Integer
    Const sngRate As Single = 0.25

    intSqft = InputBox("Enter square footage")

    'Output fees
    MsgBox ("HOA fees are: " & Format(intSqft * sngRate, "Currency"))

End Sub
```

CODE WINDOW 3.33

k. Close the VB Editor, display the frmDashboard, and then click the **HOA FEES button** to test the code.

l. Close the database and exit Access. Based on your instructor's directions, submit v3m2HOA_LastFirst.

Beyond the Classroom

Debug a Recordset Procedure

The Mountain Top Lodge would like you to calculate the total guests in each service category. You created a standard module and added a new procedure. The procedure is producing an error. Try to debug the error, run the procedure, and then verify the total in each party. To begin, open the *v3b1Lodging* file, and then save the database as **v3b1Lodging_LastFirst**. Open the VB Editor, and then run the procedure. Debug the error, and then fix the procedure. Run the procedure again, and then verify the number of total guests in ServiceID 1. Based on your instructor's directions, submit v3b1Lodging_LastFirst.

Create a Recordset Using ADO

All of the recordsets that you have created in this chapter were created using the DAO object library. In this exercise, you will create a recordset using the ADO object library. Open the *v3b2Doctors* file, and then save the database as **v3b2Doctors_LastFirst**. In the new database, open the Doctors table, and then review the data. Open the VB Editor, click **Tools** on the menu bar, and then click **References**. Add a reference to the Microsoft ActiveX Data Objects 2.8 Library. Search Help and the Internet to find an example of how to create a recordset using ADO. Create a recordset that changes all records with zip code 33070 to 33099. Close the database and exit Access. Based on your instructor's directions, submit v3b2Doctors_LastFirst.

Capstone Exercise

You have been hired as an account manager for Quantum technical support, an IT company that specializes in computer maintenance for consumers and small businesses.

You were asked to add several enhancements to the company's current database. You will create a custom function that will calculate the payment date based on credit rating, create an event that will display a prompt when a record is being edited, and add a procedure that allows the user to run reports based on a specified account number. Your last step will be to add error handling to your work.

Create a Function

Your first task is to create a function that calculates a customer's payment due date, based on their credit rating. **A** credit receives a due date of 90 days from the current date, **B** credit receives 60 days from the current date, and **C** credit receives 30 days from the current date.

a. Open the *v3c1TechSupport* database.

b. Save the database as **v3c1TechSupport_LastFirst** and click **Enable Content**.

c. Open the VB Editor and insert a module named **Function**.

d. Add the code, as shown in Code Window 3.34.

```
Function DueDate() As Date

    'Declarations
    Dim dtmDate As Date
    Dim intDuration As Integer

    dtmDate = Date

    'If statement to determine duration
    If Forms("AccountDetails").Credit = "A" Then
        intDuration = 90
    ElseIf Forms("AccountDetails").Credit = "B" Then
        intDuration = 60
    Else
        intDuration = 30
    End If

    DueDate = dtmDate + intDuration

End Function
```

CODE WINDOW 3.34

e. Save the code and exit the VB Editor.

Call the Function

After creating the custom function, you will create an On Click event for the Account Details form that calls the function and displays the results in a message box.

a. Open the AccountDetails form in Design View.

b. Add an On Click event to the cmdTotal (labeled Payment Due Date) command button.

c. Type the following code starting on **Ln6**, **Col5**: **MsgBox "Payment is due on" & Format(DueDate(),"mm/dd/yyyy")**.

d. Save the procedure and exit the VB Editor.

e. Switch to Form View and click the **Payment Due Date button**.

f. Verify the calculations are correct in the message box and click **OK**.

Create Save Warning

The Account Details form contains a command button to create a new account. Currently when pressed, the button creates a new record. You would like to add additional functionality by displaying a text box with a save message while an account is being created or edited. The text box should only appear when the form is being edited.

a. Open the AccountDetails form in Design view and create a new text box below the Account Details label.

b. Delete the label that was created with the text box.

c. Name the text box **txtSaveWarning** and enter the following text with red Font Color =**"***Please Save Changes***"**.

d. Add a new On Current event to the form and enter the following code: **Me.txtSaveWarning.Visible = False**

e. Add a new On Dirty event and enter the following code: **Me.txtSaveWarning.Visible = True**

f. Add a new AfterUpdate event and enter the following code: **Me.txtSaveWarning.Visible = False**

g. Save the code and exit the VB Editor.

h. Click the Create New Account button and add a new customer to the database with the account number **B-1111** to test the new save warning message.

i. Save and close the form.

Set a Report Record Source Based on Form Properties

Your next task is to add a procedure to the existing Customers report that will enable the user to select an account from the AccountLookUp form to populate the report.

a. Open the AccountLookUp form in Design View.

b. Name the combo box **cboLookUp**. Save and close the AccountLookUp form and open the Customers report in Design View.

c. Add an On Open event and type the code as it appears in Code Window 3.35.

```
Private Sub Report_Open(Cancel As Integer)

    'Declare variables
    Dim strPurpose As String
    Dim strRS As String

        'Use combo box to filter report
        strPurpose = Forms![AccountLookUp]![cboLookUp]

        'Set the record source = the filtered products table
        strRS = "SELECT Accounts.* FROM Accounts WHERE Account = '" & strPurpose & "'"
        Me.RecordSource = strRS

End Sub
```

CODE WINDOW 3.35

d. Save the code and exit the VB Editor.

e. Open the AccountLookUp form. Look up an account such as **B-30494** to test your work.

f. Close the report preview.

Add an Error Routine

You need to add an error routine that will display a simple, user-friendly message if an error occurs.

a. Return to the VB Editor, add the code **On Error GoTo Error_Routine** underneath the first line of the Report_Open procedure.

b. Starting at **Ln 18, Col 1**, add the code, as shown in Code Window 3.36.

c. Save the code and click **Form_AccountLookup** in the Project Explorer to view its code.

d. Modify the code as displayed in Code Window 3.37 to complete the error handling for your project.

```
Private Sub Report_Open(Cancel As Integer)
On Error GoTo Error_Routine

    'Declare variables
    Dim strPurpose As String
    Dim strRS As String

        'Use combo box to filter report
        strPurpose = Forms![AccountLookUp]![cboLookUp]

        'Set the record source = the filtered products table
        strRS = "SELECT Accounts.* FROM Accounts WHERE Account = '" & strPurpose & "'"
        Me.RecordSource = strRS

Exit_Routine:
    Exit Sub

Error_Routine:
    If Err.Number = 94 Then
        MsgBox "Account number cannot be blank.", vbCritical, "An error has occured."
        Cancel = True
    Else
        MsgBox Err.Number & " " & Err.Description & vbCrLf & _
            "Contact your technical support staff.", vbCritical, "An error has occured."
    End If
    Resume Exit_Routine
End Sub
```

CODE WINDOW 3.36

```
Private Sub cmdAccount_Click()
On Error GoTo Error_Routine

    DoCmd.OpenReport "Customers", acViewPreview

Exit_Routine:
    Exit Sub

Error_Routine:
    If Err.Number = 2501 Then
        'Do Nothing
    Else
        MsgBox Err.Number & " " & Err.Description & vbCrLf & _
            "Contact your technical support staff.", vbCritical, "An error has occured."
    End If
    Resume Exit_Routine

End Sub
```

CODE WINDOW 3.37

e. Save the code and exit the VB Editor.

f. Click the **Look Up Account button** to test your work.

g. Close the Customers report, save all database objects, and then exit Access. Based on your instructor's directions, submit v3c1TechSupport_LastFirst.

Glossary

A1 style A referencing style that is used commonly in Excel.

ADO (Active X Data Objects) An object library that enables your client applications to access and manipulate data from a variety of sources through an OLE DB provider.

After Update An event that is triggered after a record is saved.

And operator A logical operator that requires all conditions included in the statement evaluate to True.

Argument A value in the form of a constant, variable, or expression that provides necessary information to a procedure or function, similar to how arguments provide necessary data for Excel functions.

Before Update An event that is triggered before a record is saved.

Bound control A control that is connected to a data source in the host application.

Calling procedure A procedure that calls a function.

Caption property A property that controls the text that appears on the form's title bar.

Cells method A method that allows you to reference a cell by using its index or R1C1 style address.

CheckBox control A control that allows the user to select one or more options at the same time.

Chr Function A function that requires an integer as its argument and then returns a character associated with that integer.

Class Module A module enables you to create an object template along with the properties and methods that decide how the object behaves.

Code Window A workspace text editor for writing and editing VBA programming statements.

Collection A group of objects with similar characteristics.

CommandButton control A control that displays a button to execute some action when the user clicks it.

Comment A remark or text that documents or explains what a section of code does.

Concatenate A technique of combining two values by using the ampersand character (&) or plus sign (+) to join two values.

Condition An expression that uses a relational operator (such as = and <=) to compare two values (through variables, constants, or expressions) and determine whether the result of the comparison is true or false.

Conditional compiler constant A constant defined in the host application.

Constant A value that is specified at design time and that remains the same (or constant) while the application is running.

Control Used in forms for entering data, displaying information, or evoking events.

ControlSource property A property that defines the cell to which the control is bound.

Counter variable A variable that is used to count the number of times a loop repeats.

DAO (Data Access Objects) An object library specifically created to work with Access databases.

Data type The type of data the variable or constant can hold and how the data is stored in the computer's memory.

Data validation The process of checking data entered by a user to ensure it meets certain conditions.

Decision structure A programming structure that makes a comparison among values, variables, and/or constants. Based on the result of that comparison, the program executes statements in a certain order.

Declaration A statement that assigns a name and data type and allocates memory to store a value for the variable or constant.

Design time The mode for designing or creating programming code.

Do...Loop structure A structure to execute a block of statements while a condition remains true or until a condition is true.

Edit A method that enables a change within a record set.

Enabled property A property that determines if a control can receive focus or attention and if that control can respond to the user.

Error trapping The process of intercepting and handling errors at run time.

Event An action that occurs when the code is running, such as a button click.

Focus In VBA, when a control has focus, it is active.

For...Next structure A structure that repeats a loop—a set of statements or a procedure—a specific number of times.

Format function A function that uses predefined formats to change the appearance of text.

Frame control A control that displays a frame or border around related controls on the form to increase readability for the user.

Function procedure A procedure that performs an action and returns a value, similar to how functions return values in Excel.

If...Then structure A decision structure that performs a logical test; if the test evaluates to True, the program code specifies what action to take.

If...Then...Else structure A decision structure that tests for a condition and specifies one action to take if the test evaluates to True and another if it evaluates to False.

Input box A dialog box that displays on the screen to prompt the user to enter a value.

InputBox function A function that prompts the user to enter a value that the application needs to perform an action.

Integral data type A data type that stores only whole numbers.

Intrinsic constant A constant specific to an application, such as Microsoft Excel or Microsoft Access.

IsNumeric function A function that checks a text string and determines whether it evaluates as a number.

Iteration One execution of the loop.

Keyword A word or symbol particular to a programming language and with a specific purpose.

Label control A control that indicates the purpose of other controls because those controls do not have Caption properties.

Line-continuation character A a space followed by an underscore (_) that allows for the continuation of a statement on more than one line in the code window.

ListBox control A control that display a list of items from which the user may select.

Logical operator An operator that uses Boolean logic to test conditions.

Logical Test A comparison that uses relational operators.

Loop A set of statements or a procedure that is repeated.

Message box A small dialog box that contains a title bar, a message, an icon, and one or more buttons.

Method An action pertaining to an object.

Module A container to organize programming code.

MoveNext A method used to advance through the records of a record set.

MsgBox function A function that displays a message on the screen and returns an integer value indicating which button the user clicked in the message box.

MsgBox statement A statement that displays a message box onscreen with optional buttons, icons, and title bar text.

Name property A text string to identify an object that is used in VBA.

Object An object represents an element, such as a worksheet, cell, chart, or form.

Object library Various collections of objects in Microsoft Office that support VBA.

Object model The object model organizes all objects into an object hierarchy, which defines how objects are related to one another.

Object-oriented programming language A programming language that uses methods that revolve around objects and actions that manipulate those objects.

On Current An event that is triggered by a record being loaded into a form.

On Dirty An event that is triggered when the record is being edited.

On Enter An event that is triggered when the insertion point is placed in a text box.

On Error statement A statement that directs the code to skip to a particular line in the procedure (usually at the bottom) where the appropriate message is displayed and any corrective action can be taken.

Operator A character or combination of characters that accomplishes a specific computation.

Option Compare Database A statement that is used in a module to declare that string comparisons are not case sensitive when data is compared.

Option Explicit A setting that requires you to explicitly declare a variable before assigning a value to it.

Option Explicit A statement that is used in a module to require that all variables be declared before they are used.

Or operator A logical operator requires that any one of the conditions evaluate to True for the expression to be true.

Order of precedence The order in which arithmetic expressions are performed.

Post test Used after entering a loop to perform a test to check conditions.

Pretest Used before entering a loop to perform a test to check conditions.

Private procedure A procedure available only to a specific object or module.

Procedures Named sequences of statements that perform a series of actions for a defined task.

Programming structure The sequence in which the program statements execute at runtime.

Project A collection of modules and objects needed to run an application.

Properties Window A pane that displays the properties or attributes for the selected object in the Project Explorer.

Properties Attributes for the selected object.

Property procedure A procedure that creates or manipulates a custom property.

Public procedure A procedure that is available to any object in an application; the code for an object anywhere in the application can use the code statements.

R1C1 Style A referencing style used in Visual Basic for Applications that references the row number then the column number.

Recordset A set of records selected from a table or query loaded in the random access memory of your computer.

Relational operator An operator that compares the relationship between two values.

Repetition structure A programming structure that repeats the execution of a series of program statements.

Resume Exit_Routine statement A statement that directs the code to jump to the exit routine.

RowSource property A property that specifies a range that contains a list of the items that will appear in the list box or combo box control at run time.

Runtime The mode during which a program is being executed.

Scope Specifies which program statements can access the value stored in the variable or constant.

Select Case structure A decision structure that compares an expression or a value to a case block, which is the set of cases that might apply.

Sequence structure A structure in which a program executes statements in the order in which they appear.

Standard module A module that stores procedures that can be used by any object in the application.

Step value The amount by which the counter is incremented or decremented during each cycle of a loop.

Sub procedure A procedure that performs an action but does not return a specific value.

Symbolic or user-defined constant A constant created by a programmer.

Syntax error An error that occurs when you misuse or misspell a keyword, use incorrect punctuation, have not defined a procedure, or violate any other programming rules specific to the language.

TabIndex property A property that determines the order in which controls receive the focus.

TabStop property A property that determines whether the control receives the focus when the user presses Tab.

TextAlign property A property that specifies the horizonal alignment of a caption appearing in a label.

TextBox control A control that enables the user to enter data in a form.

Toolbox A palette that contains the standard controls.

Unbound control A control that is not connected to data in the host application.

Update A method that saves changes and closes the edit process of a record in a record set.

Val function A function that converts a text value into numeric data for calculations.

Variable A programmer-defined name that stores values that can change while the application is running.

VBA debugger A tool that enables the programmer to suspend the execution of VBA code momentarily so that it can be debugged.

Visual Basic for Applications (VBA) A programming language that you can use to create and customize Office applications to enhance their functionality.

Index

Italics indicate illustrations, tables, sidebars, or photos.